CSA Guide to Cloud Computing

CSA Guide to Cloud Computing

Implementing Cloud Privacy and Security

Raj Samani

Brian Honan

Jim Reavis

Vladimir Jirasek, Technical Editor

AMSTERDAM • BOSTON • HEIDELBERG • LONDON
NEW YORK • OXFORD • PARIS • SAN DIEGO
SAN FRANCISCO • SINGAPORE • SYDNEY • TOKYO

Syngress is an imprint of Elsevier

SYNGRESS.

Acquiring Editor: *Chris Katsaropoulos*
Editorial Project Manager: *Benjamin Rearick*
Project Manager: *Punithavathy Govindaradjane*
Designer: *Mark Rogers*

Syngress is an imprint of Elsevier
225 Wyman Street, Waltham, MA 02451, USA

Library of Congress Cataloging-in-Publication Data
Samani, Raj, author.
  CSA guide to cloud computing: implementing cloud privacy and security / Raj Samani, Brian Honan, Jim Reavis; Vladimir Jirasek, technical editor.
    pages cm
  ISBN 978-0-12-420125-5 (paperback)
  1. Cloud computing. 2. Cloud computing–Security measures. 3. Computer security. I. Honan, Brian, author. II. Reavis, Jim, author. III. Jirasek, Vladimir, editor. IV. CSA (Organization) V. Title. VI. Title: Cloud Security Alliance guide to cloud computing.
  QA76.585.S376 2014
  004.67′82–dc23
                    2014031206

British Library Cataloguing-in-Publication Data
A catalogue record for this book is available from the British Library

ISBN: 978-0-12-420125-5

> For information on all Syngress publications,
> visit our website at *store.elsevier.com/Syngress*

Working together to grow libraries in developing countries

www.elsevier.com • www.bookaid.org

Contents

Forewords

Our dependency on technology has grown almost as fast as new acronyms and buzzwords are introduced to the industry. Cloud computing equally represents a remarkable illustration of this dependency. While the term "cloud security" is new, the basic concept has been around for many years. Almost every Internet user is now leveraging some form of cloud computing and in certain cases not even realizing that they are using the cloud, or more importantly understanding their dependency on cloud services. This, of course, represents a wonderful opportunity to all of us, the ability to leverage incredible technical resources without the burden of having to buy, set up, secure, and maintain systems. Add to this, that we only have to pay for the resources we need, there is no question that cloud computing not only acts as wonderful resource to support our technical lives, but also a great driver for innovation and economic growth.

There are many excellent examples of the economic benefits of cloud computing for individuals, small businesses, large enterprises, and the public sector alike. However, as our dependency on cloud computing grows so do the increased risk around security and privacy. With such a concentration of system resources and customers, the impact of a major outage will have greater ramifications than ever before. An outage affecting only one organization means that the impact will affect only that organization and their stakeholders. With cloud computing however, an outage or major incident will not only affect one customer, but potentially an entire industry.

Herein lies the risk; as our dependency on cloud computing grows so does the potential impact of any incident. These risks go beyond cyber of course, with natural disasters, bankruptcy, and even law enforcement action against providers those do not undertake appropriate due diligence on what their customers do. Without the requisite transparency, end customers for cloud computing may be completely unaware of such risks until it is too late. Indeed many examples exist where customers realize something is wrong only when they can no longer gain access to their resources.

This book is critical in building the necessary levels of assurance required to protect such valuable resources. Of course the level of assurance will vary, but having the necessary tools is imperative. The Cloud Security Alliance and the authors of this book have provided a comprehensive view of the salient points required to protect assets with cloud service providers with appropriate references to external sources for more detail. Such measures are imperative as we have seen with the advent of the US FedRAMP, but also a multitude of other certification schemes established to build the confidence we all expect when using the cloud.

Cloud computing is here to stay. It promises tremendous opportunities that benefit each and every one of us. This is not lost on cyber criminals, and the need for protecting, or the benefits of, such critical assets has never been so great.

By
Honorable Howard A. Schmidt,
Partner, Ridge Schmidt Cyber,
Former Cyber Security Advisor for
presidents George W. Bush and Barack Obama

Throughout history, great inventions and innovations have been underestimated and even ridiculed, only to exceed all expectations and change the world. The Internet clearly falls into the category of wildly successful innovations, a research network that languished in obscurity for years, only to burst onto the scene in the 1990s and become a pervasive part of business and society. At the same time, many contemporaneous technology trends have failed to fulfill their promise. With the hype that has surrounded cloud computing over the past several years, it is easy to fall into the same complacent thinking—Is not cloud just a new characterization of preexisting computing technologies, such as the mainframe and the World Wide Web?

Cloud computing indeed has a heritage in many familiar computing concepts. Like many transformational technologies, timing is everything. Cloud is transforming computing into a utility—the most powerful utility yet conceived. The idea that any person on Earth, rather than a privileged few, can have access to an unlimited amount of computing power, on demand, is startling in its possibilities. The idea that sophisticated new software-driven businesses can be built in the cloud in days rather than years is mind boggling. With each passing day, Cloud Security Alliance (CSA) receives new evidence that the cloud revolution is upon us. Global enterprises tell us that they are "all in" with the cloud. Financial institutions tell us they have opened their last internal data center. Software companies tell us that in the future, all of their products will exist in the cloud. Entrepreneurs are challenging every existing industry and dreaming up new ones, powered by the cloud. The time for cloud is now. Many of humanity's most difficult and pressing problems will someday be solved by the power of cloud computing, if we can trust it.

At the CSA, our mission is to build the trusted cloud ecosystem and deliver a broad portfolio of security best practices to enable that trust. We are a nonprofit organization with our presence in many countries. As the CEO of Cloud Security Alliance, I am pleased to provide an introduction to the *CSA Guide to Cloud Computing: Implementing Cloud Privacy and Security*. I would like to thank Brian Honan and Raj Samani for their vision and efforts in breathing life into this guide. Through their research, skilled writing, and sheer determination, they have produced an eminently readable guide, appropriate for anyone with a career in information technology, information security, and beyond. I would also like to thank the many volunteers within CSA who helped review and edit this publication. Please enjoy this guide with our best wishes.

By
Jim Reavis,
Chief Executive Officer,
Cloud Security Alliance

About the Authors

RAJ SAMANI

Raj Samani is an active member of the information security industry, through involvement with numerous initiatives to improve the awareness and application of security in business and society. He is currently working as the Vice President, Chief Technical Officer for McAfee EMEA, having previously worked as chief information security officer for a large public sector organization in the UK and recently inducted into the Infosecurity Europe Hall of Fame (2012).

He previously worked across numerous public sector organizations, in many cyber security and research orientated working groups across Europe. Examples include the midata Interoperability Board, as well as representing DIGITALEUROPE on the Smart Grids Reference Group established by the European Commission in support of the Smart Grid Mandate. He is also author of the recent Syngress book *Applied Cyber Security and the Smart Grid*.

In addition, Raj is currently the Cloud Security Alliance's chief innovation officer and previously served as Vice President for Communications in the ISSA UK Chapter where he presided over the award of Chapter Communications Programme of the Year 2008 and 2009. He is also Special Advisor for the European CyberCrime Centre, also on the advisory council for the Infosecurity Europe show, Infosecurity magazine, and expert on both searchsecurity.co.uk and Infosec portal, and regular contributor to multiple media outlets across the globe. He has had numerous security papers published, and appeared on television commenting on computer security issues. He has also provided assistance in the 2006 RSA Wireless Security Survey and part of the consultation committee for the RIPA Bill (Part 3).

BRIAN HONAN

Brian is recognized internationally as an expert in the field of information security and has worked with numerous companies in the private sector and with government departments, in Ireland, Europe, and throughout the United

Kingdom. Brian has also provided advice to the European Commission on matters relating to information security. He is also on the advisory board for a number of innovative information security companies.

Brian is the author of the well regarded book *ISO 27001 in a Windows Environment* and coauthor of the book *The Cloud Security Rules*. Brian, also been regularly published in many respected trade publications, is a prolific blogger on items relating to information security and blogs for information security magazine. He is also European Editor for the SANS NewsBites newsletter which is published twice a week to over 500,000 information security professionals worldwide.

Brian's expertise on Information Security is recognized both domestically and internationally and he speaks regularly at various industry conferences. Brian has addressed events such as the RSA Europe Conference, BRUcon, Source Barcelona, BsidesLondon Security Event, IDC IT Security Seminar, and the ICS Data Protection Seminar, to name but a few.

JIM REAVIS

For many years, Jim Reavis has worked in the information security industry as an entrepreneur, writer, speaker, technologist, and business strategist. Jim's innovative thinking about emerging security trends have been published and presented widely throughout the industry and have influenced many. Jim is helping shape the future of information security and related technology industries as cofounder, CEO, and driving force of the Cloud Security Alliance. Jim was recently named as one of the Top 10 cloud computing leaders by SearchCloudComputing.

About the Cloud Security Alliance

The Cloud Security Alliance (CSA) is a not-for-profit organization with a mission to promote the use of best practices for providing security assurance within cloud computing and to provide education on the uses of cloud computing to help secure all other forms of computing. The CSA is led by a broad coalition of industry practitioners, corporations, associations, and other key stakeholders.

HISTORY

The issues and opportunities of cloud computing gained considerable notice in 2008 within the information security community. At the ISSA CISO Forum in Las Vegas, in November of 2008, the concept of the Cloud Security Alliance was born. Following a presentation of emerging trends by Jim Reavis that included a call for action for securing cloud computing, Reavis and Nils Puhlmann outlined the initial mission and strategy of the CSA. A series of organizational meetings with industry leaders in early December 2008 formalized the founding of the CSA. Our outreach to the information security community to create our initial work product for the 2009 RSA Conference resulted in dozens of volunteers to research, author, edit, and review our first white paper.

Acknowledgments

We would like to thank the volunteers and staff at the Cloud Security Alliance (CSA) who have not only made this book possible, but also the cutting edge research produced by the CSA family. We are truly indebted to their support and expertise that has allowed the publication of research that keeps our modern digital society safer.

A huge thanks goes to Vladimir Jirasek (Research Director for the CSA UK Chapter) who was an excellent technical reviewer, and also Said Tabet, Neha Thethi who provided a thorough review of the text. We would also like to thank Peter Kunz, Evelyn de Souza, Paavan Mistry, and many more who pointed us in the direction of the latest industry research.

We would also like to thank our families that have provided us with the support required to take on an undertaking required to write this book.

Many thanks and we hope you enjoy.

Brian, Jim, and Raj

CSA Guide to Cloud Computing—Introduction

Now that the 2014 FIFA World Cup is over, we can get back to the hottest topic of the day—cloud computing. A little too much perhaps? Well consider that almost every Internet citizen uses the cloud even if they do not even know it (see Chapter 1). Furthermore, cloud computing is being advertised not only within technology-related press but on mainstream media such as billboards, television, to name but a few.

Cloud computing is truly ubiquitous and its growing list of benefits provides an explanation as to why; Particularly by providing customers the opportunity to focus on their core business while the difficult task of buying and managing the technology is done by somebody else. Add to this the ability to pay for only the service when needed and without the added burden of large operational expenditure, then we can see why cloud computing is not only a hot topic but also a fundamental shift in the way organizations work today with technology. In his book entitled 'Hackers, Heroes of the Computer Revolution[1]', author Steven Levy wrote about many of the pioneers of modern computing, in particular, those students based at the Massachusetts Institute of Technology (MIT). These pioneers "harbored the kind of restless curiosity which led them to root around campus buildings in search of ways to get their hands on computers." These individuals were members of a model railroad club (known as the Tech Model Railroad Club, TMRC). "There were two factions of TMRC. Some members loved the idea of spending their time building and painting replicas of certain trains with historical and emotional value, or creating realistic scenery for the layout. The other faction centered on the Signals and Power Subcommittee of the club, and it cared far more about what went on under the layout. S&P people were obsessed with the way The System worked, its increasing complexities, how any change you made would affect other parts, and how you could put those relationships between the parts to optimal use."

In a little over 50 years, tomorrow's pioneers are provided with (almost) unlimited access to computing resources to satisfy this internal technical curiosity,

---

[1]Steven Levy. "Hackers, heroes of the computer revolution". November 1996 [cited July 2014].

without the added burden of having to buy any hardware, manage operating system licenses, or even have to speak to anybody. The ease and speed with which anybody can test any new idea, and all for less than a cup of coffee (okay the last part may depend on the level of resources sought) provides an incredible opportunity for businesses, entrepreneurs, and everybody else for that matter.

With this in mind, we become ever more reliant on cloud computing. What was originally used to host our email is now hosting applications that will keep the water clean, what was originally used to store our movie collection is now used to store personal and sensitive data about each and every one of us. The need for 'cloud security' has never been more important, and as our dependency on cloud computing increases the need to further innovate and develop better, faster, and more efficient security controls is imperative. The bad guys are continuously innovating, consider for one moment that it was a little over 10 years ago that we were concerned about malware that spread by offering a picture of a female tennis player, and less than nine years later malware was able to compromise a nuclear plant by impacting the integrity of centrifuges. Volunteers within the Cloud Security Alliance (CSA) dedicate their time for the continuous innovation of security (and privacy) measures that help protect these critical assets. This book is intended to present the research within the multitude of CSA working groups, as well as incorporate the research and findings across other relevant sources. It should be used as a reference for CSA research and also a broader cloud security reference guide. We would also hope that this publication acts as a springboard. A springboard for you, the reader to get involved; whether this is for the reader to get actively engaged with the CSA community or to adopt some of the research and apply it to your own cloud story. Therefore please enjoy the book, tell us what you think, but more importantly become a part of the community. The need to secure the cloud has never been more important, and we need your help.

HOW THIS BOOK IS STRUCTURED

We have presented 11 chapters for this book. The aim was to try and incorporate as much of the research working groups within the CSA, all of which are important. Therefore, just because one particular research may be referenced more than another does not make that group any less or more important. The following defines the chapters within this book;

- *Chapter One: Cloud Computing, What is it and What's the Big Deal?*—In order to secure a cloud, we need to have a common agreement on what it actually is. This chapter will provide a definition, but also consider its benefits and the importance that cloud computing plays within the Internet economy.

- *Chapter Two: Selecting and Engaging with a Cloud Service Provider*—Selecting a cloud service provider will need to consider a number of key criteria, price being only one of these. This chapter will consider the available mechanisms to measure the security deployed by prospective providers.
- *Chapter Three: The Cloud Threat Landscape*—In the third chapter there will a thorough assessment of the top threats to cloud computing. This will include references to CSA research as well as third parties that have evaluated the threat landscape.
- *Chapter Four: Secure Cloud for Mobile Computing*—The devices we use to access cloud resources is also changing, none more so than our dependency on mobile devices. In this chapter we will look at the threats to mobile computing for the cloud.
- *Chapter Five: Making the Move into the Cloud*—Following two chapters considering the threats to cloud computing, we will turn our focus to the steps that end customers need to consider in order to make the move to the cloud.
- *Chapter Six: Certification for Cloud Service Providers*—While the previous chapter presents the security controls to mitigate the threat, the reality is that for many end customers their ability to influence the security measures will be limited. Indeed, even the level of transparency into the controls deployed will be limited. This is why cloud certifications will be so important, they are used more and more as the vehicle to provide assurance regarding the security deployed by providers to potential customers.
- *Chapter Seven: The Privacy Imperative*—The discussion about privacy associated within the cloud is one of the most contentious issues within technology. This chapter will consider the overall debate and provide mechanisms for both providers and end customers to address many of these concerns.
- *Chapter Eight: Cloud Security Alliance Research*—As mentioned earlier, our intention is to provide a singular reference for all CSA research. This chapter will provide the reader with an overview of the various working groups within the CSA, and details of their current findings.
- *Chapter Nine: Dark Clouds, What to Do In The Event of a Security Incident*—With corporate resources now stored and managed (to some extent) by third parties, the need to have a strong security incident management policy is imperative. This chapter will recommend the steps required to address the fundamental question: *What happens when something does go wrong?*
- *Chapter Ten: The Future Cloud*—Cloud computing is evolving, and this chapter considers its role within critical national infrastructure, as well as what will be required to secure such critical assets. It is intended to view into the components required to secure the cloud of tomorrow.

Authors of most technology books have to contend with the reality that almost as soon as the book hits the shelves (virtual or physical), their content is already somewhat dated. This book will of course be no different, but we have aimed to present the foundations of cloud security, which we anticipate to be fundamental whichever month or year you consider using cloud services. However, more important is that we welcome change, because that means that working groups are continuing their excellent work, and hopefully this text has helped more incredibly talented experts to push the topic even further.

Enjoy the book, and we hope to see you within the CSA community real soon.

Brian, Jim, and Raj

CHAPTER 1

Cloud Computing, What is it and What's the Big Deal?

In fact, I think the Cloud is critical to Europe's growth, and essential for making the best Internet available to all... Getting the cloud right will mean the Internet can continue to be a generator of innovation, growth and freedom. If we get it wrong our infrastructure will fail to meet our appetite for access to data and our fragile digital economy could be knocked about badly. To help get it right I've started work on a European Cloud Computing Strategy. I want to make Europe not just "cloud-friendly" but "cloud-active."[1]

Neelie Kroes, European Union Digital Agenda Commissioner

INFORMATION IN THIS CHAPTER

- Defining cloud computing
- Economic opportunities
- The cloud is "not" secure

Such a ringing endorsement for cloud computing would lead many to believe that such a phenomenon would be well understood by everybody, after all it would appear critical to the economic growth of so many nations and regions across the globe.

Well, not quite!

A recent survey proved there is considerable confusion regarding cloud computing, indeed the results from the survey[2] found that the majority of respondents believed that the cloud is an actual cloud (fluffy white thing that floats around in the sky) or associated with the weather (29%). Indeed only 16% said it was a computer network to "store, access, and share data from Internet-connected devices."

Despite such a lack of understanding, the majority of respondents were actually cloud computing users (95%), despite 54% claiming to never use the cloud. The survey therefore clearly demonstrates that cloud computing is not just in widespread use, but indeed ubiquitous. However, most people have no idea what it is, even when they are using it. This may not necessarily be a bad thing, after all one of the many reported benefits of cloud computing is to allow its customers to focus on their daily activities while leaving the technology and security to specialist providers. In fact, this particular message forms the backbone of many cloud provider sales messaging; Salesforce, for example, state "With cloud computing, you eliminate those headaches because you're not managing hardware and software—that's the responsibility of an experienced vendor."[3]

Despite the lack of understanding among the general public, the most telling statistic is that 95% of respondents are cloud users (even if they did not know it). This reveals an appetite for computing resources that cloud computing appears to be fulfilling. However, in order to evaluate the economic benefits of cloud computing, and indeed more broadly some of the concerns raised, we must agree on some common definitions.

DEFINING CLOUD COMPUTING

One of the biggest challenges is defining cloud computing, because much like other big buzzwords within the technology industry (e.g., Web 2.0) everyone has their own definition. Based on the Cloud Security Alliance (CSA) "Security guidance for critical areas of focus in cloud computing" (v3)[4] cloud computing can be defined as

> Cloud computing is a model for enabling ubiquitous, convenient, on-demand network access to a shared pool of configurable computing resources (e.g., networks, servers, storage, applications, and services).

Of course, the general view that cloud computing does not vary greatly from traditional computing models does hold some merit; there are, however, some distinct characteristics as defined from National Institute of Standards and Technology (NIST) 800-145[5]:

- *On-demand self-service*: Consider traditional computing models, where the need for additional computing resources leads to the acquisition of new hardware, installing an operating system, ensuring that all of the licenses are installed, etc. With cloud computing, the customer is able to provision additional computing resources in an automated fashion without having to engage with customer service personnel from each cloud service provider (CSP). In practice, for many CSPs, the sign-up, payment, and deployment of applications are completely on demand and driven from their Web site without the need for any human interaction. This, however, is not always the case: in 2012, the Web site CloudSleuth[6] investigated how many CSPs actually fulfilled this characteristic. Their research found that "*of the* 20 companies we selected in this round, only 11 were fully self-serve, 9 required some level of sales interaction, and, astoundingly, 3 of those 9 simply didn't respond to our requests." This particular characteristic also applies to those implementations reserved for internal use (we will cover the private cloud later). For example, consider a business unit looking to build resources for an internal project; historically this would have involved calls, e-mails, and countless meetings to scope, define, and implement the resources to support this project. Examples of these benefits were realized by Intel IT, in their white paper entitled "Implementing On-Demand Services inside the Intel IT Private Cloud."[7] Within this example, the current web and database provisioning process undergoes a total of 38 different steps resulting in 12–16 days throughput time. Through the use of an on-demand self-service process, this is reduced to 13 steps and takes a total of 3 h. Equally, the latter process is entirely automated, as opposed to the current model that is manual with workflow automation. This is graphically illustrated in Figure 1.1.

- *Broad network access*: Cloud resources should be available over the network and through multiple devices. Equally the resources should be available using "standard" mechanisms. This characteristic focuses on the accessibility of cloud resources, without the need for any specific device or proprietary software. Typically, the resources are available via a web browser using protocols such as HTTP, XML, Java, or other protocols that are "standard."
- *Resource pooling*: One of the key selling points for cloud computing is the potential reduced cost for customers. This is largely driven by the characteristic defined as resource pooling by NIST, where CSPs are able to utilize economies of scale to reduce the overall cost of the solution. Meeting this characteristic is achieved using a multitenancy model, whereby an instance of computing resources such as hardware,

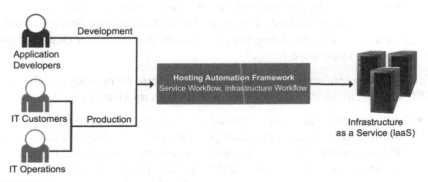

FIGURE 1.1

On-demand self-service through a self-service portal.

operating system, and database are able to serve different customers (tenants), but remain isolated from each other. It is also important to note that within this characteristic the customer may have neither knowledge nor control of the exact physical location of the resources. This may be acceptable, however, should the resources host personal data, or other regulated data, and this may breach specific compliance requirements. This issue of "data sovereignty" is seen as one of the major barriers toward the adoption of cloud computing. Subsequently, many providers allow for greater transparency and control to customers in terms of the specific location of resources. This particular issue is covered in detail later in the book.

- *Rapid elasticity*: Almost any potential cloud computing customer faces resourcing dilemmas in terms of what to do during times of peak demand. Consider a bookshop: During the three months leading up to Christmas, it faces an increase in demand for those customers wishing to buy books via its Web site by 300%, does it buy three times as many servers just to support one-quarter of its business? This particular characteristic of cloud computing aims to address this quandary by providing cloud customers the ability to rapidly provision or release resources. Equally, this particular characteristic can also be achieved automatically, for example, by utilizing cloud provider monitoring tools to manage the capacity of resources as required by the workload. This may be to automatically provision 10 more servers until the load decreases.
- *Measured service*: Cloud systems automatically control and optimize resource use by leveraging a metering capability at some level of abstraction appropriate to the type of service (e.g., storage, processing, bandwidth, and active user accounts). Resource usage can be monitored, controlled, and reported, providing transparency for both the provider and consumer of the utilized service. What this effectively means is that the provider will monitor utilization to ensure that resources are optimized. If we consider the bottom-line benefits of the cloud as potentially delivering cost savings, this particular characteristic becomes imperative.

While the above characteristics are essential for cloud computing as defined by NIST, the CSA includes multitenancy as an important element.

- Multitenancy: Although we briefly touched on the concept of multitenancy, it is an important point that warrants further clarification. Within multitenancy an application or resource can be used by other customers of the CSP. This could be a different department, or indeed another organization completely unrelated to other customers using the same resources or application as depicted in Figure 1.2. Multitenancy

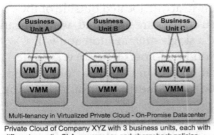
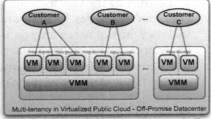
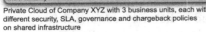

Private Cloud of Company XYZ with 3 business units, each with different security, SLA, governance and chargeback policies on shared infrastructure

Public Cloud Provider with 3 business customers, each with different security, SLA, governance and billing policies on shared infrastructure

FIGURE 1.2

Multitenancy.

therefore maximizes the resources by allowing shared access to resources. This is demonstrated by Salesforce.com (cited in 2010) with "72,500 customers supported by 8–12 multitenant instances in a 1:5000 ratio."[8] This means that each multitenant instance is capable of supporting 5000 tenants that share the same database schema. Such a level of efficiency can be achieved through an architecture where instances are isolated. Alternatively, instances of database/application may not be isolated, and access control methods are utilized to restrict access to resources (e.g., data, or the application).

Although such characteristics are important to define cloud computing, the level of importance placed on these particular characteristics are dependent on the specific model deployed.

Cloud Models

In addition to the broad definition of cloud computing, it is important to define the various cloud models available. These models are based on two characteristics:

1. based on ownership/sharing, for example, public, private, hybrid, community
2. based on cloud architecture, for example, Software as a Service (SaaS)

If we consider the various different ownership/sharing models, there are four distinct categories:

1. Public Cloud: Often, when the topic of cloud is brought up, the public cloud is usually referenced. This is because the most well-known and popular cloud services are public in nature. Typical examples include e-mail services, such as Hotmail, Apple iCloud, or storage services such as Dropbox. These services are made available to the general public, who can access services via the Internet. The infrastructure is managed

and owned by the CSP with the infrastructure located outside of the customer's premises. In addition, customers are untrusted, which means that they are not necessarily part of a single organization and will likely not even be aware of other cloud customers whatsoever. While many customers from one organization may in fact use a public cloud service, the very nature of the public model means it is available to any customer.

2. Private Cloud: While the public cloud uses an infrastructure for multiple customers, the private cloud is that reserved for a single customer. Within the private cloud deployment, the infrastructure, platform, software, etc. may be managed and owned either by the end customer or the CSP. Equally, the infrastructure may be located either on or off premise; however, the customer will have control over its specific geographic location. This particular point makes the private cloud a preferred model for hosting data that is regulated (for example, personally identifiable information), and as such may have restrictions on where it can be hosted. Unlike public cloud models, those within a private cloud are "trusted," or at least known. This means that the company that has commissioned the private cloud will know the users using the service, and will be able to define their level of access.

3. Community Cloud: A community cloud extends the concept of the private cloud to incorporate multiple customers with a shared concern. As such, it has some similar characteristics to that of the private cloud. One particular example of a community cloud is that which is realized within health care. As reported by TechTarget,[9] collaboration between the Open Science Data Cloud and the University of Chicago's Institute of Genomics and System Biology, Center for Research Informatics, and Institute of Translational Medicine established the Bionimbus Protected Data Cloud (PDC). The PDC is a cloud-based infrastructure built to manage, analyze, and provide researchers an easy access to large data sets under The Cancer Genome Atlas (TCGA). The TCGA uses techniques to find mutations that cause cancer, and the PDC allows researchers, once authorized by the National Institutes of Health, to access TCGA data. This is an excellent example of the community cloud; there is a collaboration of stakeholders with a common interest, and through the authorization process only trusted parties are provided access to the data.

4. Hybrid Cloud: Somewhere in between the private cloud and public cloud is the hybrid cloud. This category is there to catch those implementations that fall in between, where there is an element of public cloud and private cloud. A good example is the M-Cloud implementation in Moldova,[10] which is intended to utilize a single cloud platform and provide a central platform from which public services will be delivered. This approach

will utilize a single data center as opposed to the 100 disparate centers currently providing public services. It is a hybrid approach as some of the services are public in nature, such as those providing resources for citizens to access public services (and therefore accessible via the Internet); other resources are only for use by other public departments, and as such not directly accessible via the Internet. This is just one example of hybrid cloud using "Accessible and Consumed by" as detailed by the CSA Guide 3.0. There are other attributes such as Managed by, Owned by, and Located by (see Figure 1.3).

The various terms are often used interchangeably, and there is often some confusion in their description. Defining the differences between public/private/hybrid cloud models should not solely focus on their accessibility; there are other factors that can be used to differentiate, as depicted in Figure 1.3.

Another key point of differentiation between the various cloud models is the architectural design, often referred to as X-a-a-S. In other words, "something as a Service." While there are three main categories described below, the market is adding almost every possible concoction into an as a Service, hence the term X-a-a-S.

- Infrastructure as a Service (IaaS): IaaS is the foundation of cloud services whereupon other as-a-Service models are built. This particular implementation provides the customer with fundamental computing

	Infrastructure Managed By[1]	Infrastructure Owned By[2]	Infrastructure Located[3]	Accessible and Consumed By[4]
Public	Third Party Provider	Third Party Provider	Off-Premise	Untrusted
Private / Community	Or Organization / Third Party Provider	Organization / Third Party Provider	On-Premise / Off-Premise	Trusted
Hybrid	Both Organization & Third Party Provider	Both Organization & Third Party Provider	Both On-Premise & Off-Premise	Trusted & Untrusted

[1]Management includes: governance, operations, security, compliance, etc...
[2]Infrastructure implies physical infrastructure such as facilities, compute, network & storage equipment
[3]Infrastructure location is both physical and relative to on organization's managemet umbrella and speaks to ownership versus control
[4]Trusted consumers of service are those who are considered part of an organization's legal/contractual/policy umbrella including employees, contractors, & business partners. Untrusted consumers are those that may be authorized to consume some/all service but are not logical extensions of the organization.

FIGURE 1.3
Cloud computing models.

resources, such as storage, servers, network, and operating systems. Consider the earlier example of the M-Cloud; within this scenario, any public department that required a server for internal purposes would traditionally acquire hardware, install the software, and host this within their data center. With the M-Cloud, they could simply complete an online form, define the operating system they need, and this is then commissioned and provided from the single data center. This model describes IaaS, whereby the basic infrastructure is provided as a service allowing the end customer to customize.

Within this implementation, the customer does not control the underlying infrastructure (for example, the hardware), but has management control over the operating system, applications, and possibly selected limited network components. With management control over the operating system and application, the responsibility for patching is likely to fall under the customer. This particular nuance is important to note, in terms of ensuring that patches are deployed, and possibly it could become a key point should a security incident occur that leverages an unpatched operating system/application.

- Platform as a Service (PaaS): Building upon IaaS is the PaaS model. There is considerable flexibility offered to the IaaS customer, much of this is removed within a PaaS environment. For example, within the PaaS environment, the CSP manages storage, operating system, and network but the customer has the ability to build or develop customized applications.

  Examples of PaaS platforms today include AppEngine from Google, Microsoft Azure, and WaveMaker, SimpleDB, S3, DynamoDB, SQS, and SQF from Amazon.

- Software-as-a-Service (SaaS): While the IaaS and PaaS platforms offer a degree of flexibility to the end customer, the SaaS model is a simple proposition with very limited flexibility. Consider a typical example of SaaS as an e-mail service (e.g., Gmail) that is provided over the Internet, the customer signs up for the service and in effect does not really care about the type of server hardware, operating system, or indeed the ability to extend the functionality of the service. What is provided is the application over the Internet. In some instances, a degree of flexibility is provided from within the application; however, the degree of configuration available to the customer is considerably more limited than the PaaS and IaaS models.

The various categories of service models and architectures are graphically depicted in figure 1.4.

In fairness, to the preceding paragraphs, the descriptions themselves are entirely valid; however, the market itself has progressed with many more models and

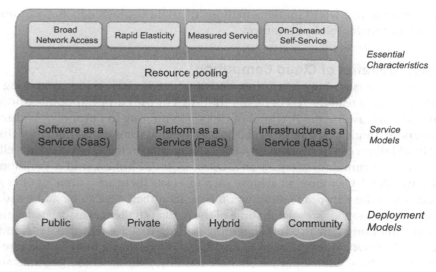

FIGURE 1.4
National Institute of Standards and Technology (NIST) visual model of cloud computing definition.

variances of architectures appearing. Indeed, even the term cloud computing itself is somewhat blurred, with many definitions existing. However, having an agreed set of grounding principles clearly defined is imperative to enable further innovation, and of course dialogue.

A good example of this was realized within the excellent work conducted by the European Network and Information Security Agency, and in particular with the work undertaken to understand security concerns associated with the cloud. Within these working groups there was no time wasted arguing various definitions, as the grounding already existed. It is for that matter the start of this particular book has focused in restating such definitions, which, while may be frustrating for those of you already familiar with such principles, is important.

ECONOMIC OPPORTUNITIES FOR CLOUD COMPUTING

Recent comments by David Mundell, the Under Secretary of State for Scotland, claimed that cloud computing is vital for Scotland's economic growth.[11] In fact, his comments are not isolated, as many others in public office across the globe see the potential benefits that cloud computing can have on the macroenvironment such as the economic conditions for an entire nation. This not only refers to the potential cost savings that the technology can have on prospective customers, such as those highlighted in the M-Cloud implementation, but also includes the wealth generation (including new jobs) by such services. It is intended to focus on the macro benefits that cloud can bring, and then analyze some real-world implementations of cloud deployments to focus on the micro benefits felt by customers.

Macro Benefits of Cloud Computing

To really understand the level of expectation placed upon cloud computing, one only has to read the recent report published by the European Commission entitled "Unleashing the Potential of Cloud Computing in Europe."[12] Within this report, it anticipates the potential impact of cloud computing could result in "EUR 45 billion of direct spend on Cloud Computing in the EU in 2020 as well as an overall cumulative impact on GDP of EUR 957 billion, and 3.8 million jobs, by 2020." Of course, to achieve such forecasts there are a number of key actions that the European Commission have identified need to be addressed. This includes not only resolving some of the market challenges associated with cloud computing, but also implementing policies that are regarded as "cloud friendly." This includes the need to establish a digital single market. It is forecasted that the implementation of cloud-friendly policies would generate an estimated EUR250bn in gross domestic product (GDP) by 2020, whereas failure to implement such policies would yield a return of EUR88bn. Further, the cumulative impact of implementing such policies equates to EUR940 between 2015 and 2020; this is in contrast to EUR357bn with a no-intervention strategy. Such estimates are based on research conducted by the International Data Corporation (IDC) on behalf of the European Union in the report entitled "Quantitative Estimates of the Demand for Cloud Computing in Europe and the Likely Barriers to Take-up."[13]

In terms of the specific policy actions required to realize such enormous economic benefits within Europe, the following have been identified as enabling a "cloud proactive environment":

- Harmonizing data protection and privacy protection regulation across the European Union, so that CSPs and users are sure that the same regulations are respected, no matter where the data are
- Clarifying data jurisdiction regulation and providing European Union-wide guidelines about which laws apply to data stored in the EU MS
- Promoting common standards and interoperability of cloud systems, so that portability of data and processes between cloud vendors is possible and lock-in in proprietary systems is prevented
- Establishing clear and harmonized principles around CSPs' accountability and liability for security breaches, no matter which country they are from
- Developing European Union-wide certification of cloud service vendors on their security and data protection arrangements and compliance with main regulations, to build trust in the offerings; this is specifically requested by the public sector, where ensuring compliance is a priority.

Subsequent chapters will focus on many of these requirements in greater detail; however, these concepts are introduced here to highlight the potentially enormous macro benefits the cloud can yield. Indeed, outside of these staggering sums of money, the potential benefit in terms of jobs can be as much as the creation of 2.5 million extra jobs.

Such a positive economic forecast shows exactly why in Europe so much attention has been placed on the creation of a cloud-friendly environment.

The macro economic opportunities that cloud computing represents is of course one potentially benefitting many geographies, and not only Europe, and its importance on the future economic prosperity has led to the development of policies enabling it a cloud proactive environment. Other government bodies that have focused their efforts on maximizing the benefits of cloud computing include the Australian Government. In their May 2013 "National Cloud Computing Strategy,"[14] three core goals were identified in order to realize the "promise of cloud computing." These three goals are

1. Maximizing the value of cloud computing in the government
2. Promoting cloud computing to small businesses, not-for-profits, and consumers
3. Supporting a vibrant cloud services sector

Modeling cited within the strategy expect that the "increased adoption of cloud services across the Australian economy would grow annual GDP by $3.3 billion by 2020."

What this and other cloud computing strategies published by government bodies demonstrate is that the cloud will generate economic opportunities for nations. Although the number of cloud-related jobs is expected to increase, it is worth noting that fulfilling such roles may prove somewhat problematic. The reason for this was demonstrated by a recent study undertaken by the IDC and sponsored by Microsoft that showed over 1.7 million jobs related to cloud computing were unfulfilled at the end of 2012.[15] Indeed, further detail[16] into the research confirms the expectation that the number of jobs within cloud computing will increase significantly in the years ahead. Demand for information technology (IT) professionals who are "cloud ready" is expected to grow by 26% annually to 2015. Such growth will be experienced in specific geographic regions, in particular the emerging markets (Latin America, Central and Eastern Europe, the Middle East, and Asia Pacific), which are expected to account for 40% of all cloud-related jobs, and are predicted to grow at 34% annually to 2015. In Europe, Middle-East, Africa (EMEA), the growth is also impressive, with jobs expected to grow by 24% annually to 2015. Although it is predicted to account for a total of 1.4 million jobs, it is somewhat off the target set by the European Union (this of course can be attributed to the fact the European Union cited their potential growth to 2020, and as a best case scenario with the development of a cloud friendly environment). In North America, growth for cloud-related jobs is expected to reach 22% per annum from 2012, to 2.7 million jobs by 2015.

The potential lack of skills represents a significant risk with regards to the realization of such global employment gains. In terms of the types of skills/competencies sought, respondents within the study were asked to rate the most important. The findings are rated in terms of importance:

- Risks and consequences of cloud computing
- Clouds impact on IT service management
- Steps to successful adoption of cloud computing
- Business and IT perspectives of cloud computing
- Business value of cloud computing
- Technical alternatives in cloud implementation

What this clearly shows is that the skills related to risk management, and ultimately securing cloud, are cited as the most important competencies for prospective cloud customers. This bodes well for the reader, because the intention of the book is to put forward the controls required to secure cloud computing. Consider the number of new roles, and the fact that determining the risk associated with cloud implementation is the most sought after competency, and the decision to buy, and read this book can be seen as an excellent investment.

While the previous studies have largely focused on the expected number of open jobs related to cloud computing, and indeed within certain geographies, we should provide evidence on the global demand for cloud computing. There are of course a multitude of reports forecasting varying degrees of growth; therefore, we were somewhat spoilt for choice in the proceeding paragraphs.

In 2011, Morgan Stanley published their Blue Paper examining the growth within cloud computing.[17] Forecasts from within the research identified the following.

Public cloud adoption: It is predicted that the workload within the public cloud could increase at a compound annual growth rate (CAGR) of 50% within the next 3 years. This prediction is based upon a series of interviews undertaken by the research team of 300 decision makers, whereby 51% expect to use public cloud within 3 years. This is up from the current 28%.

Server growth shifts to the cloud: More servers are expected to be shipped into public cloud infrastructures, an earlier forecast for example predicted at an annual compound growth rate of 60% (to 2013). This of course will be based on the transition of workloads from on-premise to public cloud environments. To give an example of the scale, in 2013, then Microsoft Chief Executive Officer (CEO) Steve Ballmer provided a rare insight into the operations of the largest cloud providers: "We have something over a million servers in our datacenter" he went on to say "Google is bigger and Amazon is a little bit smaller."[18]

Now of course this top-level figure fails to provide a breakdown over the specific functions of the servers. This does, however, put the scale of operations behind the likes of popular cloud services such as Hotmail, Azure, and Office 365 into context. Another way of looking at the scale is presented by Sebastian Anthony: "At roughly 200 watts per server, plus perhaps another 50 watts of overhead (cooling, distribution losses, routers), that's a total power consumption of 250 megawatts—or around two terawatt-hours (TWh) per year. That's about the same amount of power used by 177,000 average US homes (at 11,280 kWh per year). Assuming each server costs on average $1000 (some will be beefy, some will be wimpy), that's $1 billion of capital expenditure— and that's before you build the data centers. Data centers are usually priced by the megawatt, with modern data centers coming in at around $10 million per megawatt. 250 megawatts, then, equates to $2.5 billion."

On-premise server growth on decline: Respondents anticipate spending on servers for on-premise installations to reduce by 8.6% over the next 3 years.

Beyond these forecasts, which of course by the time the book is published are likely to have been proven right or wrong, is also predicted continued growth for cloud computing. Analyst firm Gartner[19] anticipates a CAGR of 17.7% through to 2016, which would mean the market is expected to grow from $76.9 billion in 2010 to $210 billion in 2016. Examining the growth of public cloud even further, it is anticipated that growth will be mainly experienced within the infrastructure-related services, which will include IaaS. Indeed, IaaS will be the fastest category of growth experiencing a CAGR of 41.3% to 2016. In comparison, PaaS is forecasted a CAGR of 27.7%, and SaaS 19.5%. In terms of geographic regions most likely to adopt such services, North America leads the way accounting for 59% of all spending, followed by Western Europe (24%).

These forecasts are not likely to surprise many. During the research for this book, we found many varying examples forecasting the growth of the cloud across many, many sources. However, there are a number of potential barriers that threaten to derail the considerable growth of cloud computing. One of the major barriers according to a number of studies is security. A study by IDG Enterprise, for example, found that "two-thirds of IT decision makers see security as the primary barrier to cloud adoption."[20] This is a recurring theme, with countless other studies all commenting on security as the major barrier to cloud adoption. The only difference between the various studies is often the total number surveyed, or the percentage that sees security as the main barrier, the one constant is that security is usually at the top of the list.

Cloud Computing—the Concerns

Developing a business case for cloud computing or any project will invariably call for practical information to measure the likely success of migration. This includes the return on investment and the total cost of ownership; more on these shortly.

Failure to accurately incorporate such information and indeed ensure that the implementation of the solution meets the expectations set out in the business case is likely to result in some very uncomfortable conversations. There does appear to be an entire industry overselling the benefits of the cloud, and failure to undertake appropriate diligence and relying solely on the marketed benefits is not the best approach.

Such a business case should not only address the business metrics, but also consider that many businesses have identified a number of barriers toward cloud adoption. Many of these barriers are documented in the KPMG report entitled "Breaking through the cloud adoption barriers"[21] and are based on a survey of 179 CSPs to understand the perceived barriers to cloud adoption. As mentioned previously, the presentation of supporting figures underlining the financial benefits of cloud computing is imperative in the development of a business case, and indeed the findings from the survey would support this theory. Providers certainly believe that cost reduction is the single most important factor in any decision toward cloud adoption, with 60% of providers believing this being the main goal. Perhaps more insightful than this statistic is that only 39% of providers believed that customer expectations on cost reduction is realistic, which again reinforces points raised earlier.

While much of this chapter has focused on the benefits of cloud computing, there is no doubt that many concerns do exist. The survey identifies that many of the barriers toward cloud adoption surround security and privacy. This reinforces many earlier studies in which security is perceived as the greatest barrier toward cloud adoption, and explains why cloud security skills are perceived as so important. The top 10 perceived barriers are detailed in Table 1.1.

Table 1.1 Perceived Barriers toward Cloud Adoption

Loss of control	48%
Integration with existing architecture	41%
Data loss and privacy risks	39%
Not sure the promise of a cloud environment can be realized	28%
Implementation/transition/integration costs to high	28%
Risk of intellectual property theft	27%
Lack of standards between cloud providers (interoperability)	25%
Legal and regulatory compliance	22%
Transparency of operational controls and data	22%
Lack of visibility into future demand, associated costs	21%

While the perceived barriers are likely to include some of the well-known concerns, the order may surprise many. Indeed, if we compare the perceived barriers with those that are reported by end customers, not only are there certain barriers not included within the top 10 above, but also their order in terms of importance does vary.

Security plays a recurring concern within multiple end-customer surveys regarding concerns/barriers toward cloud adoption, as do concerns about data privacy. Based on a survey of 489 "business leaders," the PwC report entitled "The Future of IT Outsourcing and Cloud Computing"[22] asked a series of questions to respondents across multiple geographies, industry verticals, and company sizes relating to cloud adoption.

When asked about concerns regarding data security, respondents believed it represented the biggest risk to infrastructure in the public cloud. Indeed, 62% of respondents believed data security as either a serious or an extremely serious risk. In comparison, other concerns were not rated nearly as highly, with the next risk only garnering 40% of the overall response, which interestingly was data and systems interoperability. These findings align rather closely with the view of CSPs; however, the subsequent risks did not correlate as well. In particular, the next risks were data portability (41%), viability of third parties (40%), IT governance (39%), and service level agreements (35%). The third risk relating to data and systems portability is well documented within cloud computing, whereby the concern that migrating to one provider will lead to the customer being locked into that provider for the long term, which of course is very much related to the viability of the provider. What this means is that once a customer has moved to one particular cloud provider, and spent time and money transitioning their services to this provider, they will find it very difficult to move those services elsewhere. The motivation to migrate from a cloud provider may be due to a number of reasons: whether the provider is not meeting the expectations of the customer, has gone out of business, or for any other reason. History is littered with multiple examples where either these or other scenarios have resulted (we present a large number of these throughout this book) in the customer having to find an alternate provider. This concern may be the last thing potential cloud customers think of when considering which provider to engage with, because the Web site of the provider seemed so convincing, or the customer service team at the provider was so responsive and helpful, but it is important to consider the what if scenario.

Viability of Provider

This exact same scenario was played out for customers of Pano Logic, a provider of virtual desktop infrastructures and other cloud-related services. It was reported in late 2012[23] that customers had no indication or prior warning that any problem existed, that was until they could no longer access the services that they had paid for. According to journalist David Marshall who reported on the story,[24] there was no formal announcement, and customers took to social media asking whether a problem did indeed exist. The concern was raised shortly after October 22, 2012, when the company sent their final tweet regarding a customer who was using their technology. Thereafter, there was complete silence. This led to rumors and conjecture with many voicing questions about the company, where customers took to social media with tweets such as "is panologic dead??" and "hello are you still with us?" Both Twitter and Facebook were used to ask questions about the company "because e-mail and phone calls were evidently going unanswered." In fact, comments from the community seemed to suggest that there was indeed a problem, with one individual stating they had driven to the company's headquarters only to discover it was "all closed up." What we do now know is that the company failed in October of 2012, and in early 2013, another organization confirmed they had secured the rights to support Pano Logic customers, and will "help transition the customer base to a new platform."[25]

This example demonstrates why the viability of the third-party provider can be considered such a major barrier toward cloud adoption, and does indeed go some way to explain the number one perceived barrier toward cloud adoption (as indicated by providers), which is the loss of control. If you are hosting services on-premise, then at the very least you will (or should) know that there are potentially some difficulties that may impact service. When migrating any service to a third party, whether that is a cloud provider or a traditional outsourcing company, there is always the risk that you have zero visibility as to the state of the provider as Pano Logic customers can attest to. However, financial considerations are not the only reason that the viability of a CSP can be impacted, as customers of MegaUpload can attest to.

Established in 2005 in Hong Kong, as an online file storage (and viewing) service, MegaUpload garnered an enormous user base. At the time of its service being shutdown, it was able to boast 180,000,000 registered users and at its peak was the 13th most visited site on the Internet. However, the service ceased amidst accusations the service facilitated large volumes of illegal downloads of copyrighted material, costing the owners of such copyrights at least $500 million in lost revenue. While we could dedicate this chapter, and indeed many of the proceeding chapters on the case, the impact on the end customer when its cloud provider is no longer viable is the focus of this particular section.

When the service was shut down by the US Department of Justice on January 19, 2012, authorities reportedly seized 25 petabytes of data. For customers, however, the issue was compounded when it was reported that a Dutch hosting company deleted data stored on 630 servers rented by MegaUpload, which led to founder Kim Dotcom calling it a "huge disaster."[26] For those cloud customers breathing a sigh of relief in the belief that their data was not among the purge, attempts by MegaUpload to acquire 1103 servers owned by Carpathia Hosting have at the time of writing not proven successful. In April 2013, MegaUpload reached an agreement with Carpathia to buy the servers and ultimately preserve the data stored. However, this was reported to have been blocked by authorities, forcing founder Dotcom to issue the following statement:

> "The destruction of the LeaseWeb servers demonstrates the urgent need to reach a workable solution for data preservation as soon as possible, lest the 1103 servers currently in Carpathia Hosting's possession meet the same fate," it concludes. "We therefore respectfully urge the Court to reconvene the interested stakeholders and renew negotiations as quickly as the Court's schedule permits."[23]

What this and the earlier example clearly demonstrate is that when utilizing any third-party services, there is undoubtedly a loss of control, and should such providers experience financial issues, or indeed face the ire of regulators, the customer may indeed be the last to know. While, of course, there are many CSPs that remain entirely financially viable, and are nowhere near facing the actions undertaken by authorities as in the case of MegaUpload, there is no doubt that the attention these examples received has resulted in serious concerns. After all, as a cloud customer, the implications of not being able to access data could be the death knell for a business, and something Kyle Goodwin can attest to. Goodwin used MegaUpload as a backup service for his business as an Ohio videographer. However, the combined actions of US authorities and a hard drive failure have meant that Goodwin has lost "valuable commercial footage" and is forced to undergo a number of court hearings to recover these data. Despite the fact that his case is supported by the Electronic Frontier Foundation (EFF), it does demonstrate as a spokesperson for the EFF cited as "the virtually insurmountable burden on innocent users seeking to get their files back by asking the court to do a slow-walking, multi-step process that takes place in a faraway court. Most third parties are not in a position to attend even one court appearance, much less the multiple ones the government envisions."[27]

Once We Choose, We Are Locked-in

Viability of a provider does not necessarily have to result in the said provider going out of business or facing scrutiny from authorities. In fact, simply increasing the prices of provisioned services can be equally debilitating. What may be unacceptable to senior management is the need to stay with the costly provider because the cost of transitioning to another vendor (or even bringing back to an on-premise solution) is far too high, or complicated. In an interview reported in NetworkWorld, CEO of RedHat stated on the subject of vendor lock-in as "Once users get stuck in something, it's hard for them to move,"[28] before unveiling measures his company were undertaking to tackle the issue. The interview does concur that lock-in comes in many forms, which can broadly be divided into three categories:

- Platform lock-in: The provider will leverage a specific virtualization platform, and the transition to an alternate provider and its preferred platform can be both complicated and costly.
- Data lock-in: This is very much related to the loss-of-control concern raised earlier, but the question remains who ultimately owns the data once stored on the cloud? Furthermore, how can the end customer retrieve the data should they wish to migrate to another provider? This particular concern is echoed by Bill Gerhardt, director of Cisco Systems' Internet solutions group's service provider practice, "We need to sort out data portability. Customers ask: 'If I give you all this data, how do I retrieve that data if I want to go somewhere else?' Many cloud companies don't have a clear exit route."[29] In addition to data retrieval, there are also concerns about data structures and architecture. For example, if I get .csv (comma separated value) files from my provider, I will need to understand data field relationships in order to migrate to a new Customer Relationship Management (CRM) system.
- Tools lock-in: This particular type of lock-in is considered the most common, and refers to the various tools to manage, provision, and monitor the hosted services.

Point of note: There is considerable concern regarding the aforementioned lock-in scenarios, and we certainly agree that these concerns should be considered when selecting a cloud provider (more on the selection of a CSP in Chapter 2). It should be noted that lock-in scenarios with specific vendors also exist in the on-premise world, and indeed at home.

David Linthicum summarizes the lock-in concerns in his Cloud Computing article published by InfoWorld[30]: "The reality is that using any technology, except the most primitive, causes some degree of dependency on that technology or its service provider. Cloud providers are no exception…As long as technology and their service providers' profitability and intellectual property value trump data and code portability, this issue will remain. It's not a new situation." Moreover, it is also worth noting that the market should punish vendors that use overt mechanisms to lock-in customers. Such market forces are recognized by vendors and operators as is highlighted by Oracle CEO Larry Ellison[31] in this interview appropriately entitled "Larry Ellison Debunks Myth of Oracle Cloud Lock-in": "But we cannot have lock-in; lock-in is a very bad idea. Once we lock someone in and charge high prices, you get mad at us, and you look for a way to break away from us. We watched IBM do that, and we think that's a very bad strategy. We get LAZY; if we don't give you choice, then we think we don't have to compete, we don't have to work so hard, we don't have to advance our technology. As long as we give you choice, you're not locked in."

THE CLOUD IS "NOT" SECURE

Depending on whose survey you read, the concern over security is probably one of the biggest concerns related to cloud computing. Perhaps we should not have included the results from the KPMG survey then!

Indeed, whenever we (not wishing to speak for my coauthor here, so perhaps using I would be more appropriate) present any topic on the concept of cloud computing, the first slide that is always presented includes the following quote:

> According to IDC,[32] 87% of respondents cite security as the greatest worry with regards to cloud computing.

According to the survey, concerns regarding security trump availability (83.5%), performance (83%), and even interoperability (80%). However, one has to really question whether such a concern is even valid. Indeed, this entire book is dedicated to presenting research and mechanisms that hopefully answer this question in the negative, but we have to ask whether rather than security being the concern, really the issue is about transparency.

Let us take Google as the case in point. Consider that, in 2012, it was reported[33] that Gmail (SaaS-based e-mail) had 425;million customers and Google Apps had 5;million customers. The belief that security is a major barrier to cloud adoption infers that the CSP has an unacceptable level of security. However, the opposite is likely and indeed in the case of Google one can argue Google deploys stronger security measures than those using their services. That of course does not mean that cloud is more secure than on-premise, nor does it mean that on-premise is more secure than cloud. This is because there is no "the cloud" per se. There are many companies that have a service termed as such that may not meet the NIST definition (as CloudSleuth demonstrated). The use of cloud computing involves entrusting third parties with corporate/personal data, and to do so with less transparency into the security controls than internally provisioned services. The use of on-premise providers will generally provide greater transparency regarding the security controls deployed than the use of cloud providers. Imagine the following scenario, for example: senior management asks you about the level of physical security protecting the company's intellectual property.

For an on-premise deployment, this is likely to involve a trip to the company's security office, a likely visit to the data center, and possibly the human resources department. Perhaps an oversimplification, but there will be some internal processes, and indeed accountable and responsible individuals who can provide the information or facilitate a tour. For the CSP, this level of transparency is not possible (or rather unlikely). Giving intricate details about the physical security is likely commercially sensitive (e.g., you would not want your provider sharing physical security plans with other customers), and providing a clause that gives customers a "right to audit" is unsustainable where there is a high volume of customers. The concept of transparency was introduced by Gartner analysts Jay Heiser and Mark Nicolett in their 2008 research paper entitled "Assessing the Security Risks of Cloud Computing."[34] It clarifies that the degree of transparency offered by the provider will determine the ability to undertake a risk assessment. Indeed, the best practices for cloud computing will include high transparency, with "the less information that is hidden the easier it is to trust the provider."

Whether the issue is security, or indeed transparency, what is clear is that there is a demand from customers to have assurance about the service provider. This includes not only the security controls deployed by the provider, but also their viability, and whether the use of their services will result in breaching regulations that govern their business. These are of course only a small subset of the assurance requirements that end customers will demand from third parties, and the cloud is no different.

Cloud computing does, however, have some nuances that do not necessarily present themselves within traditional outsourcing relationships when potential customers are attempting to determine the level of security implemented. This begins with the potential customer's journey in identifying and selecting a CSP. The reality of course is that the journey long before any review of the potential providers begins with the identification of internal business operations that are seen as suitable candidates for migration. The level of work to identify such processes/applications will be entirely subjective and out of scope of this book, as our focus will be on cloud security challenges and solutions; however, it is worth noting that as Dave LeClair, Senior Director of Strategy at Stratus Technologies, states, "Companies need to take a hard look at which applications they are putting in the cloud, then, consider what's involved in managing this shift from a resource, skillset, cost and complexity standpoint...we know first-hand these considerations are not a one-size-fits-all answer and rewriting applications for the cloud will not be the solution in many cases."[35]

END NOTES

1. *Today's Quote: Cloud Computing Is Crucial for Europe. Tech Assets* [document from the Internet] (April 2011), [cited August 2013]. Available from: http://techasset.wordpress.com/2011/04/15/todays-quote-cloud-computing-is-crucial-for-europe/.

2. *Most Americans Confused By Cloud Computing According to National Survey* (Citrix, August 2012), [document from the Internet] [cited August 2013]. Available from: http://www.citrix.com/news/announcements/aug-2012/most-americans-confused-by-cloud-computing-according-to-national.html.

3. Salesforce.com, *What is cloud computing?* [cited July 2014]. Available from: http://www.salesforce.com/uk/cloudcomputing/.

4. *Cloud Security Alliance* [document from the Internet] (2011), [cited August 2013]. Available from: https://downloads.cloudsecurityalliance.org/initiatives/guidance/csaguide.v3.0.pdf.

5. Peter Mell and Timothy Grance, National Institute of Standards and Technology (NIST), *The NIST definition of Cloud Computing* [document from the Internet] (September 2011), [cited August 2013]. Available from: http://csrc.nist.gov/publications/nistpubs/800-145/SP800-145.pdf.

6. *CloudSleuth. Friction In The On-Demand Self-Service Cloud* (April 2012), [cited August 2013]. Available from: https://cloudsleuth.net/blog/friction-demand-self-service-cloud.

7. Intel IT, *Implementing On-Demand Services Inside the Intel IT Private Cloud* (October 2010), [cited August 2013]. Available from: http://www.intel.co.uk/content/dam/doc/white-paper/intel-it-private-cloud-on-demand-services-paper.pdf.

8. Sreedhar Kajeepeta, ComputerWorld.com, *Multi-tenancy in the cloud: Why it matters* (April 2010), [cited August 2013]. Available from: http://www.computerworld.com/s/article/9175079/Multi_tenancy_in_the_cloud_Why_it_matters_?taxonomyId=154&pageNumber=2.

9. Nicole Laskowski, TechTarget.com, *Community cloud could fix data crunching dilemma for cancer research* [cited August 2013]. Available from: http://searchcio.techtarget.com/opinion/Community-cloud-could-fix-data-crunching-dilemma-for-cancer-research.

10. Centrul de Guvernare Electronica, *The M-Cloud Platform is officially launched in the Republic of Moldova* (February 2013), [cited September 2013]. Available from: http://www.egov.md/index.php/en/communication/news/item/1371-the-m-cloud-platform-is-officially-launched-in-the-republic-of-moldova#.UiMQp-BOTww.

11. CloudPro.co.uk, *Cloud computing key for Scottish economic growth, claims Minister* (August 2013), [cited September 2013]. Available from: http://www.cloudpro.co.uk/cloud-essentials/5910/cloud-computing-key-scottish-economic-growth-claims-minister.

12. European Commission, *Unleashing the Potential of Cloud Computing in Europe* (September 2012), [cited September 2013]. Available from: http://ec.europa.eu/information_society/activities/cloudcomputing/docs/com/com_cloud.pdf.

13. IDC.com, *Quantitative Estimates of the Demand for Cloud Computing in Europe and the Likely Barriers to Take-up* (October 2012), [cited September 2013]. Available from: http://www.idc.com/getdoc.jsp?containerId=prIT23744212.

14. Australian Government; Department of Broadband, Communications and the Digital Economy *The National Cloud Computing Strategy* (May 2013), [cited September 2013]. Available from: http://www.wto.org/english/tratop_e/serv_e/wkshop_june13_e/national_cloud_comp_e.pdf.

15. Mohana Ravindranath, Washington Post *Analysts expect growth in cloud jobs* [cited September 2013]. Available from: http://www.washingtonpost.com/business/on-it/analysts-expect-growth-in-cloud-jobs/2013/08/14/56d5715a-04fb-11e3-a07f-49ddc7417125_story.html.

16. Cushing Anderson, John F. Gantz, *Climate Change: Cloud's Impact on IT Organizations and Staffing* (November 2012), [September 2013]. Available from: http://www.microsoft.com/en-us/news/download/presskits/learning/docs/IDC.pdf.

17. Morgan Stanley, *Cloud Computing Takes Off* (May 2011), [cited September 2013]. Available from: http://www.morganstanley.com/views/perspectives/cloud_computing.pdf.

18. Sebastian Anthony, Extreme Tech, *Microsoft has one million servers – less than Google, but more than Amazon says Ballmer* (July 2013), [cited July 2014]. Available from: http://www.extremetech.com/extreme/161772-microsoft-now-has-one-million-servers-less-than-google-but-more-than-amazon-says-ballmer.

19. Louis Colombus, Forbes.com, *Gartner Predicts Infrastructure Services Will Accelerate Cloud Computing Growth* (February 2013), [cited September 2013]. Available from: http://www.forbes.com/sites/louiscolumbus/2013/02/19/gartner-predicts-infrastructure-services-will-accelerate-cloud-computing-growth/.

20. Michael O'Dwyer, Tech Page One, *Reluctance to change: a barrier to cloud adoption?* (January 2014), [cited July 2014]. Available from: http://techpageone.dell.com/technology/reluctance-change-barrier-cloud-adoption/#.U6bWR_1tc6U.

21. KPMG, *Breaking through the cloud adoption barriers* [cited September 2013]. Available from: http://www.kpmg.com/Global/en/IssuesAndInsights/ArticlesPublications/cloud-service-providers-survey/Documents/cloud-service-providers-survey.pdf.

22. PwC, *The future of IT outsourcing and cloud computing* [cited September 2013]. Available from: http://www.pwc.ru/en/technology/publications/the-future-of-it-outsourcing.jhtml.

23. Michael O'Dwyer, Your Online Content, *Cloud Service Provider abandons customers?* (December 2012), [cited September 2013]. Available from: http://www.youronlinecontent.com/2012/12/posts/news-articles/cloud-service-provider-abandons-customers/.

24. David Marshall, Infoworld.com, *VDI startup Pano Logic closes shop but keeps it a secret from customers* (November 2012), [cited September 2013]. Available from: http://www.infoworld.com/d/virtualization/vdi-startup-pano-logic-closes-shop-keeps-it-secret-customers-206275.

25. Wikipedia, *Pano Logic* [cited September 2013]. Available from: http://en.wikipedia.org/wiki/Pano_Logic.

26. Andy Chalk, The Escapist, *MegaUpload blames U.S. Government For Massive Data Wipe* (July 2013), [cited September 2013]. Available from: http://www.escapistmagazine.com/news/view/125712-Megaupload-Blames-U-S-Government-For-Massive-Data-Wipe.

27. Timothy Lee, Arstechnica, *Government: "Innocent" Megaupload user uploaded pirated music* (October 2012), [cited September 2013]. Available from: http://arstechnica.com/tech-policy/2012/10/government-innocent-megaupload-user-uploaded-pirated-music/.

28. Mikael Ricknäs, NetworkWorld, *Red Hat's CEO: Clouds can become the mother of all lock-ins* (June 2010), [cited September 2013]. Available from: http://www.networkworld.com/news/2010/060210-red-hats-ceo-clouds-can.html.

29. Barb Darrow, GigaOm, *Fear of lock-in dampens cloud adoption* (February 2013), [cited September 2013]. Available from: http://gigaom.com/2013/02/26/fear-of-lock-in-dampens-cloud-adoption/.

30. David Linthicum, InfoWorld, *2 more cloud myths busted: Lock-in and locked up* (April 2012), [cited September 2013]. Available from: http://www.infoworld.com/d/cloud-computing/2-more-cloud-myths-busted-lock-in-and-locked-191670.

31. Bob Evans, Oracle, *Larry Ellison Debunks Myths of Oracle Cloud* (July 2012), [cited September 2013]. Available from: https://blogs.oracle.com/TheInnovationAdvantage/entry/larry_ellison_debunks_myth_of.

32. Robert Mullins, Computing for IT by IT, *IDC Survey: Risk in the Cloud* (June 2010), [cited September 2013]. Available from: http://www.networkcomputing.com/cloud-computing/idc-survey-risk-in-the-cloud/229501529.

33. Frederic Lardinois, TechCrunch.com, *Gmail Now Has 425 Million Users, Google Apps Used By 5 Million Businesses And 66 Of The Top 100 Universities* (June 2012), [cited September 2013]. Available from: http://techcrunch.com/2012/06/28/gmail-now-has-425-million-users-google-apps-used-by-5-million-businesses-and-66-of-the-top-100-universities/.

34. Jay Heiser, Mark Nicolett, *Assessing the Security Risks of Cloud Computing* (Gartner, June 2008), [cited September 2013]. Available from: http://www.gartner.com/id=685308.

35. Thor Olavsrud, *How to evaluate moving legacy mission-critical apps to the cloud* (July 2013), [cited July 2014]. Available from: http://www.cio.com/article/736898/How_to_Evaluate_Moving_Legacy_Mission_Critical_Apps_to_the_Cloud.

CHAPTER 2

Selecting and Engaging with a Cloud Service Provider

The cloud service provider that you selected has just gone out of business. A letter has arrived at your door from administrators of the provider warning you that unless you provided a large upfront cash payment by close of business today then the data center will close, oh and by the way, if you do not want to pay and simply get your data back, it will probably take up to four months!

This may sound like a hypothetical worst case scenario, but it is exactly the position customers of 2e2 recently found themselves in.[1] Administrators were hoping to raise a total of £960,000, with smaller users expected to contribute £5000 each. Failure to meet the required total would likely prove devastating to many if not all customers:

> We have received a number of requests from customers seeking to gain access to their data immediately. Unfortunately, the levels of data held in the companies' datacentres are such that this process could take up to 16weeks and we will need to ensure that the integrity of third-party data and security is maintained.

Consider the impact this type of scenario can have not only on *your* business, but also on *your* career and credibility within *your* place of employment. After all, *you* did undergo appropriate due diligence did *you* not? There is no suggestion that 2e2 customers failed to undertake appropriate due diligence, and indeed the cause of the issue was financial and not as a result of a security-related incident. However, it is presented as a warning, that selecting and engaging with a cloud provider demands due diligence to satisfy not only appropriate regulatory bodies (where applicable), but also the internal organization, and in a worst case scenario the media and irate customers. This due diligence will likely include not only the security maturity of the provider, but also their financial viability (wherever possible), possible analysis into the directors of the company, etc. One option would be to adopt a modified Know Your Customer (KYC) principle adopted by financial institutions. The KYC controls typically include the following[2]:

- Collection and analysis of basis identity information.
- Name matching against lists of known parties.
- Determination of the customer's risk in terms of propensity to commit money laundering, terrorist finance, or identity theft.
- Creation of an expectation of a customer's transactional behavior.
- Monitoring of a customer's transactions against their expected behavior and recorded profile as well as that of the customer's peers.

While a like for like approach is unrealistic as this application is so very different to selecting a cloud provider, a comprehensive assessment is advisable as recommended by the Federal Financial Information Examination Council.[3] In their 2012 statement, they stated that "Cloud computing may require more robust controls due to the nature of the service. When evaluating the feasibility of outsourcing to a cloud computing service provider, it is important to look beyond potential benefits and to perform a thorough due diligence and risk assessments of elements specific to that service."[3] Some of the steps that should be considered under the Know Your Cloud Service Provider process should include the following, according to a paper by Peak the Cloud entitled "Tips for Selecting Your Cloud Provider"[4]:

- Solid reputation: This will involve checking for references from the provider's existing clients, and whether these implementations relate to the service prospective clients are considering. This should also include whether their implementations align with industry/geography where relevant.
- Best of breed technology partnerships: It is advised to determine whether the prospective provider has the appropriate partnerships with technology providers that align with the potential service.
- Financial stability and growth: This measure will determine the financial viability of the provider, and will ultimately determine on the willingness of the provider to discuss their financial state. This may be feasible if the accounts are publicly accessible, and will allow potential customers to determine if the provider has a history of stability and growth.
- Enterprise-grade data centers and state-of-the-art equipment: Where possible the potential customer should ensure that the infrastructure is capable of supporting the overall business. This will be a difficult measure to ascertain as the right to audit is generally unavailable.
- Compliance, availability, and performance: These measures will be covered in further detail later in this chapter.

Many of these tips address those that relate to the business viability and as such are out of scope of this book, with security and privacy considerations the focus of this publication. Further, dependent on the service sought not all of these measures will be required as the level of due diligence should be commensurate with the level of risk the organization is willing to tolerate. For example, where a provider is sought to host commercially sensitive data then the level of due diligence should be higher than if noncommercially sensitive data are being hosted. There is no magic formula with regards to the level of due diligence that should be undertaken, nor is there any specific methodology that must be followed, although certain frameworks for regulated data may either be advisable or required (for example, the Privacy Impact Assessment for personal data). Determining these factors will be entirely subjective; therefore, the following should be used as guidance and tailored according to the business (and business function).

SECURITY, TRUST AND ASSURANCE REPOSITORY INITIATIVE

One option afforded to potential end customers is to engage with each and every potential cloud service provider to determine the security controls implemented. In fact, in discussions with many providers today this appears to be the default method used by potential customers. Although such a method is likely to receive a response, it is an incredibly inefficient method for both provider and customer. For this reason, the Cloud Security Alliance launched the Security, Trust and Assurance Repository (STAR) in 2011.

As discussed in Chapter 1, one of the greatest challenges associated with cloud computing is the lack of transparency regarding the level of security deployed by the provider. In an effort to address this issue, STAR was launched to provide a central repository where potential customers can freely access to determine the level of security deployed by providers it allows. This provides a level of transparency that historically would have required more than likely multiple e-mails/calls to each and every provider under consideration. Now potential customers not only have a single place to go to understand the security employed by multiple providers, it also allows for comparisons to be made providers therefore improving assurance in the cloud.

The registry itself is based on three layers:

1. *Self-assessment*: The first layer publishes the result of the Consensus Assessment Initiative Questionnaire (CAIQ) and/or the Cloud Controls Matrix (CCM). As the name suggests, this particular layer has been filled out and completed by the provider. Therefore, entries on this layer

provide less assurance and transparency than subsequent layers. Please note that from March 2014, providers were given the option of using either CCM v1.4 or CCM v3. The opportunity to use both standards will remain until February 2015, whereupon all providers will be assessed against CCM v3.

2. *Third-party assessment-based certification*: The second layer publishes the results of an assessment undertaken by a third party on the cloud service provider against the CCM and International Organization for Standardization (ISO)/ International Electrotechnical Commission (IEC) 27001 (please refer to Chapter 6 for more details on ISO/IEC standards), or American Institute of Certified Public Accountants (AICPA) Service Organization Control (SOC) 2. Results within this layer provide a greater level of assurance, in that they are verified by a third party.

3. *Continuous monitoring-based certification*: Results within this layer are published in a continuous fashion. While previous layers would update the registry based on the audit or certification cycle (usually annually) of the provider, continuous monitoring leverages the Cloud Trust Protocol (CTP) to update as the name suggests, continuously! As the results are provided even outside of annual audits, end customers are given the greatest transparency and assurance regarding the security maturity of the provider. Please refer to Chapter 6 for more detail on CTP.

A review of the various layers would suggest to the end customer that it would always be prudent to use providers that fall into the third category. However, as mentioned earlier in the chapter, the level of due diligence should be commensurate with the level of risk an organization is willing to tolerate. Equally, this level of risk will depend on the value of what is being hosted with a third party. So the hosting of nonsensitive data could well suffice with providers that only offer self-assessment, but the hosting of sensitive data will likely require a greater level of assurance.

Accessing the STAR Registry

The STAR registry is currently located at the following URL: https://cloudsecurityalliance.org/star/.

A snapshot of the repository is included under Figure 2.1. As detailed earlier, the entries within the repository provides the potential end customer with a simple interface that includes the name of the provider, URL, an overview of the company, and when the submission was made.

There also includes details of the type of submission made; as the examples in Figure 2.1 demonstrate, the two providers have undertaken a self-assessment as well as certification. At present, there are four methodologies that providers can use to assure end customers; these methodologies, however, fall into the

Amazon AWS

https://aws.amazon.com/

 Amazon Web Services provides a highly reliable, scalable, low-cost infrastructure platform in the cloud that powers hundreds of thousands of businesses in 190 countries around the world. With data center locations in the U.S., Europe, Brazil, Singapore, and Japan, customers across all industries are taking advantage of the following benefits: Low Cost, Agility and Instant...

Read More..

Submission Info

Data Listed: July 20, 2012

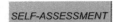

| SELF-ASSESSMENT | CERTIFICATION | ATTESTATION | CONTINUOUS |

Aria Systems

http://www.ariasystems.com

The Aria Subscription Billing Platform enables companies – from small businesses to enterprise organizations – to make the most of their digital commerce opportunities.

Read More..

Submission Info

Date Listed: December 22, 2012
Last Modified: July 30, 2014.

Additional Info   What is this?

Service category: *Backoffice*
× Service supports enterprise identity.
× Service supports file sharing.
× Service supports a mobile app.

FIGURE 2.1
CSA STAR registry.

three levels described previously. Certification and attestation both fall within the second level:

Level One
- STAR self-assessment: There exist a large number of cloud providers that have made self-assessed contributions to the STAR registry. This includes contributions based on the CAIQ, or alternatively the CCM. Both are referenced in this chapter, but with further detail included in Chapter 6.

Level Two
- STAR certification: For end customers looking for additional assurance, the opportunity exists to utilize level-two submissions where the security of the provider has been independently verified by a third party. Of the two options available under level two, STAR certification leverages the ISO/IEC 27001:2005 standard, in conjunction with the Cloud Security Alliance (CSA) CCM. As the ISO standard has been first published in 2005, ISO/IEC 27001:2005 replaces BS 7799-2:2002, which contains a

Table 2.1 ISO/IEC 27001:2005

Control Domain	Objectives	Controls
Security policy	1	2
Organization of information security	2	11
Asset management	2	5
Human resources security	3	9
Physical and environmental security	2	13
Communication and operational management	10	33
Access control	7	25
Systems development and maintenance	6	16
Information security and incident management	2	5
Business continuity plan	1	5
Compliance	3	10
	39	**134**

total of 134 controls that support 39 control objectives. Each of these controls and their corresponding objectives are divided into 11 domains (as depicted in Table 2.1). The standard has long been used by organizations looking to develop a formal security management program (Information Security Management System (ISMS)), and as such by incorporating the standard into STAR allows providers to leverage existing investments when demonstrating the security deployed to potential customers.

The third-party assessment can only be carried out by organizations that are certified by the Cloud Security Alliance. The assessment itself will indicate a score that indicates the management capability against the domains of the Controls Matrix, which will ultimately result in the allocation of a level that will either be classed as No, Bronze, Silver, or Gold.

- Attestation: While STAR certification focused on ISO/IEC 27001:2005 combined with the CCM as the framework by which the security is measured, attestation utilizes Type 2 SOC attestations supplemented with the CCM. Many readers are likely to be familiar with Statement on Auditing Standards (SAS) 70 auditing standard that preceded Statement on Standards for Attestation Engagements (SSAE) 16. Issued by the AICPA, the SSAE 16 provided three SOC reports for Certified Public Accountants (CPAs) to report on the controls at a service organization. An assessment by the CSA on the standard was conducted and published in the report entitled "CSA Position Paper on AICPA Service Organization Control Reports."[5] The assessment found "for most cloud providers, a type 2 SOC 2 attestation examination conducted in accordance with AT section 101 of the AICPA attestation standards is likely to meet the assurance and reporting needs of the majority of users of cloud services, when the criteria for the engagement are supplemented by the criteria in the CSA CCM. AT 101 provides the following key strengths for the cloud industry's consideration:

- AT 101 is a mature attest standard (it serves as the standard for SOC 2 and SOC 3 reporting).
- Allows for immediate adoption of the CCM as additional criteria and the flexibility to update the criteria as technology and market requirements change.
- Provides for robust reporting on the service provider's description of its system, and on the service provider's controls, including a description of the service auditor's tests of controls in a format very similar to the now obsolete SAS 70 reporting format, and current SSAE 16 (SOC 1) reporting, thereby facilitating market acceptance."

As with STAR certification, the benefit for providers is to leverage existing investment that they may have had with the AICPA SSAE 16 standard. By supplementing with the CCM (as with those that used ISO/IEC 27001:2005), the provider is able to demonstrate their security to potential customers without adoption of an entirely new framework. Moreover, for potential customers looking to migrate to cloud services, they can be assured that the framework used to assess security of potential providers is tailored specifically to cloud services.

Level Three

- Continuous: As previously mentioned, those providers that provide assurance via continuous methodology utilizing CloudAudit will be classified as continuous. This level is seen as providing the highest level of assurance because as the name implies it is continuous and not based on a point in time assessment. At present, this particular level is not available, and is expected to be available in 2015.

ENGAGING WITH THE CLOUD SERVICE PROVIDER

Once the decision is made of which cloud provider to use, the challenge for the end customer will be ensure that the security controls are clearly defined. Clearly defining these requirements within a formal contract is imperative, as it clearly delineates the responsibilities expected of the provider. Further, having these clearly defined will be important in the event the end customer feels the provider has not fulfilled their obligations, and should further action be required.

Service Level Agreements

The typical approach for organizations to define the requirements they expect of the outsourced provider will be to leverage a series of service level agreements

(SLAs). According to the European Commission's publication "Cloud Computing Service Level Agreements,"[6] an SLA is defined as

> A Service Level Agreement (SLA) is a formal, negotiated document that defines (or attempts to define) in quantitative (and perhaps qualitative) terms the service being offered to a Customer. Any metrics included in a SLA should be capable of being measured on a regular basis and the SLA should record by whom

These SLAs are likely to incorporate many more requirements than security, but should be detailed to define not only the expectations, but also how monitoring of these SLAs are achieved. According to the European Network Information Security Agency (ENISA) in their 2012 report entitled "Procure Secure, A Guide to Monitoring of Security Service Levels in Cloud Contracts,"[7] there is a difference in the ability of the end customer to negotiate SLAs with the provider: "It is important to differentiate between small projects, in which the customer will simply make a choice between different types of service and their SLAs (service level agreements) offered on the market, and large projects, where the customer may be in a position to negotiate with providers about the kind of service or SLA required."

Regardless of whether the end customer has the ability to negotiate service levels, as a minimum it is important to understand how the security controls will be deployed and monitored. Of course, the level of due diligence undertaken will be dependent on the value of data being hosted/processed by the provider. The guidance provided within the ENISA guidance provides "the most relevant parameters which can be practically monitored"; these are defined as follows:

1. Service availability.
2. Incident response.
3. Service elasticity and load tolerance.
4. Data lifecycle management.
5. Technical compliance and vulnerability management.
6. Change management.
7. Data isolation.
8. Log management and forensics.

It may not be necessary for the end customer to define, or even review, all of the above service levels defined by the provider. This will be entirely dependent on the type of service being sought; for example, within an IaaS environment, the end customer will likely be responsible for ensuring security patches are deployed on the operating system and applications. Subsequently, it is recommended to ensure that the scope of the project and customer expectations are clearly defined before any provider is engaged. This will allow any potential negotiation to be concluded more effectively, and where negotiation is not possible for the review of services to be more effective. It is recommended for the ENISA guidance to be reviewed to obtain further detail on the aforementioned parameters. Of course, that is the recommendation, and all cloud customers follow the recommended guidance, do they not?

Sadly, the reality is that many cloud customers fail to undertake the appropriate level of due diligence when defining the security service levels they expect from their providers. In a survey conducted by ENISA, and subsequently published in "Survey and analysis of security parameters in cloud SLAs across the European public sector"[8] the results revealed that, while availability is often covered, many security parameters are rarely covered. This survey requested content from information technology (IT) officers within the European public sector, and therefore the results reflect the implementation of cloud or IT projects for the European public sector.

The following are the key findings:

- *Governance frameworks/security standards*: While ISO 2700x and Information Technology Infrastructure Library (ITIL) were the frameworks/standards used by the majority of end customers, ensuring alignment with their third-party providers is rarely done. For example, only 22% of respondents stated that their IT providers are obliged to adhere to the same standards. Indeed, almost one in five (19%) of providers were not obliged to comply with their customers. Although it is suggested that this may undermine the ISMS of the end customer, not having consistency will likely increase the cost of managing (e.g., hiring subject matter experts to understand the standards used by the provider), as well as the efficiency of managing security.
- *Availability*: The majority of SLAs (50%) referring to availability ensures that the "service is reachable by all clients"; however, 1 in 10 have not defined availability. This is rather surprising as this particular requirement would be the easiest to measure and would be an important requirement regardless of the type of service provisioned. This would explain why just over the same percentage (11%) of respondents did not know what the requirements actually were. The majority of SLAs (37%) referring to availability dictated two nines or 99%, which would suggest that the majority of externally provisioned services were not particularly critical (only 8% required four nines or 99.99%). Equally, the majority of providers (70%) are obliged to report downtime within a given timeframe. Please see Table 2.2 for the percentage calculation, with the results from the ENISA survey.
- *Security provisioning*: While there is a degree of consistency with most respondents defining requirements for availability, security is less well defined. To an extent, this is not hugely surprising, as the services that are provisioned externally are not particularly critical (with only 8%

Table 2.2 Downtime Calculation

Availability	Downtime p/year	Downtime p/month	Downtime p/week	Survey Result (%)
99% (two nines)	3.65 days	7.2 h	1.68 h	37
99.9% (three nines)	8.76 days	43.8 min	10.1 min	19
99.99% (four nines)	52.56 min	4.32 min	1.01 min	8

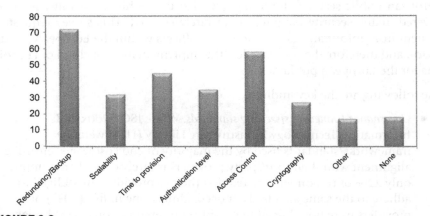

FIGURE 2.2

Aspects explicitly defined in SLAs.

dictating very high availability), but nonetheless the level of disparity among respondents is still surprising. Figure 2.2 shows the disparity regarding the components explicitly defined with the SLA.

- Security incidents: One example of a requirement that is not defined as consistently as availability is security incidents. A total of 42% of respondents commented that SLAs did not include a classification of incidents, and a further 32% stated they only briefly commented on how the schema works. Although other categories are entirely subjective in their necessity (e.g., take cryptography is unlikely to be required when the data managed by the third party is not sensitive), there is no question that the need to have consistency regarding security incidents will be important to all customers. In addition, only half of respondents confirmed that providers were obliged to notify of security incidents within a given timeframe, and in only 43% of cases did the SLAs specify a recovery time for incidents where the provider faced penalties for not recovering within the time specified. To put this into perspective, less than half of providers were obliged to notify customers that their data/ systems had experienced a security incident and even if they did the provider was not financially incentivized to recover in the time specified!

This sounds remarkable, and one could easily point the finger at the provider, but sadly this demonstrates that, although the customer is ultimately responsible for ensuring such measures are clearly defined, they are on the whole failing to do so. This could of course be because the service that is being provisioned is of so little value to the end customer that any form of interruption is acceptable (however, reviewing the responses regarding availability we know this is not entirely the case).

- Service levels: Building upon the lack of penalties applied to providers in the event of a security incident, the survey revealed that almost one in four end customers do not define penalties in the event the provider fails to meet service levels.

Message from Said Tabet (CSA Co-Chair of the SLA Working Group), "Within the CSA we recognize the value in SLAs as they relate to cloud computing. We are therefore conducting a lot of work within this space, and the reader is encouraged to understand the areas of focus for our working group."

When engaging with a cloud provider, it is recommended for the SLAs to reflect the security requirements of the end customer. The level of flexibility afforded to the end customer will be limited, according to the Cloud Buyer's Guide[9]: "A typical cloud contract will have little flexibility in negotiating terms and penalties — the only real option in a true cloud implementation will be a credit for downtime, with no enhancements for loss of business critical functionality." Subsequently, undertaking the appropriate due diligence in determining the security controls provided is imperative, this should be followed up with the SLAs, which according to the buyers guide "The single most important aspect of any liability and warranty statement revolves around breach of security and loss of personal data. The average cost per user of a data breach is approximately $215, so the liability language in the contract should ensure that the insurance coverage provided by the provider could cover the total fees for a breach where the provider is at fault. This liability clause must ensure that the provider WILL and MUST allow for a third party to perform a root cause analysis and be bound by the findings of the party. This may need to be negotiated prior to the execution of a contract."

END NOTES

1. Graeme Burton. Computing.co.uk. 2e2: *pay up £1m now or we close the datacentre*. (February 2013), [cited May 2014]. Available from: http://www.computing.co.uk/ctg/news/2242625/2e2-pay-up-gbp1m-now-or-we-close-the-datacentre.

2. Wikipedia. *Know your customer*. [cited June 2014]. Available from: http://www.wikipedia.org/wiki/Know_your_customer.

3. Emmanuel Olayaoe. Reuters. *U.S. Bank Regulators warn on due diligence in using cloud computing services*. (July 2012), [cited July 2014]. Available from: http://blogs.reuters.com/financial-regulatory-forum/2012/07/13/u-s-bank-regulators-warn-on-due-diligence-in-using-cloud-computing-services/.

4. Peakcolo in the Cloud. *Tips for selecting your cloud service provider.* [cited June 2014]. Available from: http://www.poweredbypeak.com/wp-content/uploads/2013/08/PeakColo-Whitepaper-Tips-for-Selecting-Your-Cloud-Provider-Peak-Branded-v1-1.pdf.

5. David Barton. Cloud Security Alliance. *CSA Position Paper on AICPA Service Organization Control Reports.* (2013), [cited May 2014]. Available from: https://downloads.cloudsecurityalliance.org/initiatives/collaborate/aicpa/CSA_Position_Paper_on_AICPA_Service_Organization_Control_Reports.pdf.

6. European Commission Directorate General Communications Network. *Cloud computing Service Level Agreements.* (June 2013), [cited June 2014].

7. ENISA. *Procure Secure, a guide to monitoring of security service levels in cloud contracts.* (2012), [cited June 2014]. Available from: http://www.enisa.europa.eu/activities/Resilience-and-CIIP/cloud-computing/procure-secure-a-guide-to-monitoring-of-security-service-levels-in-cloud-contracts.

8. ENISA. *Survey and analysis of security parameters in cloud SLAs across the European public sector.* (December 2011), [cited July 2012]. Available from: http://www.enisa.europa.eu/activities/Resilience-and-CIIP/cloud-computing/survey-and-analysis-of-security-parameters-in-cloud-slas-across-the-european-public-sector.

9. CSC. *Cloud buyers guide.* [cited June 2014]. Available from: http://assets1.csc.com/cloud/downloads/2647_13_CloudBuyerGuide_v8.pdf.

CHAPTER 3

The Cloud Threat Landscape

- The cloud threat landscape
- Notorious nine
- Additional threats

Outsourcing any workload to a third party will introduce risk, although whether the overall risk increases is entirely dependent on the provider and the security deployed within the internally provisioned service. Regardless of whether the service is provisioned internally or externally, there will always be an element of risk; this is because while the workload can be outsourced, the risk rarely is. As discussed in Chapter 1, security is seen as a major barrier in the adoption of cloud computing. Many of these security concerns would also apply to internally provisioned services and traditional outsourcing; there are, however, some threats that are specific to cloud computing.

In this chapter, we will review the security threats for the cloud based on the research conducted by the Cloud Security Alliance (CSA) Top Threats Working Group. It is worth noting, however, that the security considerations for cloud computing extend beyond those presented within the findings of the working group and are published as "The Notorious Nine":

1. Data breaches
2. Data loss
3. Account or service traffic hijacking
4. Insecure interfaces and application programming interfaces (APIs)
5. Denial of service
6. Malicious insiders
7. Abuse of cloud services
8. Insufficient due diligence
9. Shared technology vulnerabilities

The end of the chapter will include references to additional sources that define the threats to cloud computing. Many of the security considerations are "traditional threats," in other words, those that would exist both in internally provisioned services and within a cloud implementation. For example, the requirement to introduce appropriate physical security controls would exist in both internally provisioned services and cloud implementations. Within a cloud deployment, however, the customer will not have the same level of transparency regarding the level of security deployed by the provider. Subsequently, the controls deployed will likely be articulated as part of the security certification(s) and reviewed by the customer as part of the process of selecting a provider (see Chapter 2). Furthermore, the level of flexibility afforded to end customers regarding the implementation of security controls is generally lower with cloud computing (as was discussed in Chapter 2).

THE CLOUD THREAT LANDSCAPE

Utilizing the cloud provides organizations with many business benefits, but with these benefits come a number of threats. Some of these threats are the traditional threats that we are accustomed to while others are unique to the cloud. By better understanding the various threats that can face our data and services in the cloud we are better prepared to determine how best to secure them.

Before examining the various threats, it is important that we first understand what a threat is. There are many different interpretations and definitions for threats in the context of computer security. The Oxford English Dictionary defines a threat as

> (noun) (1) a stated intention to inflict injury, damage, or other hostile action on someone. (2) a person or thing likely to cause damage or danger. (3) the possibility of trouble or danger

In security fields we tend to focus on the second definition "a person or thing likely to cause damage or danger." However, we need to focus further into what exactly a threat is, particularly in relation to information security.

According to the International Organization for Standardization 27001 Information Security Standard, a threat is defined as

> a potential cause of an unwanted incident, which may result in harm to a system or organization.

Under the Payment Council Industry's Data Security Standard a threat is described as

> Condition or activity that may cause information or information processing resources to be intentionally or accidentally lost, modified, exposed, made inaccessible, or otherwise affected to the detriment of the organization.

The National Institute of Standards and Technology definition of a threat is given in SP 800-301 and defines a threat as

> the potential for a threat-source to exercise (accidentally trigger or intentionally exploit) a specific vulnerability

While the above definitions seem to be more relevant to the information security, the definition supplied by the European Network and Information Security Agency (ENISA) probably provides the most apt definition, in particular when taking cloud computing into account.

According to the ENISA,[1] a threat is

> Any circumstance or event with the potential to adversely impact an asset through unauthorized access, destruction, disclosure, modification of data, and/or denial of service.

Having understood what a threat is, it is important to appreciate how threats against computer systems have evolved over the years. This is not just so we can better understand today's threats but also so we can appreciate that as computing technology evolves and our business and personal use of it also evolves, so too will the threats.

Evolution of Cyber Threats

Since we first started using computers they have been under threat. Those threats come from various sources whether they are from those with malicious intent, from well-intentioned people making mistakes, man-made failures such as power outages, or indeed natural disasters. As our use of computers and the Internet has grown over time so too has the number and the sophistication of the threats facing those systems.

In the early years of computing, the main source of threats against computer systems were mainly from internal threats such as disgruntled or unhappy employees, or from the well-meaning user who makes a mistake. The other threats faced by these systems were from natural sources or man-made sources such as hardware failures or software bugs. This low level of threats was due to many such computer systems being isolated from other systems outside their own organization's offices and buildings. As a result, the threats against these systems were mostly limited to those with physical access to those systems or from disasters in the locale.

Over time, access to these systems became more and more frequent with companies employing modems and wide area networks to allow remote offices and users to connect to them. While enabling remote users to gain from the benefits of these systems, it also opened up these systems to threats from external parties.

At this stage in the evolution of computing, the external threats posed to organizations' systems were restricted to mainly individuals who broke in and explored these systems out of curiosity to determine how computers, networks, and systems worked. In the main, there was no malicious intent in this type of activity with the primary motive being curiosity.

In the 1980s, we witnessed the introduction of personal computers and their subsequent growth not just in home use but also within corporate environments. Over time, and as a result of these developments, companies and organizations saw their staff becoming more and more productive as they moved from a centralized computing model to a distributed one. The growth in use of personal computers saw data being moved from being stored and managed on a central location onto individual computers located throughout organizations.

In parallel to this growth in the use of Personal Computers, there was also the growth in the use of the Internet. With the growth of the Internet, many organizations took advantage of its openness and global spread to enable them to promote their services, products, and their brands to existing and potential customers. Other Internet-based technologies also enabled workers to share information with others and to be more productive and effective.

All these new technologies brought many advantages to organizations and indeed to society and the economy in general. However, legitimate businesses and organizations were not the only ones taking advantage of these new technologies. Those with malicious intent also saw the opportunities in this brave new world.

In the early stages, the number of attackers looking for financial gain from stealing information from systems also started to increase. While the majority of online attacks still came from those with curiosity as their main motive, many others saw the Internet as a way to promote their political cause or other activism by attacking and disrupting systems to raise awareness of their cause, or by defacing an organization's Web site and posting their messages online.[2]

The threat posed by those with looking to gain financially also increased as they looked to extort money from organizations by defacing their Web sites and extorting payment from them to stop their Web site from being defaced again, or by stealing information from their systems.

With the dawn of the twenty-first century, we saw an explosion in organizations rushing to store and transmit more and more data on their computer systems, we also saw a surge in the use of the Internet by organizations to promote and sell their products and services. As companies rushed to benefit from computers and the Internet so too did those with malicious intent. As the value of information grew and the ability to steal that information through insecure systems equally grew, we witnessed a change in the online criminals. No longer a niche arena for individuals, or small numbers of like-minded people, cyber-crime now attracted traditional organized criminal gangs as they saw many new opportunities to make vast sums of money by exploiting weak computer security with relative low risk of being prosecuted.

This evolution in online threats was also mirrored by the growth in sophistication of computer viruses of the same timeline. The early computer viruses were not very sophisticated[3] and were primarily designed to disrupt the operation of the systems they infected, often in amusing ways, such as the cascade[4] and ping-pong[5] viruses. As these viruses were easily detected due to their disruptive nature, they could be eliminated with the appropriate security tools or by rebuilding the system. Today, however, most viruses are specifically designed to go undetected as their raison d'être is no longer to cause disruption. Instead, criminals create these viruses to go undetected on infected systems so they can be used to steal valuable data such as sensitive financial data, logon credentials to financial systems, or valuable information such as an organizations' intellectual property.

The modern computer virus is also designed not to just steal information but also to enable online criminals use infected computers in other criminal enterprises such as spending spam e-mails, infecting other computers, and extorting money from companies by using the infected computers under their control to take part in a distributed denial of service (DDoS).

Computer viruses are also being developed as advanced weapons to silently attack targets. The Stuxnet[6] virus is a prime example of how a computer virus can be used to silently disrupt the operations of critical target. We will no doubt see further advances in the complexity and capabilities of computer viruses in the future.

As our use of computer systems has evolved so too have the threats facing those systems; moving to the cloud is just one more evolution in our use of computers, networks, and applications and while the traditional threats facing those systems still remain, there will be other threats that will evolve specifically against cloud computing.

Knowing and understanding what these threats are will make it easier to develop strategies, solutions, and systems to counter and manage those threats.

NOTORIOUS NINE

Data Breaches

Cited as the number one security threat for cloud computing, data breaches refer to the loss of confidentiality for data stored within a particular cloud instance. It is of course worth noting that such a threat is likely to exist even within an on-premise solution, or traditional outsourced solution.

The concern over the loss of confidentiality is entirely understandable, as the potential financial and reputational cost can be significant. This will be entirely dependent on the data that have been stolen; organizations will have many types of data ranging from intellectual property and sensitive business information to personal data (e.g., customer data). For personal data, according to the "2013 Cost of Data Breach Study"[7] conducted by the Ponemon Institute, a data breach (referred to as the theft of protected personal data) can cost up to $200 per record. This cost is entirely dependent on the country in which the surveyed company resides, and as depicted in Figure 3.1.

In terms of deriving the cost per record, costs were divided into two categories, direct and indirect. Direct costs are those that refer to "the expense outlay to accomplish a given activity such as engaging forensic experts, hiring a law firm or offering victim's identity protection services. Indirect costs include the time, effort and other organizational resources spent during the data breach resolution." Dependent on the country in which the surveyed company resided, the costs varied in terms of direct versus indirect. For example, companies surveyed in the United States experienced 32% direct costs compared with those in Brazil where direct costs rose to 59%. According to insurance company Beazley[8] in their small business spotlight, the greatest direct cost associated with responding to a data breach is the notification required. This of course is more relevant to those businesses that have a requirement to notify affected customers. In the United States, for example, and as of the time of writing, and according to Bloomberg Law[9] there are only four states without a data breach notification law; these are Alabama, Kentucky, New Mexico, and South Dakota. However, the data notification requirements across the various states do differ, with varying requirements such as notification triggers and method of notification.

Now of course, the United States is not the only country where data breach notification laws exist; under the European Union's Regulation on the notification

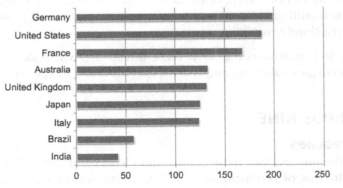

FIGURE 3.1

Estimated cost of breach per record (in USD).

of personal data breaches,[10] providers of publicly available electronic communications services are obligated to notify customers about data breaches. This notification must be done within 24 h to the national competent authority. Moreover, impending legislation, in particular in the European Union, is likely to increase the notification requirements for organizations that experience a data breach.

Notification is one cost associated with data breaches; however, as recent public data breaches have demonstrated, those affected companies have many other costs to contend with, and these may be either direct or indirect. Additional costs can include direct technical costs to identify the cause of the breach, and any remediation work to close vulnerabilities and prevent the issue from reoccurring. In addition, there are likely to be costs associated with the breach itself, such as the potential loss of business. Following the 2006 data breach experienced at the TJX Corporation in which $45 million credit and debit cards were stolen,[11] it was reported that the retailer had faced costs of over $256 million (these figures do vary greatly dependent on source; therefore, the more conservative figure is quoted here), despite initial estimates attributing the costs at a "mere" $25 million. While this level of data breach is certainly at the higher level of examples, it does provide an illustration of the impact an organization faces when experiencing a data breach, and subsequently validates the reason why it is rated as the number one concern when migrating to cloud computing. A large proportion of the costs from the TJX breach was related to the offer of services to its customers; this included credit monitoring services as well as identity theft protection. A breakdown of the estimated costs, and associated activities were presented in an article published by Wired[12] in 2007; while the actual figures in Table 3.1 may be disputed, it does provide an insight into the associated costs related to a data breach.

What these figures, or rather what these activities, clearly demonstrate are that the costs associated with a data breach can be significant, and any potential breach is quite rightly seen as a major concern. In addition, it is worth noting that some of these figures seem low and therefore it is assumed they are per record (e.g., cost per call is $25, but is likely per customer). From a cloud perspective, it is worth noting that as the risk is not outsourced, the remediation costs will be borne by the customer and not the provider. As discussed in Chapter 7, the data controller will almost always be the end customer and therefore they will be responsible for ensuring that not only is the appropriate due diligence undertaken but their own customers (data subjects) will look to them to remedy the situation. It may be possible to point the finger at a provider, but the truth is that the data subjects (whose records have been stolen) are not direct customers of the cloud provider and their decision to no longer work with the company they trusted to look after their data will affect the bottom line of the data controller. This is referred to as the abnormal churn rate, which can be as high as 4.4% dependent on geography and likely sector.

Table 3.1 Assumed Costs Related to TJX data Breach

Number of client records breached	45,600,000
Cost of detection and determination of response	$319,200,000
Internal investigation ($3.00 per record)	$136,800,000
Legal and external advice ($2.50 per record)	$114,000,000
Public relations and Investor relations ($1.50 per record)	$68,400,000
Cost of customer remediation	$1,140,000,000
Letters, e-mails, and phone calls	$25
Call center to address response ($5.00 per record)	$228,000,000
Cost per call	$25
Percentage of clients that call	20
Credit watch per year	$50
Years of credit watch	2
Percentage of clients that request credit watch	20
Cost of corporate remediation	$630,000
Fines	$150,000
Increased cost of audit/assessment oversight	$200,000
Legal defense and investigation	$100,000
Systems remediation	$180,000
Cost of down time	$100,000
Value per day of down time	$100,000
Number of days	1
Cost of brand impact	$700,000
Lost existing customers	500,000
Lost new customers	200,000
Cost of fraudulent use of data	$228,000,000
Average cost per compromised record	$50
Percentage of client records that result in fraudulent use	10
Total cost of breach	$1,688,630,000
Average cost per client record	$37
Probability of a breach	33%
Expected value based on probability of a breach	$557,247,900

Small caveat to the above statement: the provider could also experience a loss of trust if the breach is significant and public enough to negatively impact the trust of other customers, both potential and/or existing.

Other types of data can also have a significant financial impact. Research conducted by the Centre for Strategic and International Studies identifies the following categories in its report entitled "Economic Impact of Cybercrime"[13]:

- Intellectual property: "The cost to companies varies from among sector and by the ability to monetize stolen data (whether it is IP or business confidential information). Although all companies face the risk of loss of intellectual property and confidential business information, some sectors—finance, chemicals, aerospace, energy, defense, and IT—are more likely to be targeted and face attacks that persist until they succeed." From a cloud perspective, while personal data will demand due diligence, the hosting of data classed as intellectual property should be commensurate to its value. This should include not only the cost of the research, but also the opportunity costs such research represents to the business.

- Financial crime: "Financial crime usually involves fraud, but this can take many forms to exploit consumers, banks, and government agencies. The most damaging financial crimes seek to penetrate bank networks, with cybercriminals gaining access to accounts and siphoning money." The migration of cloud services, particularly for financial services will witness greater focus from nefarious actors looking to commit fraud by targeting systems hosted by external providers. This renewed focus was reported by CNBC when "cybercriminals acting in late 2013 installed a malicious computer program on the servers of a large hedge fund, crippling its high-speed trading strategy and sending information about its trades to unknown offsite computers." Admittedly, these types of attacks are not solely targeted at cloud computing, but demonstrate the threat landscape for financial fraud involves malicious actors that are very technically adept and well resourced.

- Confidential business information: "The theft of confidential business information is the third largest cost from cybercrime and cyberespionage. Business confidential information can be turned into immediate gain. The loss of investment information, exploration data, and sensitive commercial negotiation data can be used immediately. The damage to individual companies runs into the millions of dollars."

The loss of confidentiality for an organization can have a significant impact regardless of whether the data are hosted externally or are an internally provisioned service. Using cloud computing can have enormous efficiency gains, but as the example of Code Spaces (more detail under Data Loss) demonstrates, the need for security remains and indeed one can argue that with the volume and complexity of threats increasing the need for security has never been more important. Ultimately, the loss of confidentiality will impact the cloud customers significantly, and also be to the detriment of the provider.

Data Loss

Unlike data breaches, loss of data refers to the unavailability of data stored within the cloud for the end customer. We touched on the subject briefly in the first chapter using MegaUpload as the example; however, the legal status of the provider is only one example that may potentially impact the service.

Provider Viability

What do you do when our cloud service provider (CSP) goes bankrupt? This was a question that customers of Nirvanix faced[14] when they were notified they had 2 weeks to migrate their data. Posted on their Web site on September 30, 2013, customers were advised they had until the 15th of October to ensure their data had been removed.

Two weeks. It is hardly a sufficient time frame to analyze alternate providers, conduct due diligence, and then implement a migration plan despite the company providing a list of recommendations. Indeed, reports[15] suggest that the provider had many customers with over a petabyte of data and while official notice was provided it was a full 10 days after the reports began to appear in the mainstream press.

Recognizing the impact of a provider going bankrupt has led to the introduction of legislation that allows the end customer a legal right to claim back data from a bankrupt provider. Introduced in July 2013, the European country Luxembourg introduced Article 567 p2, of the Code of Commerce.[16] This allowed the end customer the opportunity to recover "intangible and nonfungible movable assets" under the following conditions:

- "The bankrupt company must not be the legal owner of the data but only hold it;
- The claimant must have entrusted the data to the bankrupt company or be the legal owner of the data;
- The data must be separable from the other intangible and non-fungible movable assets of the company at the time of the opening of bankruptcy proceedings."[9]

The associated costs of the recovery of the data will be the responsibility of the claimant; therefore, while the law provides the means to recover data the cost of recovery will need to be factored in. Although of course the law does include cloud computing providers, its scope is considerably wider and includes any third parties entrusted with customer data. Although a significant legal document, its global scope is limited to Luxembourg; however, it serves as an indicator that the legal framework is focusing attention on the viability of providers.

Insufficient Disaster Recover (DR)/Business Continuity Planning (BCP) Practices

The benefit of migrating to the cloud is that defining the level of availability is as simple as a line entry in the contract. This really sounds simple does it not? By stating availability as 99.999% and then sitting back to use the service safe in the knowledge that the likelihood of the service going down is so unlikely (because there is the safety of a sentence in the contract). Sadly the reality is very far from this perfect world.

What happens when the service level agreement regarding the availability of service is not met? Invariably, the response as defined within the contract results in credit being issued to the end customer. Depending on the provider this is likely to be a tiered model, with greater compensation/credit being provided depending on the amount of downtime experienced. While receiving credit may be an appropriate level of compensation for many provisioned services, for many customers getting 10% credit for an hour's downtime may not compensate the loss of service. This loss of service itself is most likely to be a result of a power outage, according to recent research.[17] Of the 27 publicly reported outages in 2012, the main cause for the outage was power loss, as depicted in Figure 3.2.

What was particularly interesting within the research was that the average time to recover the services from the outage was 7.5 h, and the examples used within the research used some of the biggest names in cloud computing.

Errors

While the examples of malicious actors involve a conscious decision to affect the availability of services, not all actions are a direct result of someone malicious intentionally looking to impact the availability of a paid service. There could be something as simple as a human error, for example, an operator inadvertently deleting something or powering down an important asset. While the action may be an accident, the result is likely to be the same, namely, the unavailability of data to the end customer.

Such an example was reported by ZDNet in 2011,[18] whereby a software bug resulted in the deletion of customer data. The status page from Amazon Web Services (AWS) at the time reported the following:

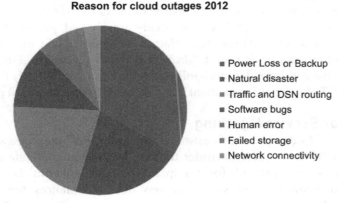

FIGURE 3.2
Research into reasons for cloud outage.

> Independent from the power issue in the affected availability zone, we've discovered an error in the EBS software that cleans up unused [EBS] snapshots...During a recent run of this EBS software in the EU-West Region, one or more blocks in a number of EBS snapshots were incorrectly deleted.[10]

The power issue in the status update refers to lightning that impacted European operations of AWS. Despite the power issue, the software bug resulted in a number of customers being without access to their data for a period of time. While the issue itself was not malicious the net result would appear to be exactly the same.

While these examples of potential threats to a cloud service can be mitigated by employing a secondary service, or with the requisite assurance that the provider employs sufficient business continuity practices, such costs should be factored in. Therefore, the cost presented by the provider is unlikely to be the total cost of ownership for the provision of an outsourced solution. Equally, the aforementioned examples are only a small snapshot of some of the reasons for data loss, one glaring omission are the actions of malicious actors, or "hackers" if we adopt the media definition. The recent case of Code Spaces provides a stark warning to organizations looking to leverage cloud computing without implementing the appropriate level of security. In June 2014, it was reported[19] that the company was "forced to close its doors after its AWS EC2 console was hacked." The company faced a DDoS attack in June 2014, and also an "Amazon Web Services (AWS) Elastic Compute Cloud (EC2) console and left messages instructing the company's management to contact them via email." Although they were able to change their passwords, the intruder leveraged backup accounts created in the intrusion. However, the "hacker removed all Elastic Block Storage (EBS) snapshots, Simple Storage Service bucks, AMIs, and some EBS and machine instances. Most of the company's data, backups, machine configurations and off-site backups were either partially or completely deleted, leaving Code Spaces unable to operate." Of course, this particular example could have applied to internally provisioned, just as easily as to those hosted with a CSP. However, as Nathan McBride, Chief Cloud Architect for AMAG Pharmaceuticals, puts it, "if you're going to put your eggs in the AWS basket, you have to have the mechanisms in place to really solidify that environment."[20] To be fair, this statement could be made about any cloud provider.

Account or Service Hijacking

As the case of Code Spaces demonstrates, knowledge of one's password can have serious repercussions. Consider the implications of someone knowing your social media password, for example, Twitter or LinkedIn. These issues have played themselves out with some very notable instances, for example, in early 2013, the Twitter account of Burger King was compromised and the attacker, in addition to sending tweets under the guise of Burger King, changed the logo of the account to that of its competitor McDonalds.[21] This of course is one of many examples and is not specific to cloud computing.

In a cloud environment this threat was one that was realized by Wired journalist Mat Honan who wrote of his experience in an article entitled "How Apple and Amazon Security flaws led to my epic hacking."[22] The article demonstrated the ease with which hackers were able to take control of key cloud-related services using simple social engineering techniques leveraging information that the journalist describes that "anyone with an Internet connection and a phone can discover." Indeed this information (at the time in 2012, and as reported by the journalist) consisted of a billing address and the last four digits of a credit card to encourage the vendor to issue a new password, and ultimately allow a malicious individual access to the target's iCloud account. According to an interaction with an individual the journalist believes was party to the hack, they then proceeded to outline the manner in which they accessed these two critical pieces of information to enable a reset of the Apple ID. A billing address in this example was straightforward as the journalist had a personal Web site, and registered the domain to this particular address. Therefore, a simple WHOIS search provided the billing address.

The last four digits of the credit card was garnered through a social engineering technique to the Amazon call center, and with that the attacker(s) had all of the information necessary to carry out a call to the Apple call center. What this example demonstrated is the ease with which the password mechanism was circumvented through a simple social engineering technique (the journalist confirms they repeated the social engineering tricks the attacker outlined with equal success). Clearly, stronger authentication mechanisms would have posed more of a problem for the attacker.

According to penetration tester Peter Wood,[23] the ease with which cloud credentials can be hacked is exasperated by the ability to log in from anywhere as the content is primarily delivered through a browser. He continued to highlight that "Spear phishing is massively increasing as a primary entry point technique," and noted the increasing use of social engineering techniques (such as those experienced by Honan). "We get social engineering attacks by telephone almost every week," said Wood. Of course, the rise of spear phishing attacks are being made simpler due to the relative ease in being able to research the target. With social media profiles offering attackers a veritable banquet of valuable information, delivering an attractive e-mail to the target to induce a click is really very simple. Indeed, such is the prevalence of spear phishing that according to security firm Trend Micro, "In an analysis of targeted attack data, collected between February and September 2012, Trend Micro found 91% of targeted attacks involved spear phishing."[24]

We could quite easily spend the rest of this chapter, and beyond, to dive into the rise and psychology behind spear phishing attacks. Tempting really does distract from the purpose of focusing on the specific threats impacting cloud computing. However, it is worth noting that broadly speaking, the majority of spear phishing threats will look to leverage the influencing levers. According to psychologist Robert Caldini, there are six principles of influence[25] that are used to convince others. In today's spear phishing attacks, it is not uncommon to see these principles being used, some of course will be more prevalent than others:

- Reciprocation: By carrying out a favor to someone, they invariably feel obligated to return the favor. Consider social media, when writing a recommendation does that individual feel obligated to return the favor?
- Scarcity: Something is more attractive when it becomes scarce; with many social engineering attacks using e-mail this principle is used. For example, warnings that an account may be closed unless verification is provided (e.g., entering personal data) use scarcity principles.
- Consistency: Once we have committed to something we are more likely to see this through.
- Liking: We are more likely to be influenced by those we like.
- Authority: A sense of duty of obligation exists to those in authority. We will invariably see this principle used through the use of e-mails that purport to be from financial institutes, for example, with attackers making great efforts to appear the communications are coming from the legitimate institute.
- Social validation: There is greater safety in numbers, and social validation looks to leverage this belief.

To meet this particular threat, of course, user education is an important approach. However, organizations leveraging cloud services should not only consider using stronger authentication principles, but also ensure that the service management (e.g., resetting passwords/access) have, and enforce strong validation against callers.

Insecure Interfaces and APIs

APIs within cloud environments are used to offer end customers software interfaces to interact with their provisioned services. There are multitudes of APIs available within a cloud environment; these can include provisioning new hardware and monitoring the cloud services, as just two examples. According to API Management Company, Mashery, there exist three categories of Cloud APIs[26]; these are

- Control APIs: APIs that allow the end customer to configure their cloud provisioned service. Amazon EC2 provides a multitude of APIs that allow customers to configure their services, as defined within the Amazon Elastic Compute Cloud: API Reference.[27] Examples include the allocation of internet protocol (IP) addresses, creating/editing of access control lists, or monitoring of specific instances.

- Data APIs: APIs within which data may flow into or out of the provisioned service. Such data flows can also be into alternate cloud providers, so that data can flow from one provider and into the provisioned service provided by an alternate provider.
- Application functionality APIs: Although the earlier APIs provide the ability to transfer data between alternate providers, or indeed management of the overall solution, the application functionality APIs can provide considerably more functionality that the end customer can interact with, ranging from the simple availability of shopping baskets to integration with social networking solutions, and considerably more in between.

While the flexibility of cloud APIs is not in question, and indeed depending on the source considered one of the driving forces behind the widespread adoption of cloud computing, there does remain considerable security considerations.

Indeed, these security considerations may not even be malicious, whereby an administrator may inadvertently invoke an action that may have significant repercussions. Consider the command available for EC2 customers entitled ec2-terminate-instances. As you can likely guess, this command will terminate an EC2 instance, the implication of this action is that the data stored within the instance will also be deleted.

In order to reduce the risk of such an action being inadvertently carried out, there is an opportunity to implement a safeguard to prevent inadvertent deletion using a feature available through the AWS console, command line interface, or API. Such a feature provides protection against termination with the DisableApiTermination attribute; this controls whether an instance can indeed be terminated using the console, Command Line Interface, or an API.

While such a feature, or rather attribute, is an important step in preventing accidental deletion of a particular instance, it is only one example of where an accidental action can have significant repercussions. A simple error such as mistyping the IP address for an instance is equally likely to result in the unavailability of the provisioned service, and does not have the luxury of an attribute to protect against the error. While of course the latter example is a simpler fix than the deletion of an instance, these examples do demonstrate some of the challenges facing the use of cloud APIs.

Other challenges facing cloud end customers, and their use of APIs, are also malicious attempts to circumvent authorized process. In a recent article published by DarkReading,[28] author Rob Lemos presents the security risks API keys present to their end customers. Such keys are utilized to identify applications utilizing provisioned services; however, should such keys fall into the hands of malicious actors they can be used to capture confidential data or rack up fees for the end customer. The issue has arisen not due to a weakness in the keys themselves, but rather the manner in which they are managed, whereby in particular implementations they are used to identify users, and as such are not protected by developers as assets that are critical to the business with examples of them being e-mailed and being stored on desktop hard drives.

Recently, the CSA chapter Switzerland (https://chapters.cloudsecurityalliance. org/switzerland) held a chapter meeting focusing entirely on service orientated architecture as it relates to cloud computing in which coauthor Raj Samani recently spoke. This meeting focused on the security challenges relating to APIs within a cloud environment and presented emerging research within this field. Emerging areas of research include the use of technology to enforce access policy, and governance rules as they pertain to the use of APIs. It is therefore recommended for the reader to coordinate with the chapter should they wish to get more detailed information about this very important (and sadly not hugely researched) topic.

Denial of Service

A Denial of Service (DOS) or its now more popular unruly child the DDoS attack is not a new phenomenon, and has plagued information technology (IT) managers for many years. It refers to an attack that aims to overwhelm the victim with network traffic or consume resources (central processing unit, Memory, for example) and subsequently prevent the processing of legitimate requests. The various types of DOS can be broadly defined into two categories:

- Infrastructure-based attacks: These particular attacks reside within layers 3 and 4 of the Open Systems Interconnection model (OSI) stack, but in effect intend to submit large volumes of traffic intended to overwhelm the target, and prevent its ability to respond to legitimate requests. It is now considerably easier to initiate such attacks. In the McAfee report entitled "Cybercrime exposed,"[29] DOS (or DDoS) services are accessible to anybody with access to a search engine, and can be purchased for as little as $2 per hour. Subsequently, the probability of such attacks occurring is increasing and this is reflected in the report published by Prolexic in their "Quarterly Global DDoS Attack report Q3 2013"[30]; compared to Q3 2012 the total number of attacks increased by 58%, with infrastructure-based attacks increasing by 48%.
- Application-based attacks: Unlike the use of traditional infrastructure-based DDoS attacks, the emerging trend has been for the use of layer 7 attacks (OSI stack). What this actually means is that rather than using network traffic to overwhelm the target, it would use traffic that appears legitimate. According to Prolexic, these particular attacks represent around 20% of DDoS attacks, but still a 101% increase on the preceding year.

When considering a DOS attack as it pertains to cloud computing, there are two main considerations: (1) the threat of DOS attacks against provisioned cloud services and (2) how cloud computing (and predominantly dedicated Software as a Service (SaaS) services) can be used to reduce the risk of DOS attacks. In this section, we will focus on the first scenario.

Denial of Service against the Cloud

The migration to a cloud computing platform should provide greater protection against such attacks than traditional internally hosted service. This at least is the view taken by the ENISA, their publication entitled "Critical Cloud Computing"[31] takes the view that "Elasticity is a key benefit of cloud computing and this elasticity helps to cope with load and mitigates the risk of overload or DDoS attacks. It is difficult to mitigate the impact of peak usage or a DDoS attack with limited computing resources."

This perspective is of course entirely valid, whereby a typical network-based DOS (or DDoS)-based attack should indeed be better mitigated leveraging a service with redundancy in its resources. Equally, with the probability for a DDoS attack against a CSP likely to increase, the provider will be expected to invest more in providing controls to mitigate the threat. Cloud provider Rackspace,[32] for example, provides specific DDoS mitigation services to customers that can be added as a subscription service, or on demand. Regardless of the pricing model, the service intends to undertake assessment against incoming traffic and in the event malicious traffic is detected transfer to a "sanitation engine" to filter the traffic and forward legitimate traffic to its intended destination. This is one example; other CSPs also offer such mitigation services but the challenge for any potential customer is the effectiveness of the documented solution. In other words, the true test of any paid (or even one that is included and marketed by a provider) solution to mitigate DDoS attacks is during an attack. Such experiences were documented by The Register[33] where code hosting provider BitBucket faced 19 h of downtime due to a DDoS attack on the infrastructure it purchased from AWS. According to Jesper Nøhr, who runs BitBucket; "We were attacked. Bigtime. We had a massive flood of UDP packets coming in to our IP, basically eating away all bandwidth to the box...So, basically a massive-scale DDoS. That's nice." Please note, that as a result of the attack "Peter DeSantis, vice president of Amazon Elastic Compute Cloud (EC2), said that they were definitely taking this lesson about the tardy detection of Bitbucket.org's problem to heart. He said, from Amazon's perspective, the black eye from that smarted, and the company would be changing its customer service playbook and network policies to prevent a reoccurrence."[34]

This encounter can lead the reader to think that the advice from ENISA is not entirely accurate, and this would not be fair. The likelihood is that if BitBucket were using internally provisioned services, and not Amazon, then perhaps their service may have been unavailable for longer, and their ability to withstand traffic not as resilient. Therefore, the ability of the provider (of course this depends on the provider) to withstand a DDoS attack should be more than that of an internally provisioned service. This is an entirely case-dependent statement. However, one risk that cloud end customers should certainly consider is the noisy neighbor concept. This particular point goes against the universally believed concept that the cloud reduces the threat of a DDoS, whereby the use of a cloud provisioned service means that the customer is sharing resources with other customers. This scenario was documented[35] by Rich Bolstridge of Akmai Technologies, who provided three cases in which the shared services approach negatively impacted cloud customers;

- Case 1: DDoS attack against Brazilian bank subsidiary
  An attack targeting the home page of a Brazilian bank's Brazilian site. However, as the Brazilian Web site utilized a shared network infrastructure, the US banking site was also negatively impacted. Somewhat ironically, the bank had invested in DDoS mitigation for the US Web site, but failed to recognize the threat of the shared network infrastructure.

- Case 2: DDoS attack against a Luxembourg customer of a US exchange
  A US exchange had a market data service used by a customer in Luxembourg to serve its clients. The application, however, came under attack, causing it to be unavailable. The service, however, was also used by the exchange's main applications for desktop clients in the United States, which ultimately failed.

- Case 3: DDoS attack against US subsidiary of European bank
  A DDoS attack against the domain name servers of a large regional bank in the United States resulted in the Web site for the bank across three continents also being impacted.

Therefore, to summarize, the threat of a DOS attack can impact not only internally provisioned services, but also that of CSPs. While the general view that the cloud computing provider should provide a greater ability to withstand such attacks, the probability of a DDoS attack will increase when using shared resources with multiple customers. To summarize, the risk will be reduced if the cloud provider has implemented the appropriate controls to withstand such an attack, but the number of attempts (some that may be successful) will increase.

Malicious Insiders

There exist multitudes of varying statistics attempting to quantify the threat of malicious insiders. While the exact number can be, and regularly is, argued, there is no question that the risk does exist; the only question is how big the threat is. According to the CERT Insider Threat Centre,[36] the malicious insider can be defined as

A malicious insider threat to an organization is a current or former employee, contractor, or other business partner who has or had authorized access to an organization's network, system, or data and intentionally exceeded or misused that access in a manner that negatively affected the confidentiality, integrity, or availability of the organization's information or information systems.

To be clear, this particular threat refers to the conscious effort to compromise information, or an information system. While of course this threat can affect individual organizations, within a cloud computing environment there are three types of cloud-related insider threats based upon the CERT Program,[37] Software Engineering Institute Carnegie Mellon University:

- Rogue administrator: An individual employed by the CSP who undertakes an action to affect the confidentiality, integrity, or availability of the service. Examples include theft of sensitive information or sabotage. Of course, there exist multiple examples of rogue administrators undertaking actions that circumvent the policy of their employer. In addition, such actions can exist even after the employee has left the organization, as was the case reported by InformationWeek.[38] The case refers to a former employee of Gucci who was accused of maintaining a Virtual Private Network (VPN) token, and using it to access the network of his former employer and "deleting virtual servers, taking a storage area network offline, and deleting mailboxes from the corporate email server." Within a cloud environment, CERT identifies four levels of administrators, each with differing levels of access, and subsequently the potential impact if they are malicious. The levels of access are, however, hierarchical, where the top-level administrators (hosting company administrators) have the greatest level of access.
  - Hosting company administrator: Has the highest level of access and therefore could cause the greatest impact such as updating the drivers of the virtual machines to compromise the images. Moreover, can implement network taps to perform man-in-the-middle attacks on all hosted systems.
  - Virtual image administrator: Could create alternate images outside of the authorized baseline, and that report they align with such baseline. Could also potentially copy virtual machines/disks, or modify individual instances of a virtual machine in a cloud so that only some of the cloud behaves the wrong way.
  - System administrators: Have the ability to conduct operating system attacks, and could update the virtual machine drivers to vulnerable instances.

- Application administrators: Have the ability to copy application data, edit the configuration of applications, potentially can gain control of the hosting platform.
- Exploit weaknesses introduced by use of the cloud: The use of cloud computing introduces vulnerabilities that the malicious insider will look to exploit. One particular example of these vulnerabilities includes a difference between the access control model between the local system and the cloud-based system. Also, another threat proposed is the replication lag exploit. In this example, the cloud environment potentially includes multiple systems that synchronize important information (such as pricing, for example). However, due to network latency, or that servers are located in different geographic locations, the replication of these data may take some time. Therefore, while the cloud environment removes the single point of failure issue compared with a single server located on premise, by understanding the replication lag issue the insider may be able to purchase items for less than the corporate agreed price. The example provided by CERT is as follows:
  - Company has server A that is authoritative for all pricing.
  - Server A replicates prices to servers B1 and B2 that have 1 and 2 s of latency, respectively.
  - Server B1 replicates prices to servers C1 and C2, these have 2 s of latency each.
  - Server B2 replicates prices to server C3 with 4 s of latency.

The attacker wishes to buy a $20 item for $10. Therefore, when a price change is scheduled, they will apply a false notice so the price is actually $10 sending to C3. Then by timing the purchase before the correct price is applied they could remove evidence of the incorrect price, and potentially evidence they circumvented the integrity of the system.

- Using the cloud to conduct nefarious activity: This example relates to a malicious insider who utilizes cloud services to conduct attacks against his or her employer. Indeed, research published by TechTarget[39] suggests that the lack of appropriate fraud detection capability within CSPs allows criminals to undertake activities on commercial providers without such activity being detected. The acquisition of services can be conducted using stolen credit cards, or as indicated earlier through account hijacking.

Abuse of Cloud Services

We briefly touched on this subject in the earlier paragraph related to malicious insiders; however, the abuse of cloud services extends beyond malicious insiders and potentially allows cybercriminals the ability to utilize such services for criminal gain. There are multiple ways in which cloud services can be used for malicious purposes.

Resource Intensive Operations—Cracking Passwords

There is no question, that for the malicious actor their job is considerably easier if their intended victims use very simple passwords. Remarkably, analysis from the breach of Adobe Systems found the most common password used was 123456,[40] and was used by 1.9 million users. Should the target not use a simple password, then the attacker will be faced with alternate means to crack a user password, which has in fact become considerably easier (or rather cheaper) with cloud computing. In particular, using the computing resources to undertake a brute force attack (repeatedly trying different passwords to find the right one), is made considerably more efficient with cloud. There have been many demonstrations highlighting the use of cloud computing to brute force passwords; in 2010, for example, German hacker Thomas Roth was reported[41] to have used AWS to have cracked passwords encrypted within a Secure Hashing Algorithm Hash. By using Amazon's graphics processing unit (GPU) instances, Roth was able crack hashes that contained passwords between one and six characters in 49 min, with the GPU instances costing $2.10 per hour at the time. GPU instances are a product designed for high-performance computing jobs that Roth describes as "known to be the best hardware accelerator for cracking passwords."

Other examples of brute forcing passwords via cloud computing include wireless network passwords; for example, in 2009, the service known as WPA Cracker was reported[42] to have checked a password against 135 million entries in 20 min for only $34. Wireless network and SHA1 passwords are, however, only a tip of the iceberg. There exists a multitude of services available offering computing resources for resource-intensive operations to brute force passwords over a cloud service. As we saw in the two earlier examples, some simply provide the core resources, but in other examples there are dedicated companies offering a simple GUI and SaaS service dedicated for the sole purpose of cracking passwords. There are also toolkits that give the potential hacker an interface into cloud resources for the purpose of using cloud services for brute forcing passwords. It is, however, worth noting that the use of commercial cloud services to crack passwords without authorization will breach the acceptable use policy for the provider.

Hosting Malicious Content

There are two elements regarding the hosting of malicious content: (1) using providers that have no issues regarding any (or almost any) hosting malicious content and (2) using providers to host malicious content circumventing the CSPs acceptable use policy.

The concept of using a provider that offers lenient acceptable use policies is known as BulletProof hosting. Such services have been used by malicious actors (e.g., those hosting content such as pornography or sending spam) for some time. However, the challenge of using such services is that they are often blacklisted by security providers and therefore the emerging trend for many malicious actors is to utilize commercial hosting services that are not blacklisted, and subsequently then able to reach all intended victims without security tools blocking the sending domains. This trend poses a challenge to commercial cloud providers as the implications of hosting malicious content could result in their operations being blacklisted, which will be to the detriment of existing customers, and ultimately impact profitability. There is also the potential for law enforcement action as we saw with MegaUpload discussed in Chapter 1 that may lead to seizure of equipment. The challenge of course will be for the cloud provider to ensure the customer is not using services for malicious purposes, this will be a challenge because signing up is automated without the need to interact with any human operator, all that is required is a credit card.

Subsequently, providers will need to establish mechanisms to determine whether fraudulent activities are taking place, but according to John Rowell of Dimension Data, "[There are] service providers that…do not have adequate fraud measures in place, and they have to be losing insane amounts of money on it. It's got to have an immense impact to their profitability as well as just the health and cleanliness of their platform.[30] However, the challenge will be the level of scrutiny toward customer operations in the provisioned service; one of the biggest selling features for the use of cloud is its ease of use. Indeed, many providers make establishing their services so simple that in many cases the IT Departments are not even aware (known as Shadow IT). By adding more checks and oversight there is the potential for customers to not see the service as simple, and to migrate to providers that may not be as onerous in their oversight. Therefore, a balance is absolutely necessary between fraud detection and ease of use.

Due Diligence

Migrating to the cloud is a simple and effective way to transfer existing workloads to an external party without the need to rush out and buy new hardware, install the operating system, hire administrators, etc. Indeed, the cloud is one of the most effective mechanisms to outsource the work for an organization; however, sadly the risk cannot be outsourced so easily as the failure to undertake appropriate due diligence will leave the end customer liable.

In particular, where personally identifiable information (PII) is hosted, there will likely be data protection legislation that demands due diligence when using third parties to host such data. In the United Kingdom, this is documented within the Data Protection Act, under Principle 7.[43] Under this principle, it demands that the end customer undertakes appropriate due diligence to ensure that the data processor (in this case the cloud provider) has the appropriate controls in place to protect the data. Furthermore, in the United Kingdom, the end customer (or data controller) will also need to ensure that under principle 8 the data are not transferred outside of the European Economic Area. While of course there are exclusions to using providers outside of this area, such as Safe Harbor, what these two examples demonstrate is that using cloud computing requires due diligence to ensure compliance against regulatory requirements, and that the risk cannot be outsourced because the end customer remains liable.

The intention may be to leverage certifications that the provider may boast to demonstrate security; however, regulators in many countries across the world have dictated this to be insufficient. The UK Information Commissioners Office recently clarified this position:

> The Data Protection Act does not stop the overseas transfer of personal data, but it does require that it is protected adequately wherever it is located and whoever is processing it, this includes if it is being stored in the cloud outside of the UK. While any scheme aimed at ensuring people's information is adequately protected in line with an organisation's requirements under the Act is to be welcomed, organisations thinking of using CSPs must understand that they are still responsible for the safety of that data. Just because their CSP is registered with such a scheme, does not absolve the organisation who collected the data of their legal responsibilities.[44]

This is only one such example from regulators reminding end customers of their obligation in undertaking appropriate due diligence when acting as data controllers. In the European Union, the Article 29 Working party published guidance[45] outlining the obligations of cloud computing customers in ensuring that providers adhere with data-protection rules. The Working Party, a committee comprising representatives from the 27 data protection authorities within the EU member states, also confirmed that cloud computing poses risks to data security, such as "loss of governance, insecure or incomplete data deletion, and insufficient audit trails or isolation failures."

Due diligence is therefore quite obviously imperative, and while the desire may be to adopt cloud computing just as quickly as the sign-up process allows, it is important to note the obligations to undertake a sufficient assessment of the risks associated with migrating to a third party whether in the cloud or not.

Shared Technology Vulnerabilities

One of the many benefits of cloud computing is the ability to leverage economies of scales by sharing resources across multiple customers. However, this very benefit also represents a significant weakness as this demands strong isolation to ensure that a vulnerability or misconfiguration in one instance does not affect other instances, and ultimately the entire cloud.

The types of risks associated with this category includes the failure of mechanisms associated with the storage memory, routing, and even reputation between different tenants of the shared infrastructure (e.g., so-called guest-hopping attacks, SQL injection attacks exposing multiple customers' data stored in the same table, and side channel attacks).

According to ENISA, the "likelihood (probability) of this incident scenario depends on the cloud model considered; it is likely to be low for private clouds and higher (medium) in the case of public clouds."

The impact can be a loss of valuable or sensitive data, reputation damage, and service interruption for cloud providers and their clients.

ADDITIONAL CLOUD THREATS

Of course, the notorious nine are the top threats as seen by experts. Potential customers should ensure that they undertake a comprehensive risk assessment to determine what "other" threats may exist. An excellent source is the ENISA Cloud Computing Security Risk Assessment[46]; this document outlines the key risks associated with cloud computing (with contributions from coauthor Raj Samani, and edited by Daniele Catteddu now of the CSA). The document outlines the following areas as the key areas of risk for cloud computing:

- Loss of governance: Where the use of cloud computing results in the end customer handing control to the CSP.
- Lock-in: Where it becomes difficult for the end customer to migrate from their cloud provider.
- Isolation failure: Relates to the risk of a failure in mechanisms that are intended to separate storage, memory, routing and even reputation between different tenants.
- Compliance risks: Migration to the cloud may result in compliance failure for the potential cloud customer, for example, the migration of personally identifiable data outside of specific regions.
- Management interface compromise: As the interface to the cloud service is externally accessible (via the Internet) and provides access to large sets of resources, the risk is therefore increased.
- Data protection: This relates to the due diligence threat as defined within the notorious nine, as it may be difficult for the end customer to "effectively check the data handling practices of the cloud provider and thus to be sure that the data are handled in a lawful way."

- Insecure or incomplete data deletion: This threat relates to the deletion of a cloud resource, particularly as it may not be possible to entirely delete the data. This may either be because the physical disk to be destroyed may store data from other clients or the additional copies are not available.
- Malicious insider: As covered under the notorious nine.

Cloud computing presents a hugely efficient and potentially cheaper option for many organizations. However, as this chapter indicates the risk to customers will always be theirs, and therefore it is imperative to undertake a thorough risk assessment to ensure that the appropriate controls are in place. As said previously, "if you are going to put your eggs in the cloud basket, you have to have the mechanisms in place to really solidify that environment."

END NOTES

1. European Network Information Security Agency, *Glossary* [cited July 2014]. Available from: https://www.enisa.europa.eu/activities/risk-management/current-risk/risk-management-inventory/glossary.

2. McCaughey and Ayers, *CyberActivism: Online Activism in Theory and Practice,* (February 2003), [cited July 2014]. Available from: http://www.amazon.com/Cyberactivism-Online-Activism-Theory-Practice/dp/0415943205.

3. Fred Cohen, *Computer Viruses: Theory and Experiments,* [cited July 2014]. Available from: http://web.eecs.umich.edu/~aprakash/eecs588/handouts/cohen-viruses.html.

4. F-Secure, *Cascade* [cited July 2014]. Available from: http://www.f-secure.com/v-descs/cascade.shtml.

5. F-Secure, *Ping-Pong* [cited July 2014]. Available from: http://www.f-secure.com/v-descs/pingpong.shtml.

6. Ralph Langner, Langer. *To Kill a Centrifuge* (November 2013), [cited July 2014]. Available from: http://www.langner.com/en/wp-content/uploads/2013/11/To-kill-a-centrifuge.pdf.

7. Ponemon Institute, *2013 Cost of Data Breach study* (May 2013), [cited October 2013]. Available from: https://www4.symantec.com/mktginfo/whitepaper/053013_GL_NA_WP_Ponemon-2013-Cost-of-a-Data-Breach-Report_daiNA_cta72382.pdf.

8. Beazley, *Beazley Small business spotlight; Data Breach costs* (January 2012), [cited October 2013]. Available from: https://www.beazley.com/.../Data%20Breach%20costs%20June%202012 .

9. Bloomberg Law, *Complicated Compliance: State Data Breach Notification Laws* Cited October 2013. Available from: http://about.bloomberglaw.com/practitioner-contributions/complicated-compliance-state-r.

10. Official Journal of the European Union, *Commission Regulation (EU) No 611/2013* (August 2013), [cited October 2013]. Available from: http://eur-lex.europa.eu/LexUriServ/LexUriServ.do?uri=OJ: L:2013:173:0002:0008:EN: PDF.

11. The Christian Science Monitor, *Data Theft: Top 5 most expensive data breaches* Cited October 2013. Available from: http://www.csmonitor.com/Business/2011/0504/Data-theft-Top-5-most-expensive-data-breaches/3.-TJX-256-million-or-more.

12. Wired.com, *Data Breach Will Cost TJX $1.7B, Security Firm Estimates* [cited October 2013]. Available from: http://www.wired.com/threatlevel/2007/03/data_breach_wil/.

13. Jim Lewis and Stewart Baker, CSIS, *Economic Impact of Cybercrime* (July 2014), [cited July 2014]. Available from: http://www.mcafee.com/hk/resources/reports/rp-economic-impact-cybercrime2.pdf

14. Wired.com, *IBM Cloud Storage Partner Nirvanix Files for Bankruptcy* (October 2013), [cited October 2013]. Available from: http://www.wired.com/wiredenterprise/2013/10/nirvanix-bankrupt/.

15. NetworkComputing.Com, *The Nirvanix Failure: Villains, Heroes and Lessons* (October 2013), [cited October 2013]. Available from: http://www.networkcomputing.com/storage-networking-management/the-nirvanix-failure-villains-heroes-and/240162664.

16. Molitor Legal, *New Luxembourg law on the right to claim back data from bankrupt IT and cloud service providers* (July 2013), [cited October 2013]. Available from: http://www.molitorlegal.lu/news/new-luxembourg-law-right-claim-back-data-bankrupt-it-and-cloud-services-providers-0.

17. GigaOm. *Power Outages are the Most Pervasive Reasons for Cloud Outages* (March 2013), [cited October 2013]. Available from: http://research.gigaom.com/2013/03/power-outages-are-the-most-pervasive-reasons-for-cloud-outages/.

18. ZDNet, *AWS cloud Accidentally deletes customer data* (August 2010), [cited October 2013]. Available from: http://www.zdnet.com/aws-cloud-accidentally-deletes-customer-data-3040093665/.

19. Beth Pariseau, TechTarget.com, *Code Spaces goes dark after AWS cloud security hack* (June 2014), [cited July 2014]. Available from: http://searchaws.techtarget.com/news/2240223024/Code-Spaces-goes-dark-after-AWS-cloud-security-hack.

20. Ibid.

21. BBC.com, *Burger King Twitter account hacked with McDonalds logo* (February 2013) [cited November 2013]. Available from: http://www.bbc.co.uk/news/world-us-canada-21500175.

22. Wired.com, *How Apple and Amazon Security Flaws Led to My Epic Hacking* (August 2012), [cited November 2013]. Available from: http://www.wired.com/gadgetlab/2012/08/apple-amazon-mat-honan-hacking/.

23. LifeHacker ITPro, *Why Cloud Services are so easy to hack* (February 2013), [cited November 2013]. Available from: http://www.lifehacker.com.au/2013/02/why-cloud-services-are-so-easy-to-hack/.

24. Warwick Ashford, ComputerWeekly.com, *FBI warns of increased spear phishing attacks* (July 2013), [cited November 2013]. Available from: http://www.computerweekly.com/news/2240187487/FBI-warns-of-increased-spear-phishing-attacks.

25. MindTools, *Caldini's six principles of influence,* [Cited November 2013]. Available from: http://www.mindtools.com/pages/article/six-principles-influence.htm.

26. Mashery, *APIs: the key to a thriving cloud* (February 2009), [cited November 2013] Available from: http://readwrite.com/2009/02/26/mashery_apis_the_key_to_a_thriving_cloud.

27. *Amazon Elastic Compute Cloud: API Reference* (October 2013), [cited November 2013]. Available from: http://awsdocs.s3.amazonaws.com/EC2/latest/ec2-api.pdf.

28. Rob Lemos, DarkReading.com, *Insecure API Implementations Threaten Cloud* (April 2012), [cited November 2013] Available from: http://www.darkreading.com/cloud/insecure-api-implementations-threaten-cl/232900809.

29. Raj Samani and Francois Paget, *CyberCrime Exposed: Cybercrime-as-a-Service* (September 2013), [cited November 2013]. Available from: http://www.mcafee.com/uk/resources/white-papers/wp-cybercrime-exposed.pdf.

30. Prolexic, *Prolexic Quarterly DDOS Threat Report. Q3 2013* [cited November 2013]. Available from: http://www.prolexic.com/knowledge-center-dos-and-ddos-attack-reports.html.

31. ENISA, *Critical Cloud Computing: A CIIP Perspective on cloud computing services* (December 2012), [cited November 201s3]. Available from: https://www.enisa.europa.eu/activities/Resilience-and-CIIP/cloud-computing/critical-cloud-computing.

32. Rackspace, *DDOS mitigation, prevention and Network security tool* [cited November 2013]. Available from: http://www.rackspace.com/managed_hosting/services/security/ddosmitigation/.

33. Cade Metz, The Register. *DDoS attack rains down on Amazon cloud* (October 2009), [cited November 2013]. Available from: http://www.theregister.co.uk/2009/10/05/amazon_bitbucket_outage/.

34. Carl Brooks, TechTarget, Amazon EC2 attack prompts customer support changes. October 2009 [cited November 2013. Available from: http://searchcloudcomputing.techtarget.com/news/1371090/Amazon-EC2-attack-prompts-customer-support-changes.

35. Rich Bolstridge, Asia Cloud Forum, *Risks underlying shared services DDoS* (August 2013), [cited November 2013]. Available from: http://www.asiacloudforum.com/content/risks-underlying-shared-services-ddos.

36. CERT, *The CERT Insider Threat Center* [cited November 2013]. Available from: http://www.cert.org/insider_threat/.

37. CERT. Insider Threats to Cloud Computing: Directions for New Research Challenges. [cited November 2013]. Available from: www.cert.org/archive/pdf/CERT_cloud_insiders.pdf.

38. Matthew Schwarz, *Fired employee indicted for hacking Gucci Network* (May 2011), [cited November 2013]. Available from: http://www.informationweek.com/infrastructure/networking/fired-employee-indicted-for-hacking-gucci-network/d/d-id/1097007?.

39. Jessica Scarpati, TechTarget.com, *For cloud providers, fraud detection is integral part of business plan* [cited November 2013]. Available from: http://searchcloudprovider.techtarget.com/feature/For-cloud-providers-fraud-detection-is-integral-part-of-business-plan.

40. BBC News, *Analysis reveals popular Adobe passwords.* (November 2013), [cited November 2013]. Available from: http://www.bbc.co.uk/news/technology-24821528.

41. Jack Clark, ZDNet, *Hacker uses cloud computing to crack passwords* (November 2010), [cited November 2013]. Available from: http://www.zdnet.com/hacker-uses-cloud-computing-to-crack-passwords-4010021067/.

42. Dan Goodin.*The Register Service cracks passwords from the cloud.*(December 2009), [November 2013] Available from:.http://www.theregister.co.uk/2009/12/07/cloud_based_password_cracking/.

43. Louise Kidney. *The Guardian. Navigating a tricky airspace: information governance in the cloud* (July 2011), [cited November 2013]. Available from: http://www.theguardian.com/local-government-network/2011/jul/14/information-governance-cloud.

44. Out-Law.com, *Certifications of cloud provider services welcome, but users cannot rely on them for own data protection compliance, says ICO* [cited November 2013]. http://www.out-law.com/en/articles/2012/july/certifications-of-cloud-provider-services-welcome-but-users-cannot-rely-on-them-for-own-data-protection-compliance-says-ico/.

45. Article 29 Working Party, *Opinion 05/2012 on Cloud Computing* (May 2012), [cited November 2013]. Available from: http://ec.europa.eu/justice/data-protection/article-29/documentation/opinion-recommendation/files/2012/wp196_en.pdf.

46. European Network Information Security Agency, *Cloud Computing Security Risk Assessment* (2009), [cited July 2014]. Available from: https://www.enisa.europa.eu/activities/risk-management/files/deliverables/cloud-computing-risk-assessment.

CHAPTER 4

Secure Cloud for Mobile Computing

INFORMATION IN THIS CHAPTER

- Mobile top threats
- Addressing the threat: mobile components for consideration

Throughout the book, we have referenced multiple sources that reference the growth in the number of devices that each of us are or will be using in the future. This of course means that we are likely to witness considerably more devices beyond the traditional computing devices such as computers and mobile phones. Such adoption of nontraditional computing devices is likely to take some time, indeed the year 2020 has been cited by multiple sources. Although this migration may take some time, one recent trend has been the massive growth of mobile devices, and in particular smartphones. According to analyst firm International Data Corporation, 2011 marked the year that shipments of smartphones exceeded those of personal computers (PCs),[1] a category that includes tablet computers. Looking forward, the sale of mobile devices will continue to rise significantly against a decline of PC sales according to Gartner[2] as depicted in Table 4.1.

Somewhat inevitably, as the number of mobile devices grows so do the threats. In terms of malware, for example, according to McAfee "new mobile malware has popped up at a faster rate than malware targeting PCs, and new malware samples on the Android OS have grown by 33% in just the past two quarters, while PC malware remained relatively flat."[3] Of course, this is only one threat vector, with a multitude of additional mobile-related threats in existence. In 2012, the Mobile Working Group within the Cloud Security Alliance (CSA) launched a research survey that included from 210 members across 26 countries to rank the top mobile threats in order of concern and likelihood. Please note that the threats presented are restricted to devices that connect to the Internet via cellular access (3G, 4G).

Table 4.1 Worldwide Device Shipments by Segment

	2012	2013	2014	2015
PC (desktop/notebook)	341,273	299,342	277,939	268,491
Tablet	119,529	179,531	263,450	324,565
Mobile	1,746,177	1,804,334	1,893,425	1,964,788
Ultramobile	9344	17,195	39,636	63,835
Total	2,216,322	2,300,402	2,474,451	2,621,678

MOBILE TOP THREATS: EVIL 8.0

The following top eight threats are ranked in order of their importance by way of concern as well as their likelihood of occurrence being either realized within a year, the following year, or not at all.

Threat 1: Data Loss from Lost, Stolen, or Decommissioned Devices
Threat Level: High

The key benefit of mobile devices is equally ranked as its greatest threat. This particular issue is exuberated by the manner in which users use such devices. For example, according to a survey 4 of 3000 consumers conducted by McAfee in early 2013, it was found that a third of consumers surveyed fail to protect their mobile device (phone or tablet) with a personal identification number. The majority of consumers in the United Kingdom and Germany, for example, "stick with the first one they were ever given. In contrast, French and American respondents are more likely to opt for their lucky number."[4]

While this approach clearly increases the likelihood of data getting into the wrong hands, the risk is compounded with the fact that only one in five respondents back up their mobile devices, which can have significant impact on the availability of data. Consider that, in 2013, Transport for London (TfL) responded to a Freedom of Information request[5] confirming that a total of 15,833 mobile phones were handed into its lost property department, with 2308 claimed by their owners, For tablets, there were 506 handed in, with 290 reclaimed by their owners.

This of course was only those devices handed into the TfL, and is a very small number compared with those mobile devices that actually go missing. In London, the Metropolitan Police estimate that up to 10,000 mobile phones are stolen every month, which when combined with those not stolen, but that are simply lost (there will likely be some overlap), the amount of data that goes missing each year across the globe will likely be significant. This of course justifies the decision to rank this particular threat as the highest. Particularly, as a third of these users are unlikely to have any form of security controls protecting the device. Not having any form of security controls will likely result in unauthorized attempts to access the data/applications on the device. In the Symantec Smartphone Honeystick project,[6] 50 smartphones were released (as lost), and in almost all instances, attempts were made to access data on the device:

- About 83% had attempts to access business apps
- About 89% had attempts to access personal apps
- About 96% had attempts to access at least some type of data
- About 50% of finders contacted the owner and offered to help return the phone

Although many organizations are likely to have some form of mobile management solution to manage mobile devices commissioned by them directly, there will be many more personal devices owned and managed by the employee. These are unlikely to have any form of security controls (based on the McAfee research this seems a fairly safe assumption), and should employees use such devices to store corporate data whether under the approval of their employer or not, then the loss of device will be nowhere as significant as the data getting into the wrong hands. In addition, the combination of these employee devices storing corporate data, and users installing apps with impunity, there is the risk with regards to the level of access such apps have to contacts, private pictures, social networking, Webmail, and passwords.

Threat 2: Information Stealing Malware
Threat Level: High

Figures 4.1 and 4.2 graphically depict the growth in mobile malware. While the numbers vary on the exact scale of the issue, what the two graphs should do is leave the reader in no doubt that here we have two organizations that compete commercially but agree that the growth of mobile malware is of significant concern.

Furthermore, mobile malware is predicted to continue growing. According to McAfee Labs,

"In the last two quarters reported, new PC malware growth was nearly flat, while appearances of new Android samples grew by 33%.

While McAfee Labs expects this trend to continue in 2014 it's not just the growth rate in new mobile attacks that will make news. We also expect to see entirely new types of attacks targeting Android."[8]

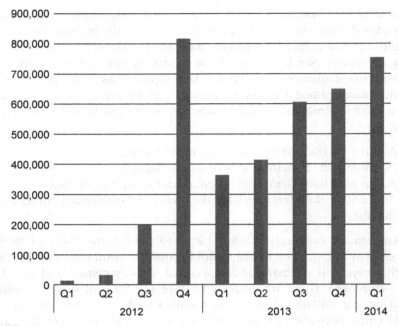

FIGURE 4.1
New mobile malware.[7]

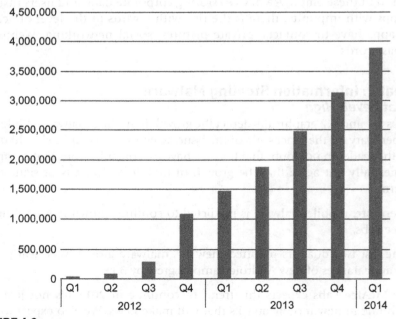

FIGURE 4.2
Total mobile malware.

The examples cited in the CSA Mobile Threats research are Zitmo, which is based on the Zeus malware intended to steal mobile transaction authorization numbers (mTANs) that are used for mobile banking. According to Kaspersky,[9] Zitmo works in the following fashion:

- Cyber criminals use the PC-based ZeuS to steal the data needed to access online banking accounts and client mobile phone numbers.
- The victim's mobile phone (see point 1) receives a text message with a request to install an updated security certificate, or some other necessary software. However, the link in the text message will actually lead to the mobile version of ZeuS.
- If the victim installs the software and infects his phone, then the malicious user can then use the stolen personal data and attempt to make cash transactions from the user's account, but will need an mTAN code to authenticate the transaction.
- The bank sends out a text message with the mTAN code to the client's mobile phone.
- ZitMo forwards the text message with the mTAN code to the malicious user's phone.
- The malicious user is then able to use the mTAN code to authenticate the transaction.

This ofcourse is merely the tip of the iceberg regarding mobile-based malware, with others not only targeting the data on the mobile device but also, in the case of NickSpy, recording conversations and uploading them to a remote server. Alternatively, in the case of Dendriod, the ability to "take pictures using the phone's camera, record audio and video, download existing pictures, record calls, send texts, and more."[10]

Of course, one of the many reasons that mobile malware is growing at such an exponential rate is the relatively low adoption rate among users for security software. According to a survey[11] conducted by the National Cyber Security Alliance, three-quarters of US respondents have not installed security software on their smartphones.

Threat 3: Data Loss and Data Leaking through Poorly Written Applications
Threat Level: Medium

How many apps do you have on your mobile device? If you can answer that question, then congratulations; that is impressive, but can you confirm what data these apps collect, and more importantly what they do with your data? It is unlikely that many can even answer the first question, let alone the proceeding questions. This of course is hardly surprising when it is estimated the average number of apps downloaded by smartphone users equals 25[12] (and a whopping 40 in South Korea).

If we take this number and then consider research by security firm BitDefender,[13] which found that based on analysis of the 836,021 applications in the Play Store (at the time of conducting the research), 1 in 20 were able to locate and open photographs on installed devices. Equally, 1 in 30 divulged e-mail addresses over the Internet, with 1749 doing so over an encrypted connection and 1661 over an unencrypted connection. In addition, the research also found that almost 10% of apps had permission to read the contact lists on the mobile device. Of course, there is no suggestion that the applications themselves are doing anything malicious, indeed for Android, the user is provided with details regarding the permissions the application is requesting. However, there is no doubt that the level of transparency regarding what happens with the data, how it is transmitted, and what happens with the data once collected does not have the same level of transparency. Indeed, if we review the data protection authorities (Canada, Netherlands) investigation into WhatsApp, there is a disparity between what was stated (regarding how long data is stored and transmitted), and what actually happened.

The issue of leaky apps is clearly a key problem, and absence of transparency about how data are stored or transmitted poses an issue. Furthermore, the issue is compounded by the fact that consumers when provided with transparency (by at least knowing what permissions exist) either do not read or understand what data are being requested by the app in question. Therefore, the challenge for organizations in mitigating this particular threat is made considerably more difficult by an audience that do not understand the implications of allowing apps almost unfettered access to their devices, and ultimately corporate data. A recently publicized example of this was demonstrated with the "Flappy Birds" application. "The following example illustrates this: com.touch18.flappybird.app (3113ad96fa1b37ac-b50922ac34f04352) is one of the many malicious Flappy Bird clones.

Among its malicious behaviors, this clone does the following:

- Makes calls without the user's permission
- Installs additional applications without the user's permission
- Allows an app to monitor incoming SMS messages, and to record or process them (undeclared permission)
- Sends SMS messages without the user's permission
- Extracts SMS messages
- Sends data to a cell number via SMS
- Allows an app to read the user's contacts data (undeclared permission)
- Extracts GPS location (latitude and longitude)
- Reads IMEI number and MAC address and transmits them to third partkies (JSON) without user's permission
- Sends user activity data to third-party sites

Allows an app to call the killBackgroundProcesses(String) (undeclared permission)."[14]

To put the issue into the context, the McAfee Labs team took a sample of 300 Flappy Bird applications, and of these, 238 was cited as malicious. This is the tip of the iceberg, but demonstrates the scale of the issue that is propagated by the simple acceptance of mobile applications without reviewing their permissions.

Threat 4: Vulnerabilities in Hardware, Operating System, Applications, and Third-Party Apps
Threat Level: Medium

Any element of technology will contain vulnerabilities, mobile or otherwise. Of course, there is no indication as to how many vulnerabilities each will likely have; however, one very rudimentary method of determining the number of likely vulnerabilities is based on the number of lines of code. In other words, the more the number of lines of code, the greater the number of likely vulnerabilities.

Known as the average defect density, according to research [15] conducted by security firm Coverity, the number of defects per 1000 lines of code is estimated to be 0.62. This figure is identical for open-source projects as they are for proprietary projects. Of course, there will be considerable debate about the actual figure, because the number of likely defects will be dependent on many other variables, such as the expertise of the programmer and quality assurance process. However, the intention of presenting these figures is to emphasize that vulnerabilities will always exist, and as we demand more features and interoperability, the risk will only get higher. Furthermore, the level of complexity associated with mobile platforms increases the likely security risk. For example, mobile applications will include the functionalities associated with desktop computing; they will, however, also include cellular communication capabilities.

There are multiple examples of vulnerabilities associated with mobile devices, operating systems (OSs), and applications. This includes those applications that are developed with information security in mind. In 2014, security firm IOActive reported [16] that the official mobile application for the RSA Conference contained half a dozen security vulnerabilities. According to Chief Technical Officer Gunter Ollman, the most significant of these vulnerabilities could allow an attacker the opportunity to conduct a man in the middle attack, inject malicious code, and potentially steal login credentials. Of course, the argument could be had that this is only an application for a conference (a security conference nonetheless), and that such vulnerabilities are unlikely to be present in applications that we use for more "important" tasks. However, research[17] conducted again by IOActive found that 90% of mobile banking applications contained security vulnerabilities:

- "A few apps (less than 20%) did not have Position Independent Executable (PIE) and Stack Smashing Protection enabled. This could help to mitigate the risk of memory corruption attacks."

- "40% of the audited apps did not validate the authenticity of SSL certificates presented. This makes them susceptible to Man in The Middle (MiTM) attacks."
- "50% of the apps are vulnerable to JavaScript injections via insecure UIWebView implementations. In some cases, the native iOS functionality was exposed, allowing actions such as sending SMS or emails from the victim's device."
- "90% [of the apps] contained several non-SSL links throughout the application. This allows an attacker to intercept the traffic and inject arbitrary JavaScript/HTML code in an attempt to create a fake login prompt or similar scam."

Of course, the above details are only the vulnerabilities associated with mobile applications, and the title with this threat includes the OS, as well as hardware. Indeed, when we consider vulnerabilities for mobile OSs, recent research would suggest that the number of identified vulnerabilities is increasing. According to Symantec,[18] 2012 saw a 32% increase in the number of documented vulnerabilities. The security flaw associated with iOS 6 as detailed by Trend Micro provides a recent example of a mobile OS vulnerability. In this example, researchers revealed that when connected to a fake charging station, the security flaw would grant complete access to an iPhone or iPad on the iOS 6 platform.[19]

This particular threat has been classed as medium because, although vulnerabilities will exist, the number of exploits (in the wild) are very low.

Threat 5: Unsecured Wi-Fi/Network Access/Rogue Access Points
Threat Level: High

Convergence. If there is any word that can be used to describe the digital phenomenon that we are all witnessing today, then convergence would most likely be the most appropriate word. What this term means in the context of technology is that now more than ever previously isolated areas of computing are merging into one, and none more so than that of wired and wireless. Historically, wired devices (e.g., desktops) would maintain separation from other devices via network segmentation. However, even with such segmentation, the ability to jump networks has been made considerably easier with the convergence between wired and wireless networks. Consider a completely isolated network segment, with multiple firewalls, data diodes, and network addressing to completely disconnect this network from unknown devices.

And now plug in a mobile device.

Indeed, the proliferation of wireless networks means that mobile devices today have a choice of networks to connect to, ranging from cellular to wireless networks.

With high international roaming charges, users are often far too willing to search and connect to any wireless network as long as it meets a very simple criteria, that it is free.

As expected, malicious actors understand this behavior and leverage rogue hotspots as a means to connect and compromise mobile devices of either passing users or to target specific individuals. According to the head of the European Cybercrime Centre, Troels Oerting, "We have seen an increase in the misuse of Wi-Fi, in order to steal information, identity or passwords and money from the users who use public or insecure Wi-Fi connections."[20] Subsequently, organizations may want to consider an appropriate policy exists regarding the use of unknown wireless hotspots and implement appropriate controls to enforce such an action on the mobile devices of employees. Other approaches to dealing with insecure networks are to assume that any network is in itself untrusted and to rely on the device and applications to protect themselves. This particular approach follows the principles of the Jericho forum.

Threat 6: Unsecured or Rogue Marketplaces
Threat Level: High
Affecting predominantly the Android platform, this particular threat relates to the availability of third-party application stores outside of the official stores. According to Digital Trends,[21] there are a number of incentives for consumers to venture outside of the Google Play App Store; these are the following:

- Free apps and promotions: Some mobile app stores provide commercial incentives to their consumers. This may be in the guise of offering a free app of the day, or aggressive discounts, as well as other offerings providing financial savings to consumers. Roughly translated, the consumer will be provided financial incentives to access this third-party app store compared with the official Google Play app store.
- App recommendations: This incentive relates to the availability of mobile applications that may not be available within the official Google Play Store.
- Curated list: A third-party app store may be able to provide a more appropriate list of applications based on the preferences for the consumer. Indeed, it has been suggested that third-party app stores provide better app discovery assistance, which means for the consumer they will be provided with a more appropriate list of recommended apps. According to the "Pfeiffer Report '2013 App Store Maturity Shootout' suggests that Amazon Appstore helps users find apps for specific activities by providing them with much more organized and sophisticated structure that includes a number of subcategories in comparison to Google Play."[22]

■ Localized portal: One particular example of a more appropriate list of available apps, as well as recommendations are stores that are country specific, and therefore in the local language of the consumer.

With such incentives, there is no surprise at the rise and popularity of third party app stores. For example, consider that the GetJar AppStore has a user base of 200 million, and the Opera Mobile Store has more than 1.8 million apps downloaded every day. These of course are a drop in the ocean compared with the actual number of stores available, and it is worth noting that, although they are used as an example to demonstrate the popularity of third-party stores, there is no suggestion that they do (or do not) host malicious content.

While there is no question that third-party stores are an attractive proposition to consumers for the reasons described earlier, they are the main delivery mechanism of malware. According to the H2 2013 Threat Report by F-Secure,[23] "the most common distribution channel for mobile malware continues to be via third-party app sites." Compare this with the Official Google Play Store where research found that only 1 in 1000 applications were classed as malware. Comparing this against third-party app stores, the level of malware increases significantly, this is depicted in Figure 4.3, which highlights the malware rate associated with a number of app stores.

This of course only tells part of the story, as malware is not the only risk associated with mobile apps. The research found both Adware[a] and Riskware[b] found in the Google Play Store, as depicted in Figure 4.4.

Equally, avoiding malware-ridden apps takes more than simply downloading only known apps. A growing trend has been to repackage known applications to offer within a third-party app store. The research found that of the top 20 most popular apps within the Google Play Store, 8 had trojanized versions available in third-party markets. For the purposes of the investigation, trojanized versions were applications that "uses the original package and application name, but also requests more permissions than the original."

---

[a]Apps are classed as Adware if they contain advertisement display functionality that potentially exposes the user to privacy or security risks, such as leakage/collection of personal details or exposure/ redirection to unsolicited or questionable applications, Web sites, or content.
[b]Apps are classed as Riskware if they include functionality that may pose a risk to the user's privacy or security if the app were misused. Note: variants in the PremiumSMS family may be classed as Riskware or Malware depending on their behavior.

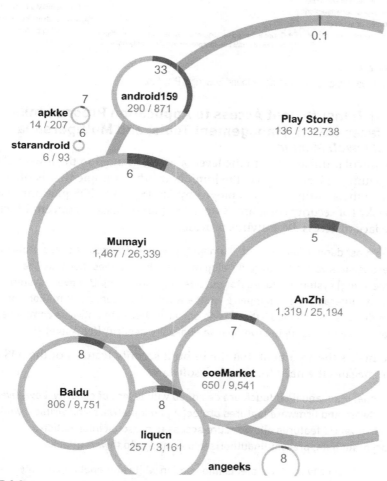

MALWARE SAMPLES RECEIVED, BY APP STORE

% of samples sourced from store classed as malware

unique malware samples / total samples received

0.1

33
android159
290 / 871

7
apkke
14 / 207

6
starandroid
6 / 93

Play Store
136 / 132,738

6

Mumayi
1,467 / 26,339

5

AnZhi
1,319 / 25,194

7

eoeMarket
650 / 9,541

8

Baidu
806 / 9,751

8

liqucn
257 / 3,161

8

angeeks

FIGURE 4.3
App stores with malware rates.

Adware	Family	Total Count	Family	Total Count	Riskware
Apps are classed as Adware if they contain advertisement display functionality that potentially exposes the user to privacy or security risks, such as leakage/collection of personal details or exposure/redirection to unsolicited or question-able applications, websites or content.	AirPush AdWo Ropin Dowgin Waps Gappusin	9,382 369 59 22 23 2	Minimob SmsReg PremiumSMS	51 4 1	Apps are classed as Riskware if they include functionality that may pose a risk to the user's privacy or security if the app were misused. Note: variants in the PremiumSMS family may be classed as Riskware or Malware depending on their behavior.

* Count is based on discrete unique samples; multiple copies of a unique sample are counted only once.

FIGURE 4.4

Count of adware and riskware samples found in Google Play Store.

Threat 7: Insufficient Access to Application Programming Interfaces (APIs), Management Tools, and Multipersonas
Threat Level: Medium

This particular threat refers to the level of access granted to the low-level func-tions within a given a device. Predominantly, the example that is often cited has been the security model deployed by Apple for the iOS platform. Eugene Kaspersky (of security company Kaspersky) raised this as a concern in relation to the lack of access for antivirus providers:

> The most dangerous scenario, I am afraid, is with iPhones. It's less probable because it is very difficult to develop malware for iPhones, because the [operating] system is closed [for outside programmers]. But every system has a vulnerability. If it happens—in the worst case scenario, if millions of the devices are infected—there is no antivirus, because antivirus companies don't have any rights to develop true end-point security [for Apple].[24]

Apple makes the argument that the in-built security features of the iOS archi-tecture negates the need for antivirus software:

> iPhone, iPad, and iPod touch are designed with layers of security. Low-level hardware and firmware features protect against malware and viruses, while high-level OS features allow secure access to personal information and corporate data, prevent unauthorized use, and help thwart attacks.
>
> The iOS security model protects information while still enabling mobile use, third-party apps, and syncing. Much of the system is based on industry-standard secure design principles—and in many cases, Apple has done additional design work to enhance security without compromising usability.[25]

Of course, the argument made by Eugene Kaspersky is that the threat of mal-ware on the iOS platform is not currently an issue; if, however, the issue does manifest itself, then addressing the problem will be considerably more difficult because of the closed nature of the platform. As the issue has not manifested itself as yet, the threat has been classed as medium, but the impact if (or when!) the risk is realized will be significant hence its inclusion.

Threat 8: Near Field Communications and Proximity-Based Hacking
Threat Level: LOW

Near Field Communications (NFC) is a wireless technology that allows for information to be shared over short distances between two devices. It allows consumers the ability to undertake a number of actions quickly and efficiently, for example, the QuickTap scheme provided by Orange allows consumers to make purchases of up to 15 GBP from up to 50,000 retailers. This is achieved by simply tapping an NFC-enabled mobile device that has an app with credit at the payment window of the retailer. Of course, payments is only example of where NFC can be utilized; use cases range from their use as boarding passes for airlines to allowing for payment with NFC-enabled parking meters and many other use cases.

While of course the benefits are well documented, and in certain cases being realized with projects across the globe, there is a growing number of risks associated with NFC. In fairness, a number of "hacks" associated with NFC have largely been proof-of-concepts, which explains why the threat has been classed as low; however, this will likely change. Examples of these "hacks" have taken place at conferences such as "Def Con"; one in particular was showcased by researchers who were able to hack an NFC-enabled device to get free transport on public services. Matteo Collura and Matteo Beccaro studied the security deployed for NFC-enabled cards in the Italian city of Turin. Attempting an NFC hack demonstrated against the San Francisco transport system at the same conference a year ago, they quickly discovered that the same issue was not present in Turin. However, upon further investigation, they found that there was a component within the ticket that is changed from 0 to 1 after each ride. By setting this sector to read-only mode, they were able to get "an unlimited-rides ticket."[26] Another issue was a timestamp, which determined whether the ticket needed to be stamped was in an area of the ticket that could be changed, and any NFC-enabled device (such as a mobile phone) could potentially overwrite this date.

Of course, this is only one such issue and is not per se an issue associated with mobile devices, but rather those platforms that leverage NFC (where the mobile device can be used as the attack vector). The issue is also compounded by the fact that there are now applications being made available to leverage the security vulnerabilities in these platforms offering the would-be mobile user free use of public transport systems: "UltraReset which takes advantage of NFC vulnerabilities in the systems used by many public transit systems, including the New Jersey Path and San Francisco Muni trains where it was tested effectively."[27]

In 2012, it was reported[28] that security researchers were able to hack into a Samsung Galaxy S3 phone that was running Android 4.0.4 through the use of NFC to send the exploit. The researchers were able to exploit a weakness in the manner in which the S3 implemented NFC, they were able to deliver a malicious file that was automatically opened by the device. Once the application was opened the researchers were able to launch a second attack and ultimately gain full rights on the compromised device.

What this and the other examples demonstrate is that there are clearly vulnerabilities in which NFC support is implemented. Moreover, there is a burgeoning security research community that are actively investing time (and money) into identifying, presenting, and in certain cases developing applications that allow anybody the ability to exploit. Subsequently, the threat level is classed as low but the likelihood is that it will not remain at that level of too long.

The threats listed above are classed as the Evil 8, and based on the research conducted by the CSA Mobile Working Group ranked as the top threats to mobile computing. In fairness, these threats are not necessarily related to mobile in relation to cloud computing, but entirely focused on mobile platforms themselves. In certain scenarios, the advent of cloud computing can be used to mitigate some of these threats; for example, threat 1 (loss of device) can be mitigated with cloud computing. Where data is automatically backed up to a cloud service, the loss of the device and ultimately data on the device is mitigated because the data is backed up to online storage. Although it is worth noting that only the risk of loss of availability is mitigated, but the loss of confidentiality still remains.

Of course, this particular point is important, those risks threats within the Evil 8 are useful to understand but without any recommendations to address they are of limited value. It is for this reason that the "Security Guidance for Critical Areas of Mobile Computing" was developed by the Mobile Working Group. This document, in addition to presenting the Evil 8, also provides mobile components for consideration. These components are those areas that organizations should consider to reduce the risk of the Evil 8 (as well as other threats) being realized at their organization.

These components, and their detail, will be presented in the proceeding section. However, much like the remainder of the book we will avoid the Control+C and Control+V shortcuts and provide additional detail while not deviating from the true spirit of the recommendations provided by the Working Group.

ADDRESSING THE THREAT: MOBILE COMPONENTS FOR CONSIDERATION

How do you address risk? In almost any formal guidance or security standard the recommendation is PPT. This of course is not through the use of Power-Point files (although we recognize the value in presenting the strategy!) but in fact Policy, Process, and Technology. For addressing the mobile risk, the very first consideration for all organizations should certainly be the mobile policy, in other words, agreeing and clearly defining the company approach in managing mobile devices (both corporate issued and employee owned).

Policy Considerations for Mobile Usage

Perhaps the first task for organizations regarding the use of mobile devices is to determine what is acceptable and what is deemed as too risky. In particular, the policy will need to be ratified (this term is particularly vague because the regulatory requirements will vary by country) by employees regarding the level of support or oversight expected on employee-owned devices.

While this may seem like the most sensible course of action; it is worth noting that recent CSA research found that one in five organizations do not have any mobile device policy in place (see Figure 4.5) according to research conducted by the CSA[29] Simply put, not having any policy in place will increase the level of risk within a given organization. This may not necessarily be security related, as any monitoring of employee devices without a formally accepted policy may open that organization up to legal action.

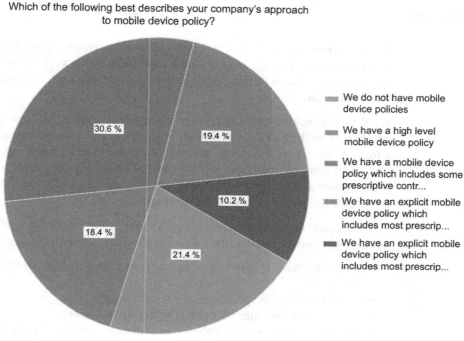

Which of the following best describes your company's approach to mobile device policy?

- 30.6 %
- 19.4 %
- 10.2 %
- 21.4 %
- 18.4 %

We do not have mobile device policies

We have a high level mobile device policy

We have a mobile device policy which includes some prescriptive contr...

We have an explicit mobile device policy which includes most prescrip...

We have an explicit mobile device policy which includes most prescrip...

FIGURE 4.5
Mobile device Policy.

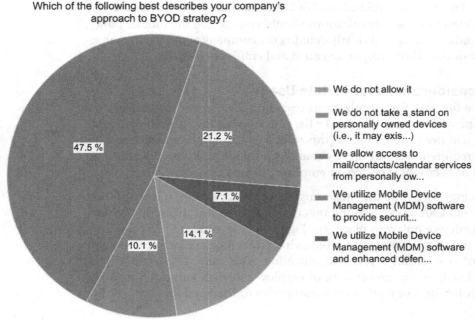

Which of the following best describes your company's approach to BYOD strategy?

- We do not allow it
- We do not take a stand on personally owned devices (i.e., it may exis...)
- We allow access to mail/contacts/calendar services from personally ow...
- We utilize Mobile Device Management (MDM) software to provide securit...
- We utilize Mobile Device Management (MDM) software and enhanced defen...

47.5 %
21.2 %
7.1 %
14.1 %
10.1 %

FIGURE 4.6
Approach to BYOD strategy.

At a minimum, the mobile device policy should determine whether BYOD will be supported within the organization. Interestingly, the majority of organizations actually allows BYOD but differ in how they manage employee devices (see Figure 4.6).

What this demonstrates is that there is no "right answer" in how to manage employees' mobile devices, although it is important to recognize that without a formal policy employees will most certainly use their own devices. However, one small caveat to the above sentence is that having a policy does "not" mean that employees will avoid using their own devices, we will discuss in detail how to enforce the policy later within this chapter.

When determining the key questions for a mobile device policy as it relates to use of employee-owned devices, the following should be considered as a minimum:

- Are employees allowed to access corporate resources using their own devices?
- Will there be any specific device restrictions?
- Under what circumstances can the device be wiped?
- Will every employee be able to participate in the BYOD program?
- What is the policy for jailbroken devices?

Table 4.2 Example of Mobile Trust Boundaries

Trust Boundary	Types of Authentication/Authorization
User to OS	Password, PIN, facial recognition
User to application	Password, social media login, two-factor
Application to application	IPC, remote methods, intents, custom URL
OS to network	NTLM, Kerberos, 802.1x
Application to OS	Application digital signatures; this will determine what an application can read/write on OS
OS to application	Application digital signatures; this will determine what the OS can read/write from application data
Application to backend	User credential, client-side credential, certificates, session keys, etc.

PIN, personal identification number; URL, uniform resource locator.

Of course, the above five policy considerations are only a snapshot into the issues that should be considered when developing their mobile device policy, and more specifically for BYOD. Further policy considerations are based on the research from the CSA Mobile Working Group. It is, however, worth considering the legal/regulatory landscape when monitoring employees; this goes beyond BYOD and even corporate mobile devise but is an area of consideration for security as a whole. Subsequently, any such policy should not be reviewed by the legal department particularly where employees across multiple geographies will be managed/monitored as it is likely that one single approach may not be appropriate.

Technical Controls for Managing Mobile Devices
Authentication

In Chapter 3, we considered cloud computing threats; we presented the notorious nine, these are the nine biggest threats associated with cloud computing. Without wishing to give the game away, the issue of authentication is presented as a major risk associated with cloud computing. However, the majority of cloud services are simply protected with single factor authentication, and the hope that attackers are unable to simply guess a password.

There is no intention here to repeat the section on authentication as a whole, but rather focus on the authentication afforded on mobile devices. Within a mobile ecosystem there will exist multiple authentication boundaries; these are the boundaries between the various components within the mobile ecosystem and the methods these components use to establish trust in verifying their identity. This is demonstrated in Table 4.2.

Of course, the authentication methods available for the trust boundaries are likely to evolve as both technology and the industry evolves. On the latter part it is worth noting the work being conducted by the Fast Identity Online

Alliance whose aim is to establish "interoperable set of mechanisms that reduce the reliance on passwords to authenticate users."[c]

The purpose of presenting the mobile authentication boundaries is to consider the levels of authentication available, and thereafter appropriate for the use case in question. For example, consider a use case where a mobile user is looking to gain access to personally identifiable customer-related data via a private cloud service. In this case, it will be appropriate to consider the mobile device boundaries, and where stronger controls can be enforced to achieve the level of assurance sought. Subsequently, the use of authentication at user to device is unlikely to be appropriate, and the level of assurance can be achieved between the user and application. Where the user is accessing data that is not personally identifiable and nonsensitive, authentication via the user to device boundary may be appropriate.

It is also worth considering that there are a number of attack vectors associated with the major authentication threats. These are listed in Appendix 1 (and taken from the CSA MWG Security guidance); this includes a series of countermeasures.

App Stores

Within the Evil 8, one of the key threats that were presented was the use of third-party app stores. In particular, one of the key issues was the repackaging of legitimate apps to contain malicious content. Within the mobile ecosystem, there exist a number of opportunities for nefarious actors to embed their malicious content within a mobile app, as depicted in Figure 4.7.

Although Figure 4.7 is an oversimplification of the process, it does demonstrate that the provision of mobile apps to the end user can take a number of routes. Furthermore, the dashed line (D3) is used to indicate a higher risk. However, the recommendation for end users and indeed the organizations that are tasked with supporting these devices is that the mobile device policy should clearly define where the end user is allowed to download apps from.

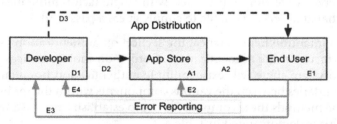

FIGURE 4.7
Channels of App distribution.

[c]For more information please visit: http://fidoalliance.org.

Some of the basic guidance end users should adopt are in the first instance to review the permission the app is requesting and determine whether the permissions requested are deemed too risky before downloading. Of course, there is no assurance that such an approach will address the issue as solely relying on people to make the right security decision can have varying results. Another option, or rather a supplementary approach for organizations is to consider utilizing whitelisting applications that an end user can download. This will demand the use of mobile device management software; however it will consume resources to test, verify, and regularly update the whitelist of approved applications.

Mobile Device Management

While the development and acceptance of a mobile device policy (and of course a risk management process that ensures that any policy satisfies the risk appetite of the organization) is the foundation for many organizations, a mobile device management solution is crucial in enforcing this policy. The key components of such a solution for both corporate-issued and employee-owned devices are depicted in Figure 4.8.

Mobile technologies continue to become a critical component to almost every organization, and as such the need to provide a safe environment for their use is essential in ensuring their use can maximize the benefit to the end user and organization. The mobile nature of such devices when combined with cloud computing allows them to be a great enabler for more productive employees. However, there is no question that the emerging focus among nefarious actors is on these devices due to their popularity. This is supported through countless

FIGURE 4.8
Mobile device management key components for BYOD/corporate devices.

studies into the threat landscape, with, for example, mobile malware growth outstripping that of traditional PCs. Subsequently, it is imperative for organizations and consumers alike to consider the threats to their mobile devices and implement People, Process, and Technology-based controls to mitigate the risk to an acceptable level.

END NOTES

1. Trevor Mogg Digital Trends, *Smartphone sales exceed those of PCs for first time, Apple smashes record* (February 2012), [cited April 2014]. Available from: http://www.digitaltrends.com/mobile/smartphone-sales-exceed-those-of-pcs-for-first-time-apple-smashes-record/.

2. Gartner Press Release, *Gartner Says Worldwide Traditional PC, Tablet, Ultramobile and Mobile Phone Shipments On Pace to Grow 7.6 Percent in 2014* (January 2014), [cited April 2014]. Available from: http://www.gartner.com/newsroom/id/2645115.

3. McAfee, *Mobile Malware Predicted to Trump All 2014 Malware Attacks* (January 2014), [cited April 2014]. Available from: http://www.mcafee.com/uk/security-awareness/articles/mobile-malware-predicted-to-top-all-2014-malware-attacks.aspx.

4. McAfee, *McAfee reveals consumers fail to protect their mobile devices* (February 2013), [cited May 2014]. Available from: http://www.mcafee.com/us/about/news/2013/q1/20130224-01.aspx.

5. Dan Worth, V3.co.uk, *More than 15,000 lost mobile phones on London underground pose security risk* (December 2013), [cited May 2014]. Available from: http://www.v3.co.uk/v3-uk/news/2318727/more-than-15-000-lost-mobile-phones-on-london-underground-pose-security-risks.

6. Scott Wright, Symantec, *Symantec Smartphone Honeystick Project* [cited May 2014]. Available from: http://www.symantec.com/content/en/us/about/presskits/b-symantec-smartphone-honey-stick-project.en-us.pdf.

7. McAfee, *McAfee Labs Threat Report June 2014* (June 2014), [cited July 2014]. Available from: http://www.mcafee.com/sg/resources/reports/rp-quarterly-threat-q1-2014.pdf.

8. McAfee Labs, *McAfee Labs 2014 Threat Predictions* (January 2014), [cited May 2014] Available from: http://www.mcafee.com/us/resources/reports/rp-threats-predictions-2014.pdf.

9. Kaspersky.com, *Teamwork: How the Zitmo Trojan bypasses online banking security* (October 2011), [May 2014]. Available from: http://www.kaspersky.com/about/news/virus/2011/Teamwork_How_the_ZitMo_Trojan_Bypasses_Online_Banking_Security.

10. Ian Barker, BetaNews, *Say cheese – new Android malware can hijack your camera*(March 2014), [cited May 2014]. Available from: http://betanews.com/2014/03/07/say-cheese-new-android-malware-can-hijack-your-camera/.

11. Infosecurity.com, *Most users have not installed security software on their smartphones survey finds* (January 2012), [cited May 2014]. Available from: http://www.infosecurity-magazine.com/view/23002/most-users-have-not-installed-security-software-on-their-smartphones-survey-finds/.

12. Zoe Fox. Mashable, *The Average Smartphone User Downloads 25 Apps* (September 2013), [cited May 2014]. Available from: http://mashable.com/2013/09/05/most-apps-download-countries/.

13. John Leydon. theRegister, *The truth about LEAKY, STALKING, SPYING smartphone applications* (January 2014), [cited May 2014]. Available from: http://www.theregister.co.uk/2014/01/31/smartphone_app_spy_risks/.

14. McAfee Labs, *Q1 2014 Quarterly Threats report* (June 2014), [cited July 2014]. Available from: http://www.mcafee.com/uk/resources/reports/rp-quarterly-threat-q1-2014.pdf

15. Brian Prince, *Open source vulnerabilities plague large organisations* (March 2012), [cited May 2014]. Available from: http://www.securityweek.com/open-source-security-vulnerabilities-plague-large-organizations.

16. Brian Donohue, Threatpost, *RSA Conference Mobile Application Marred by Security Vulnerabilities* (February 2014), [cited May 2014]. Available from: http://threatpost.com/rsa-conference-mobile-application-marred-by-security-vulnerabilities/104547.

17. Zach Epstein, BGR, *Major holes found in 90% of top mobile banking apps* (January 2014), [cited May 2014]. Available from: http://bgr.com/2014/01/14/mobile-banking-apps-security-vulnerabilities/.

18. William Jackson, GCN Cybersecurity, *iPhone has the most vulnerabilities so why is Android the most hacked* (April 2013), [cited May 2014]. Available from: http://gcn.com/articles/2013/04/19/iphone-vulnerabilities-android-most-attacked.aspx.

19. Trend Micro, *Emerging Vulnerabilities: Glitches go mobile* [cited May 2014]. Available from: http://about-threats.trendmicro.com/RelatedThreats.aspx?language=au&name=Emerging+Vulnerabilities%3A+Glitches+Go+Mobile.

20. Dan Simmons, BBC News, *Free Wi-fi hotspots pose data risks, Europol Warns* (March 2014), [cited May 2014]. Available from: http://www.bbc.co.uk/news/technology-26469598.

21. Simon Hill, Digital Trends, *Tired of Google Play? Check out these alternative Android app stores* (December 2013), [cited May 2014]. Available from: http://www.digitaltrends.com/mobile/android-app-stores/.

22. Devika Girish, Mobstac, *Boost your Android App Installs with Third-party App stores* (December 2013), [cited May 2014]. Available from: http://blog.mobstac.com/2013/12/boost-your-android-app-installs-with-third-party-app-stores/.

23. F-Secure, *H2 2013 Threat Report* [cited May 2014]. Available from: http://www.f-secure.com/static/doc/labs_global/Research/Threat_Report_H2_2013.pdf.

24. Matt Asay, ReadWrite.com, *Why your iPhone will invariably catch a virus* (September 2013), [cited May 2014]. Available from: http://readwrite.com/2013/09/05/kaspersky-the-ios-malware-dam-will-break.

25. Tom Worstall, Forbes.com, *Apple Explains Why IOS Don't Need No Steenkin Anti-virus* (April 2012), [cited May 2014]. Available from: http://www.forbes.com/sites/timworstall/2012/06/04/apple-explains-why-ios-dont-need-no-steenkin-anti-virus/.

26. Lorenzo Franceschi-Bicchierai, Mashable, *Hackers Expose Security Holes that Allow 'free Rides for Life'* (August 2013), [May 2014]. Available from: http://mashable.com/2013/08/05/mifare-ultralights-hack-def-con/.

27. Eric Limer, Gizmodo.com, *UltraReset Is an NFC-hacking App That Hands Out Free Train Rides* (September 2012), [May 2014]. Available from: http://gizmodo.com/5945669/some-nfc-hackers-managed-to-develop-a-free-train-ride-app.

28. Ryan Naraine, ZDNet, *Exploit beamed via NFC to hack Samsung Galaxy S3 (Android 4.0.4)* (September 2012), [cited May 2014]. Available from: http://www.zdnet.com/exploit-beamed-via-nfc-to-hack-samsung-galaxy-s3-android-4-0-4-7000004510/.

29. Mobile Working Group, Cloud Security Alliance, *Security Guidance for Critical Areas of mobile computing* (November 2012), [cited May 2014]. Available from: https://downloads.cloudsecurityalliance.org/initiatives/mobile/Mobile_Guidance_v1.pdf.

CHAPTER 5

Making the Move into the Cloud

A BRAVE NEW WORLD

- Cloud computing checklist
- Security for the cloud

Traditionally when organizations look to secure their data, the approach taken is a pretty conventional one. Whereupon the focus is on identifying where in the organization key systems and data are located. Once this exercise is completed, a risk assessment is subsequently done to determine what security risks are facing the organization and then selected security controls are implemented to manage those risks.

In most cases, those security controls focus on the systems and physical environment. Firewalls are placed on the network perimeters, intrusion detection systems (IDS) placed on the network, antivirus software installed on computers, and access control lists set on servers. With this model, the focus is very much on securing items such as servers, PCs, and other devices rather than focusing on the information residing on those systems. In effect, organizations mimic the security of medieval castles whereupon all access into and out of the castle is controlled and monitored with guards patrolling within the castle walls to spot any suspicious behavior.

However, just as castles have proven ineffective against many of today's threats, in the age of cloud computing so too has the traditional security model. When working in the cloud, a large amount of the control that organizations traditionally had over their infrastructure and data is no longer there. Instead organizations rely on others to secure their data and services.

This requires a radical change in approach and mind-set to security in the cloud. Instead of implementing a security model that focuses on protecting the perimeter and whatever is within that perimeter, the security model instead must shift focus to the data and where that data may be transmitted and where it may be stored, and most importantly who (person or a process) has what level of access to it.

In essence, the mind-set has to change from employing the medieval castle model for security to one more akin to an airport's air traffic control tower. In an airport, all traffic and activity in that airport is managed and controlled from the air traffic control tower. Airplanes cannot land or take off without using the air traffic control tower. Vehicles cannot move near the runways without the air traffic control tower being aware. When an airplane wants to land at an airport it must contact the air traffic control tower. The air traffic control tower will then guide that airplane to land at an appropriate runway. From there the airplane with guidance from the air traffic control tower taxis to a berth at the airport's terminal. At this berth are the support services to enable passengers to disembark from the airplane, for the passenger luggage to be unloaded, cleaning crews to enter the airplane and clean it, and catering staff to refurbish supplies and food within the galleys. Once this is done, a new set of passengers is loaded onto the plane along with their baggage. The plane is guided away from the berth and helped taxi to the right runway. When the conditions are right, the air traffic control tower allows the airplane to take off. When the airplane is in the air, it is directed safely through the airspace until it reaches the airspace for which another air traffic control tower is responsible. Control is then handed over to that other air traffic control tower to allow the airplane to continue on its journey.

In cloud computing, data is analogous to airline passengers. In order to get from one destination to another it is important to ensure the right data gets to the right place at the right time and that all supporting services are available when required. By taking the air traffic control tower analogy, organizations can focus more on the items that matter, the data and services, and leave the worry of securing the premises and the infrastructure to third parties.

In order to move to this model of securing data in the cloud, organizations need to take a number of key steps in order to ensure the appropriate data and/or services are moved to the cloud.

It should be noted that this approach is also important to identify what items can be moved into the cloud and those that for various reasons, including security, should remain on premise. There are number of reasons that this may be the case.

It may be more suitable to keep highly sensitive data on premise rather than store it in the cloud. For example, it would probably be more prudent that a company's most valuable intellectual property and/or research and development work remains on premise. However, the Customer Relationship Management system could be an ideal candidate to move to the cloud. In some specific use cases, the move to cloud may improve security, especially when company's security controls are outdated and the investment to improving those would cost more than using more secure cloud service.

Another reason not to move certain services into the cloud may be due to those services not being secured enough already. This could be due to faulty code, inappropriate access control, or poor processes. Moving these types of services to the cloud may actually make them less secure than if they remained on premise. If they remain on premise, their attack exposure may be more reduced than in the cloud. Moving an insecure service into the cloud without taking steps to secure it could make that service more vulnerable than if it remained onsite.

For an organization to successfully migrate its systems to the cloud in a secure manner requires that organization's understanding and knowing what it is that it will be moving into the cloud. This requires the organization to identify and classify its information assets.

CLOUD COMPUTING CHECKLIST

The following steps should be considered when making the move to the cloud.

Identifying Information Assets

Normally when organizations think about their assets they focus on the accountants' definition of assets. This definition tends to focus on items that hold a monetary value to the organization. In the main these tend to be physical assets such as buildings, desks, computers, printers, and, in some cases, software. This approach does not take into account the value on nontangible items such as data.

For organizations to know what data is suitable to move securely into the cloud they need to first identify what data they have, where that data is located, and finally how valuable that data is to the organization.

Organizations should identify all of the key data they employ. These data could be held in databases, in spreadsheets, on mainframe systems, or on files on a network share.

This exercise is important for organizations to complete, even more so when moving data to the cloud. It is important organizations understand what information is held in what area, not just from a security point of view, but also from a data quality point of view to prevent duplication and errors. However, when moving data into the cloud, the data identification exercise takes on even more importance to ensure that proper data is stored in the appropriate places.

Classifying the Data

Having identified what data the organization has, it then should determine how important that data is to the organization. This process is known as classifying the data or data classification. Classifying the data enables the organization to understand how critical or important that data is to the organization.

For example, the database that holds all customers' financial details would be of more value or hold more importance to the organization than the information to be published on the organization's Website.

Anyone familiar with spy novels or movies will be familiar with data classification and its advantages. Information marked Top Secret or For Your Eyes Only obviously holds more importance than information which does not. It is quite easy to determine from those labels how important the information is and how it must be secured and treated. By classifying data, organizations can ensure they are aware of what data can be moved into the cloud and which data may be more suitable to remain on premise due to its sensitivity.

There are many ways to classify data but in the main they fall into two categories: quantitative or qualitative methods. Which method an organization decides to employ will depend on many factors such as the type of industry the organization is in, how regulated the organization's industry sector is, how mature the organization is, and the time and budget the organization has to perform a classification exercise.

A quantitative method attempts to put a monetary value, or other numerical representation of value, the data has to the organization. While this exercise is relatively easy to conduct for physical assets such as computers or other items that have an actual value, it is not so easy to do for data assets. For example, how much value does an organization place on its customer database? How does it calculate that value? Does it determine the value based on the man-hours taken to generate the data, or the revenue that data brings into the organization, or is it a combination of these and other factors? While it may be difficult to do a thorough quantitative analysis of the data assets, the advantage it brings is the organization has a clear understanding of the actual impact to its bottom line that data has. This makes it much clearer and easier to determine how much budget should be spent in securing that data.

A qualitative approach to data classification is much more intuitive and may not involve, or rely as heavily upon numerical values applied to the data. In a qualitative approach, the data classification exercise determines the importance of data assets to the organization from a business perspective. The data is classified based on its criticality to the organization such as high, medium, or low criticality.

Whichever methodology is employed by the organization it is important that all involved in the data classification exercise understand the methodology used and that the results from each exercise can be consistently repeated. This is important in order to enable the organization to properly manage its data in and out of the cloud throughout the data's lifecycle.

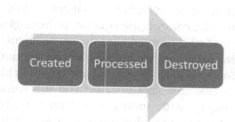

FIGURE 5.1
Information lifecycle.

Information has an inherent lifecycle. It is firstly created, and then it is processed and stored, until ultimately it is no longer needed and destroyed (Figure 5.1).

It is important to also note that as data moves through its lifecycle its classification can change. Some data that today is very sensitive may tomorrow be public information. An example of this could be data relating to an organization's stock valuation. Prior to releasing its annual report and other financial details such information would be highly sensitive and must be kept confidential as that information could be used to unfairly manipulate the organization's stock price. Once the annual report and financial information has been released then it is in the public domain and no longer needs to be treated as confidential.

Having identified and classified the data, organization can now determine what security controls it needs to implement to protect that data asset. For example, if the value of the data assets is $US25,000 then it makes good business sense to spend US$1000 to protect it. However, it does not make such good business sense to spend US$100,000 to protect the same data asset. This of course is a simplistic example as the model will need to add factors such as likelihood into any decision.

How to determine what security controls to put in place and how effective those controls will be on protecting the data asset depends on how effective the risk assessment and management process within an organization is. As data moves in and out of the cloud, it is essential that an organization regularly runs risk assessments to ensure that all risks facing that data asset are properly identified and managed.

Risk Management

Risk Management is the process by which an organization identifies the key security risks that its data assets are facing and the security controls that need to be put in place to reduce and manage those risks. Before engaging with a cloud service provider, organizations should conduct a risk assessment to ensure that the controls that will be in place by both the cloud service provider and the organization itself are effective in managing those risks. If that risk assessment determines the controls are effective in managing the level of risk, then the organization should proceed with the engagement. If that risk assessment, however, determines that the controls in place are not effective enough, then the organization needs to make the decision to put in place more controls to reduce the level of risk, to accept the risks and still engage with the cloud service provider, to engage with another cloud service provider, or to avoid engaging with a cloud service provider and run the service in-house.

Effective risk management requires that the risk assessment exercise is not run as an isolated event at the start of the engagement with the cloud service provider. Instead, the risk management process is a continuous one whereby regular risk assessments should be conducted to ensure the correct levels of controls are in place to protect the data according to its classification. An effective risk management process also helps organizations manage risks over time as the threat, technical, and business landscapes change over time. It is also important to ensure that the risk assessment process provides consistent results each time it is conducted, even when conducted by different people in the organization.

Before conducting a risk assessment it is important that an organization understands what is meant by a risk. At its highest definition, risk is a definable event that has a probability of occurrence and takes into account the impact of that event happening. In essence the risk is materialized when the identified problem or event actually happens. A simple analogy to explain this would be as follows: A weak lock on the front door of a house places the house at a risk of being burgled. However, the weak lock by itself does not guarantee the house will be burgled. Other factors come into play, such as the location of the house. If located in the middle of a forest many miles away from anyone, then the likelihood of a burglar coming across the house is much less than if the house was located in the middle of a city with a high crime rate.

It should be noted that in life risk can have a positive and also a negative outcome. Whenever a business invests money in a new marketing campaign or looks to invest in a new product, there is the risk that investment may not provide any returns. However, that investment could pay lots of dividends depending on how successful the marketing campaign or new product is. An example of this would be the Apple iPhone. There was a risk that Apple could have lost all the money it invested in the research and development it spent in producing the iPhone. As it turns out the risk of investing in the research and development of the iPhone proved to be very positive. In information security risk is often looked upon with a negative impact.

There are many different definitions of risk and in the context of information security there are a number of appropriate definitions. One definition of risk states that

Risk is the likelihood of the occurrence of a vulnerability multiplied by the value of the information asset minus the percentage of risk mitigated by current controls plus the uncertainty of current knowledge of the vulnerability.[1]

According to the ISO 31000:2009 —Principles and Guidelines[2] on Implementation, risk can be defined as the "effect of uncertainty on objectives" which translated means that risks are events that can have a negative or positive effect on the organization's objectives.

The NIST SP 800-30 Risk Management Guide for Information Technology Systems states that essentially in its simplest interpretation risk can be demonstrated as follows:

Risk = Threat × Likelihood × Impact

Effective risk management is where controls are introduced to either reduce the likelihood of the threat being realized or reduce the impact of the risk. Organizations need to acknowledge that risk cannot be fully eliminated. The purpose of risk management and risk assessments is to identify the risks and appropriate controls that will help reduce the likelihood or the impact of the risk.

Once a risk assessment to move to a Cloud Service Provider has been completed, the organization needs to look at how it will manage those risks on a continual basis. This is the discipline of risk management and is where a formal process is implemented in an organization to ensure that all risks are identified and managed. A risk register should be maintained of all the identified risks logged and recorded. A risk treatment plan should then be developed outlining the controls that may already be in place, the tasks required to implement any additional controls, and who will be responsible for ensuring each of those tasks are completed.

Having identified the risks, documented them in the risk register, and developing a risk treatment plan, the organization can then determine how best to manage the risks. A number of options exist when managing risks.

- *Risk mitigation*: Having identified the risks, risk mitigation is one wherein additional controls can be implemented to reduce the likelihood or impact of the risk. These controls may be technical controls or may involve developing new processes and procedures, or providing additional training to staff.
- *Risk acceptance*: From time to time there may be risks that the organization has no control over the likelihood of it happening or reducing the impact. There may already be certain controls in place and no additional controls may be available, or indeed there may be no cost benefit to implementing any additional controls. At this stage, the organization may decide the business benefits may outweigh the

effort to further mitigate the risk and decide to accept the risk and any consequences should it materialize.

- *Risk avoidance*: Despite all efforts by an organization, it may discover that it cannot reduce the level of risk to an acceptable level. In this case, the organization may have no choice to avoid the risk. In the cloud computing context, this would be where an organization would decide through its risk assessment process that the level of risk in moving to the cloud for a particular service is too high and therefore will stop the project or implement the solution in-house.
- *Risk transfer*: In essence risk transfer is where an organization decides to outsource the management of certain risks to a third party. In some cases this could be seeking cyber insurance[3] in the event of certain risks materializing. Alternatively it would be engaging with a third party to outsource the task or function so that third party is responsible for managing the risks. This is one of the big advantages Cloud Service Providers have over many organizations. In many cases Cloud Service Providers will have better physical and IT security in their datacenters than their customers thereby helping customers manage the risks by transferring them to the Cloud Service Provider. It should be noted though that while organizations can transfer the management of the risk to a third party, the responsibility for that risk still lies in the organization.
- *Risk deference*: Similar to risk avoidance, deferring risks is where an organization may decide not to engage in a certain activity, e.g., migrate to the cloud, due to concerns over the effectiveness of security controls. However, instead of canceling the activity entirely risk deference is where that activity is postponed until more effective controls are in place or an alternative solution can be found.

In order to determine ways of managing the identified risks, organizations need to manage the risks. The first step in the risk management process is to conduct a comprehensive risk analysis.

Risk Analysis

An organization can employ a number of risk management and analysis methodologies to identify and manage risks. It is important to note that there are no right or wrong methodologies that an organization can use, providing the methodology employed is one that can readily and easily identify the risks facing that organization based on its business and cultural needs. The European Network and Information Security Agency's (ENISA) whitepaper on Cloud Computing Security Risk Assessment[4] provides a number of examples of different types of organizations looking to engage in cloud computing and how risk assessments were achieved for each of them.

The main risk methodologies used in information security and which are applicable to migrating to the cloud are

- Operationally Critical Threat, Asset, and Vulnerability Evaluation (OCTAVE by Carnegie Mellon University, Software Engineering Institute (SEI)).[5]
- CCTA Risk Analysis and Management Method (CRAMM) from Insight Consulting.[6]
- National Institute for Standards and Technology (NIST) Risk Management Framework from the NIST.[7]
- ISO/IEC 27005:2011 Information technology —Security techniques— Information security risk management.[8]

A number of other risk assessment methodologies may be more suitable for certain organizations. The ENISA maintains a very useful list of the various risk methodologies that are available and compares them on its Inventory of Risk Management/Risk Assessment Methods and Tools[9] webpage.

Similar to data classification there are two main approaches on how to conduct a risk analysis: quantitative risk analysis and qualitative risk analysis. As with data classification which method to use is entirely down to the needs of the individual organization.

- *Quantitative Risk Analysis*: The quantitative risk analysis approach attempts to assign real numbers to the costs of safeguards and the amount of damage that can take place should the risk materialize. This approach assigns value to information assets, be they tangible or intangible assets and then estimates the potential loss per risk. Using this approach can provide real figures which can be easily translated into business speak for senior management. However, for this approach to be successful requires a lot of data to be gathered and analyzed. It also results in hard figures being assigned to intangible assets (such as data) which may lead to false assumptions.
- *Qualitative Risk Analysis*: The qualitative risk analysis approach judges an organization's risk to threats, which is based on judgment, intuition, and experience versus assigning real numbers to possible risks and their potential loss. This approach generally is easier to conduct and understand. It also does not require huge amounts of information. However, as it does not employ the rigor and discipline of assigning actual figures to assets and their potential losses, it can be hard to provide consistent and accurate results.

When selecting an approach it is important to ensure that it suits the organization's business needs and that it can be conducted regularly and consistently so that the risk management process remains effective.

Once the risks have been identified then the appropriate controls to manage the risks can be implemented. As part of the overall risk management process regular risk assessments should be completed, ideally at least on an annual basis. This process should ensure that existing controls are working as expected and that any new risks or changes to existing risks are identified and catered for (Figure 5.2).

Should there be any major changes in the technical infrastructure or business needs of the organization, a risk assessment should be completed. Similarly, should any major changes impact the Cloud Service Provider, a risk assessment should be completed to ensure all risks are maintained in accordance with the requirements of the organization.

The risk assessment process is the most critical step when migrating to the cloud. Many organizations view the cloud as a panacea to some of their internal security or indeed IT provisioning or operational issues. The assumption that many organizations have is that by migrating services and data to a Cloud Service Provider(s) who is totally focused on securing and providing that service, then logically the organization's data and/or services will also be more secure. This is not necessarily so. While it is true that because of their business model many Cloud Service Providers will invest much more time, resources, and money into securing their offerings, many security issues may not lie within the purview of the Cloud Service Provider.

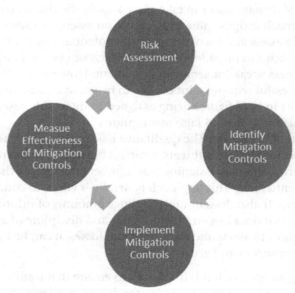

FIGURE 5.2
Risk management cycle.

If the organization has poor security processes and procedures, these will not be magically resolved by migrating to the cloud. If the application being migrated to the cloud has many security bugs and vulnerabilities, then unless the organization tackles those bugs and vulnerabilities as part of its migration to the cloud, the application will just be as insecure in the cloud as it was when onsite.

Organizations that establish and maintain a comprehensive risk management process with regard to the cloud will find they will gain many benefits and advantages from using the cloud.

SECURITY FOR THE CLOUD

Having identified the assets the organization wants to move to the cloud and having completed an appropriate risk assessment, organizations can now look to confidently migrate to a Cloud Service Provider. Depending on the type of platform the Cloud Service Provider offers will determine the security controls that can be implemented and also the amount of control the organization will have over those security controls. The main platforms to consider are

- Infrastructure as a Service—IaaS
- Platform as a Service—PaaS
- Software as a Service—SaaS.

The key differences in these platforms is outlined in the "Security Guidance for Critical Areas of Focus in Cloud Computer v3.0"[10] from the Cloud Security Alliance:

> In SaaS environments the security controls and their scope are negotiated into the contracts for service; service levels, privacy, and compliance are all issues to be dealt with legally in contracts. In an IaaS offering, while the responsibility for securing the underlying infrastructure and abstraction layers belongs to the provider, the remainder of the stack is the consumer's responsibility. PaaS offers a balance somewhere in between; where securing the platform falls onto the provider, but both securing the applications developed against the platform and developing them securely, belong to the consumer.

Organizations need to be aware of the differences between each of the platforms in order to ensure that the most appropriate and effective security controls are implemented.

In addition to understanding the different type of platforms that determine the type of security controls to deploy in the cloud, organizations need to appreciate the requirements that each of the cloud deployment models may require. In the main there are four different types of cloud deployment models. They are best described from a cloud security point of view in the "Security

Guidance for Critical Areas of Focus in Cloud Computer v3.0" by the Cloud Security Alliance.

- Public Cloud: The cloud infrastructure is made available to the general public or a large industry group and is owned by an organization selling cloud services.
- Private Cloud: The cloud infrastructure is operated solely for a single organization. It may be managed by the organization or by a third party and may be located on premise or off-premise.
- Community Cloud: The cloud infrastructure is shared by several organizations and supports a specific community that has shared concerns (e.g., mission, security requirements, policy, or compliance considerations). It may be managed by the organizations or by a third party and may be located on premise or off-premise.
- Hybrid Cloud: The cloud infrastructure is a composition of two or more clouds (private, community, or public) that remain unique entities but are bound together by standardized or proprietary technology that enables data and application portability (e.g., cloud bursting for load balancing between clouds).

Security Controls for the Cloud

When looking to implement security controls in the cloud, organizations need to consider a number of different types of controls. There are also a wide range of guidance documents that provide details on how to implement security controls in the cloud. The main reference documents in this area are

- The "Security Guidance for Critical Areas of Focus in Cloud Computer v3.0"[12] from the Cloud Security Alliance;
- The Federal Risk and Authorization Management Program (FedRAMP)[13] guidance published by the US government;
- The "Guidelines on Security and Privacy in Public Cloud Computing" published by the US National Institute of Standards and Technology (NIST)[14]; and
- "Procure Secure—A Guide to Monitoring of Security Service Levels in Cloud Contracts" published by the ENISA.[15]

Each of the above publications has a number of sections with corresponding recommendation to implement in order to secure cloud services. Please refer to Chapter 6 for further details on the certifications frameworks.

Security Guidance for Critical Areas of Focus in Cloud Computer v3.0[16]

The "Security Guidance for Critical Areas of Focus in Cloud Computer v3.0"[17] from the Cloud Security Alliance has 14 security domains where it discusses various security considerations regarding cloud security. (Please refer to Chapter 8 for more detail.)

Federal Risk and Authorization Management Program[18]

The FedRAMP[19] guidance published by the US government for use by government agencies, but equally applicable to private companies, also outlines a number of areas that should be considered when securing the cloud. Please refer to Chapter 6 for further detail.

Guidelines on Security and Privacy in Public Cloud Computing[20]

NIST's "Guidelines on Security and Privacy in Public Cloud Computing"[21] focuses on public cloud services and how best to secure them. Within its guidelines NIST looks at the following areas as being key to securing cloud services:

- Governance;
- Compliance;
- Trust;
- Architecture;
- Identify and access management;
- Software isolation;
- Data protection;
- Availability; and
- Incident response.

Procure Secure[22]

The main focus of ENISA's "Procure Secure—A Guide to Monitoring of Security Service Levels in Cloud Contracts"[23] is on how organizations should use service-level agreements (SLAs) to ensure Cloud Service Providers deliver the level of security required by the organization. It should be noted that while negotiating SLAs is best practice, this may not be possible in all cases. In some situations the Cloud Service Provider may only provide a certain service and for its own efficiency of operations or cost will not alter its SLA for individual customers. In other cases the organization may be too small, or not have the legal expertise available, to negotiate an SLA, particularly with larger Cloud Service Providers. However, as organizations will not have direct control over many of the security controls required to maintain security of their data and/or services, an effective SLA can be a major tool in securing the cloud. The areas covered by this guide are

- Service availability;
- Incident response;
- Service elasticity and load tolerance;
- Data lifecycle management;
- Technical compliance and vulnerability management;

- Change management;
- Data isolation; and
- Log management and forensics.

Each of the above publications provides valuable recommendations on how an organization can secure the cloud. While each publication has different categories and areas of focus there are a number of common controls throughout each publication. These can be categorized into the following controls areas:

- Governance and compliance controls;
- Policies and procedures controls;
- Physical security;
- Technical controls; and
- Personnel controls.

It should be noted that some controls may be applicable to more than one category but for ease of reading the category most appropriate will be used below.

Governance and Compliance Controls

- Cloud Governance Frameworks

  Organizations should ensure when engaging with a Cloud Service Provider that the Cloud Service Provider employs a cloud governance framework. By employing a cloud governance framework the Cloud Service Provider will demonstrate it takes its commitments to security seriously and has adopted industry-recognized best practices. An example would be the "Best Practices for Governing and Operating Data and Information in the Cloud" which is part of the Cloud Security Alliance's Cloud Data Governance Project.[24]

- Compliance

  One of the challenges faced by organizations with cloud computing is ensuring they are compliant with various legal, industry, customer, and regulatory requirements. Organizations based in the European Union who process personal data of individuals have to comply with the European Union's Data Protection Directive[25] while organizations in the United States that process personal medical records have to comply with the Health Insurance Portability and Accountability Act.[26] Other compliance requirements including the Payment Card Industry Data Security Standard dictate certain security requirements that organizations must comply with should they process any credit card information. Organizations that have compliance requirements will need to ensure that the Cloud Service Provider has the appropriate controls in place to ensure the organization can remain in compliance.

An example would be organizations that are obliged to comply with the European Union's Data Protection Directive. Under that directive it is illegal to export personal data outside the European Economic Area[27] unless it is to approved countries with similar privacy laws to the EU, while to the US it is to companies that sign up to the US Safe Harbor[28] Framework, or are contractually obliged[29] to protect the data in accordance with the EU Data Protection Directive's requirements. Given the nature of the cloud it can be difficult to determine exactly where data resides. It could be on a number of servers, over a number of datacenters, located in various locations around the world. The Cloud Service Provider will need to demonstrate to these organizations that their data will stored, processed, and deleted in accordance with their Data Protection obligations.

A Cloud Service Provider that has a full time compliance office, or officer, would demonstrate they take this issue seriously. Organizations engaging with a Cloud Service Provider should request details on the Cloud Service Provider's compliance function such as who is responsible in the provider for compliance, what regulations and requirements the provider complies with, and also whether or not the Cloud Service Provider has a compliance policy in place.

It should be noted that an organization is still responsible for all of its compliance requirements even when the data and/or services are provided by a Cloud Service Provider.

- Third-Party Assurances

Many suppliers, be they Cloud Service Providers or traditional IT suppliers, will assert that they provide good service and they take security seriously. While many are sincere in these proclamations, it is akin to buying a second-hand car and taking the word of the sales person that everything is okay with the car. When buying a second-hand car it is recommended to take it for a test drive and to have a trained mechanic examine it for any potential problems. Similarly when engaging with a Cloud Service Provider, an organization should consider whether or not it should take the provider at face value with regard to their assurances regarding security. Ideally, the organization should seek some independent third-party assurances as to how effective the security controls are within the Cloud Service Provider.

The ISO 27001 Information Security standard is a well-recognized international standard which is independent, vendor neutral, and covers many aspects of security. Organizations that are certified to the standard demonstrate that they have implemented the security controls within the standard that are applicable to them and that these controls have been independently verified by a trusted third party. Further details are included in Chapter 6.

Another initiative that can be used is the Cloud Security Alliance's Security, Trust & Assurance Registry (STAR)[30] initiative. The Cloud Security Alliance's STAR was launched in 2011 with the aim of improving transparency and assurance of Cloud Service Providers. Further details are included in Chapters 2 and 6.

- Data Ownership

It may seem strange to have to bring this item to the fore but it is important to ensure that when an organization moves its data into the cloud that it is clearly understood who owns the data that is migrated into the system and, just as importantly, data that is created within the cloud.

There should be no ambiguity over the ownership of the data. In order to ensure the organization meets its compliance requirements, it is essential ownership of the data is clearly understood. Should the Cloud Service Provider claim that any data held within their platform belongs to them and they can do with it what they wish, this could place the customer organization in breach of its compliance requirements.

The issue of data ownership needs to be defined in the event the customer organization decides not to engage with the Cloud Service Provider and move the service back in-house or to another provider. The customer organization will want to ensure that should they take this route the initial Cloud Service Provider does not claim ownership to the customer organization's data.

So before engaging with a Cloud Service Provider an organization must clearly agree with the provider who actually owns the data.

- Legal Interception, Court Orders, or Government Surveillance

Ever since recent revelations by Edward Snowden relating to government surveillance of Internet companies and Cloud Service Providers, the issue of government access to private data has come to the fore for many organizations. In particular, organizations that are located in one jurisdiction may have concerns whether the government from another jurisdiction can access the organizations' data because it engaged with a Cloud Service Provider that is located in that foreign jurisdiction. This issue was recently demonstrated when Microsoft were ordered by a US court to surrender email data belonging to one of its customers, even though the data was stored on a server physically located in Dublin, Ireland.[31] This has raised many concerns for some organizations as to whether or not they should store sensitive data with a Cloud Service Provider, particularly a Cloud Service Provider that is subject to court orders from a different jurisdiction.

Organizations that are considering storing highly confidential information, be they private companies with commercial or intellectual data or government bodies with sensitive information, should seek assurances from the Cloud Service Provider as to what their policy is regarding requests from government bodies or law enforcement agencies. Questions to ask include

- Will the Cloud Service Provider respond to all requests without question?
- Will the Cloud Service Provider respond only to legal court requests?
- Will the Cloud Service Provider notify the organization of any requests it received relating to the organization's data?
- Does the Cloud Service Provider provide access to customer data for intelligence agencies? If so, under what conditions?
- Under which jurisdiction and courts is the Cloud Service Provider bound?
- Does the Cloud Service Provider publish a transparency report outlining how many requests for data it has received from governments and law enforcement agencies?

Supply chain security: Many Cloud Service Providers rely on third parties to help them provide their services. These services could range from customer call center services, to technical support, to cleaning companies, to utility suppliers such as water and power, and contractor staff. Organizations engaging with a Cloud Service Provider should determine what other third party the Cloud Service Provider employs and what the security controls, protocols, and assurances that are in place with those providers.

Organizations should note that if they have any compliance requirements, in most cases those requirements not only extend to the Cloud Service Provider(s) they engage with, but also to any third parties the Cloud Service Provider uses to provide its service to the customer. Under many compliance regimes, the customer organization will retain responsibility for ensuring that the entire supply chain is compliant with the relevant regulations. Organizations therefore should ensure that the Cloud Service Provider provides full transparency with regard to its own suppliers and the security controls those suppliers have in place.

Security testing and auditing: While assurances from a Cloud Service Provider or from independent third parties can provide an organization with a certain level of confidence in the security of a Cloud Service Provider, there may be times the organization would like to verify for itself the claims being made. Traditionally in many cases this would involve allowing the organization to conduct an audit of the suppliers systems, premises, and/or services. The organization would arrange for its own internal audit team or engage with a trusted external provider to conduct an audit of the supplier.

In the traditional procurement and engagement model this approach worked in most cases, however when it comes to the cloud this model breaks down. Given that an organization's data may be located anywhere in the cloud at any time it will be extremely difficult for an auditor to conduct an audit relating to the physical location of the data. Many cloud providers have developed their own proprietary platforms and systems which many auditors will not be familiar with. Finally, many Cloud Service Providers simply do not have the manpower to facilitate every request from a potential or existing customer to audit their facilities and systems.

The issue of penetration and vulnerability tests is also an issue. A Cloud Service Provider may not wish to allow customers to perform penetration tests against their systems in the event it causes availability or other issues with the provider's services and impacts other customers. There may be legal and liability issues that could impact on the customer organization should a penetration or vulnerability test cause issues. This could extend to where customers may not wish to perform any penetration or vulnerability tests against the Cloud Service Provider's own services but simply perform such tests against their own applications. However, performing application penetration tests or application vulnerability tests may breach the Cloud Service Provider's terms and conditions.

If an organization cannot get agreement from the Cloud Service Provider for it to perform security tests or audits, it should seek agreement from the Cloud Service Provider that it will provide the organization with access to any penetration tests or audits the Cloud Service Provider engages with. While not as independent as engaging their own preferred testers and auditors, this option could help the organization determine how secure the Cloud Service Provider is.

Service-level agreements: In the world of Cloud Computing the selection, implementation, support, and ongoing management of security controls are under the control of the Cloud Service Provider and not the customer organization. The only influence and oversight the organization will have will be via the Cloud Service Provider's SLA. It is therefore vitally important that organizations spend time and energy in ensuring the SLA is suitable to their requirements and provides them with the tools and ability to manage the security of the data and services entrusted to the Cloud Service Provider.

The ENISA provides a very comprehensive guide on how to establish and manage an SLA with a Cloud Service Provider. This is detailed in the "Procure Secure: A guide to monitoring of security service levels in cloud contracts"[32] and should be referred to by any organization looking to engage with a Cloud Service Provider.

An effective SLA will provide an organization with continuous feedback on the effectiveness of the security controls being provided by the Cloud Service Provider. An effective SLA should also enable the organization to seek recompense or service credits in the event the Cloud Service Provider does not meet the goals and targets agreed in the SLA. An effective SLA can be a powerful tool in ensuring a provider continues to meet the levels of service required by the customer organization.

Policies and Procedures Controls

Processes and procedures ensure a structured approach is taken when dealing with certain tasks or practices. This is even more important when engaging with a Cloud Service Provider to ensure the security of an organization's data is not undermined or compromised by provider staff, or indeed the organization's staff, not following correct procedures. There are a number of key policies and procedures an organization should ensure the Cloud Service Provider has in place when engaging with that supplier.

- Privacy Policies

Privacy policies are important as they demonstrate to others what the company's approach is to privacy and how the company will protect the privacy of individuals. Some countries have very strict privacy regulations, such as those within the European Union, Switzerland, and Iceland, which require companies operating from them or selling to customers in them to take strict measures to ensure privacy of personal information.

When engaging with a Cloud Service Provider an organization should ensure that it first has its own privacy policy in place and then ensures that the Cloud Service Provider's privacy policy is in line with that of the customer organization.

In addition to the above the customer organization should determine what approach the Cloud Service Provider takes to building privacy controls into its services, otherwise known as Privacy by Design.[33]

The Cloud Service Provider should also have a policy of conducting Privacy Impact Assessments when it develops new services and alters or decommissions existing ones. The United Kingdom's Information Commissioner's Office provides a "Conducting Privacy Impact Assessments Code of Practice"[34] which is an excellent guide on this topic.

Change Management

All IT environments grow and change over time. New network components will be added, existing components will be upgraded or replaced, and software levels on components, services, and applications will be revised and updated. Likewise a Cloud Service Provider's environment will grow and change. It is essential that assurances are got from the Cloud Service Provider that any change to the provider's production environments are managed in a structured and controlled way to ensure minimal disruption to service.

When engaging with a Cloud Service Provider an organization should ensure it has visibility of the provider's Change Management Policy and get assurances that this policy can

- reduce the risk associated with unplanned changes;
- inform affected parties, such as the customer organization, of a planned change so that they may take appropriate action;
- minimize the effect a planned change may have on the quality or availability of services and/or data;
- minimize the overall cost and time associated with planned changes;
- provide an auditable trail for compliance, troubleshooting, and review purposes;
- facilitate continuous learning and improvement of personnel, processes, and procedures; and
- provide metrics for management decisions.

In addition the customer organization should ensure its own Change Management Policies are robust and are adapted to engage with the Cloud Service Provider. In particular the policy should ensure that

- changes made on the customer organization's infrastructure are assessed to ensure they do not impact on how the organization accesses the services provided by the Cloud Service Provider and
- any changes made on either the customer or the Cloud Service Provider's systems are assessed to ensure any coordinated changes required on both sides are completed in a timely and appropriate manner.

Patch Management
Patch management is the discipline of ensuring fixes to software bugs, otherwise known as patches, are applied in a timely manner while maintaining the service being provided. Applying patches in a timely and process-driven manner is important as

- critical bugs could cause a failure in the underlying infrastructure resulting in a prolonged outage for the cloud service or any dependent services within the customer organization's environment;
- without a formalized patch management policy it is possible that applying a patch to one element of the Cloud Service Provider's platform could have negative consequences for a system or other element that depends on the patched element; and
- critical bugs in the underlying database, services, or platform could be exploited by individuals to gain unauthorized access to sensitive data.

When engaging with a Cloud Service Provider the customer organization should make sure it is aware of what the provider's patch management policy is. In some cloud platforms, e.g., SaaS, the impact of applying a patch may have little impact on the service being provided. However, should the customer organization be integrating their own systems with the SaaS platform then the application of a patch could disrupt that interoperability. Similarly changes to a PaaS or an IaaS platform could impact negatively the services subscribed to by the customer organization.

When examining the Cloud Service Provider's patch management policies, the customer organization needs to ensure that all patches are managed in a structured manner. It is also important that the provider's patch management policy is integrated with its Change Management Policy.

The key elements an organization should look to be included in the Cloud Service Provider's Patch Management Policy are

- How often patches are applied?
- How the provider will manage emergency or critical patches?
- That the provider has outlined the level of testing that is required before applying patches
- Who within the provider authorizes the application of the patches, and will the customer organization have any input into this thought process?
- How does the Cloud Service Provider ensure patches are centrally controlled, distributed, and applied?
- The policy should also provide clarification as to roles and responsibilities for applying key patches and updates to the various systems and platforms within the service provider and where the demarcation lies for patches within the customer's systems.

Incident Response Plan

Computer security incidents are a matter of course for every organization, even more so for Cloud Service Providers given the large number of clients they have which in turn could make them a bigger and juicier target for criminals. While the Cloud Service Provider will provide many assurances that they have excellent security controls in place, it is important to recognize that there is no such thing as 100% security and that at some stage there may be a security incident.

As the party responsible for all its data, the customer organization should satisfy itself that the Cloud Service Provider has appropriate incident response plans and processes in place. It should also ensure that roles and responsibilities regarding dealing with security breaches are clearly identified, agreed, and assigned between the provider and the customer organization.

Business Continuity Plan

There are two broad aspects to business continuity: one is having the counter-measures in place to prevent a disaster happening in the first place, and the other is having the countermeasures and plans in place to minimize the effects if a disaster does occur.

Organizations migrating to the cloud should realize that simply because the data or service is hosted in the cloud, it is not a license for them to forget about business continuity. The organization is still responsible for ensuring its business can continue in the event of any interruption, be they to their own in-house systems or that of the Cloud Service Provider.

As such, the customer organization should seek reassurances that the Cloud Service Provider has a comprehensive business continuity plan in place, and the customer organization integrates that plan into its own business continuity plans. The key areas the customer organization should look at include

- Has the provider identified the business processes critical to the continued provision of its services?
- What is the priority of restoring services for the specific customer, i.e., is the cloud provider restoring the largest customers first and then small ones?
- Has the provider conducted a detailed Business Impact Analysis (BIA)?
- Has the provider conducted a detailed risk assessment upon which to formulate its Business Continuity Plan?
- Has the provider identified the staffing requirements it needs to support the provision of critical services in the event of an interruption to the business?
- What solutions has the provider implemented to restore its services in a timely manner and to minimize interruption to the customer organization's business processes?
- Has the provider identified and provisioned the facilities required to support the continuation of critical services in the event of an interruption to the business?
- What are the provider's processes and procedures for invoking the Business Continuity Plan?
- What notifications will be provided to the organization in the event the Business Continuity Plan is invoked?

As well as ensuring the Cloud Service Provider's business continuity policies, processes, and procedures are appropriate, it is equally important the customer organization revises its own plans and adapts them to the change in service delivery model. In many cases moving to the cloud can enhance business continuity for the client organization but this should not be taken for granted. The organization should review its plans to ensure the business can continue to operate should there be a business interrupting event either at their own facilities or those of the Cloud Service Provider.

Access Control

Ensuring only authorized personnel have access to the data and services stored in the cloud is another key challenge that organizations need to address. Once the data has migrated to the cloud, any authorized person with access to the Internet can theoretically gain access to that data.

It is important the customer organization has its own processes to ensure only authorized personnel have access to the cloud service based upon its security and business requirements. The organization should work with the Cloud Service Provider to ensure access to the service is provided in a manner which will protect the confidentiality and integrity of that information. This could be based on two-factor authentication solutions, restricting access to certain IP addresses associated with the organization, and/or restricting logins during certain times and from specific regions.

The organization should regularly review the access control rights to the service for users and groups of users to ensure that all access rights are appropriate for the role of the individual users.

The organization should also ensure that administrator access to the cloud service is limited to only those members of staff with a valid business requirement for such access. It should also ensure that other staff, such as developers and other application personnel, do not have administrator access to the service, except in emergencies and then with appropriate authorization.

As well as ensuring it manages the access to the service of its own staff, the customer organization should seek assurances from the Cloud Service Provider that appropriate access controls are in place regarding the provider's staff.

Forensics and eDiscovery

Computer forensics and eDiscovery are relatively mature disciplines within traditional IT environments.[35] However, when it comes to cloud computing these disciplines are still in their infancy. Cloud computing brings a number of challenges when trying to forensically capture data. Firstly there is the issue of where the data is stored and located, and how can the data be gathered in a forensically sound way. There is also the issue of the dynamic nature of the cloud and how to soundly capture threats, processes, and memory to support an investigation. In a cloud environment there is also the challenge of how to isolate logs and other critical supporting evidence for one customer's instance from all of the other customers using that Cloud Service Provider.

When engaging with a Cloud Service Provider the customer organization should ensure it fully understands what the Cloud Service Provider can, and just as importantly cannot, provide with regard to computer forensics and eDiscovery requests. With that information the customer organization should review its own computer forensics and eDiscovery processes and procedures and adapt them accordingly.

The Cloud Security Alliance's research group on Incident Management and Forensics[36] is looking to developing guidelines on Best Practices for Incident Handling and Forensics in a Cloud Environment.

Data Migration

Migrating data into a Cloud Service Provider's environment can be a timely task. Data may have to be reformatted or restructured to fit in with the architecture of the Cloud Service Provider. However, once this has been completed many organizations enjoy the benefits of managing and processing their data using the power of the cloud. Customer organizations should ensure though that when they first engage with a Cloud Service Provider that they clearly understand and agree how their data can be migrated away from the provider in the extent that provider closes business, is taken over by another service provider, or should the customer organization decide to engage with a competitor providing a similar service. It is important that the customer organization takes these steps to ensure it does not get "locked in" to the service provider simply because they cannot retrieve their data in a timely and secure manner. The customer organization should familiarize itself, and be satisfied, with the data migration policy of the Cloud Service Provider. A key thing the customer organization should consider is what format the data will take should it decide to migrate away from a service provider. Will their data be returned as a flat text file, a CSV file, or in a structured file format? Each of these formats could have implications for how easy it is to migrate the data to another platform. In addition the customer organization should ensure the Cloud Service Provider securely erases all data that is no longer required to be stored with that provider.

Physical Security Controls

For most customer organizations, migrating their data or services to the cloud will result in that data being stored in facilities that have better physical security than many of those organizations can provide on their own premises. However, this is something that customer organizations should not take for granted and when engaging with a Cloud Service Provider details of how the organization's data will secured should be throughly reviewed and accessed to ensure the controls meet the customer's requirements.

This should include the physical perimeter of the Cloud Service Provider's premises where controls are in place to prevent access by unauthorized personnel. These controls should be designed to prevent unauthorized access, damage, or interference to the services provided from that facility. Monitoring of these controls should be in place such as the use of CCTV cameras, IDS, fire detection and suppression systems, logging at all entry and exit points, and the use of security guards.

The customer organization should determine that the Cloud Service Provider has appropriate controls in place to protect against environmental issues such as fire, floods, hurricanes, earthquakes, civil unrest, or other similar threats that could disrupt services.

Other physical controls should include protection against interruption to key services such as Internet access to the data centers, power, water, humidity, heat, rodent infestation, and other such threats. There should be controls in place to not just prevent these threats from being realized but also to minimize their impact should they occur.

Technical Controls

Technical controls are key to protecting data in the cloud. It is important to note that many of the technical controls for the cloud are the same as those used in traditional IT environments. This is because even though the cloud is a relatively new evolution of how data is managed, stored, and processed, the threats that face traditional systems, such as viruses, hacking, spam, are as relevant to the cloud.

Different implementations of technical controls will provide different levels of effectiveness. Also some providers may employ alternative controls in place of those expected by the customer organization. When engaging with a Cloud Service Provider customer organizations should use their risk assessment to ensure the controls provided by the Cloud Service Provider are adequate for the customer organization's needs.

The Cloud Security Alliance's Security Guidance for Critical Areas of Cloud Computing provides excellent details of what security controls should be implemented based on the customer organization's needs and the type of cloud provider platform.

The core controls that a customer organization should ensure are in place are as follows.

Backups

Customer organizations should not assume that simply because their data is stored in the cloud there is no reason to worry about backing it up. Data can be deleted, lost, corrupted, or destroyed whether it is stored on traditional or cloud systems. When engaging with a Cloud Service Provider it is important to determine how the customer organization's data is backed up, where is it backed up to (bearing in mind any compliance requirements), how the backups are secured, and how the backups can be accessed. It is also important to determine how long backups are held for and indeed the time taken to restore either all of the data or individual files. This information will be key to the customer organization as it adjusts its business continuity and disaster recovery plans to take into account the adoption of cloud services.

Secure Deletion

Data when deleted from disks is never fully deleted. Instead references to where that data is stored are removed so the operating system knows it can overwrite those areas. As such many data recovery and forensic tools can easily restore any deleted data. As data stored in the cloud can be located across different disks, across different systems, and across different data centers, it is important that the customer organization knows when data is deleted it is done so in a way to prevent it from being recovered. This is important in situations where customers are migrating from one service provider to another and need to ensure their data are properly and securely removed from the previous provider.

Secure Development

Engaging with the cloud in many cases involved accessing services, data, and systems via an interface or application. The complexity of these applications will depend on the cloud platform. In the IaaS platform, it may simply be a control panel, whereas in the SaaS environment it will be a full blown application. It is important therefore that the customer organization has assurances that these applications, interfaces, and control panels have been developed in a secure manner and that security is built into the development cycle as early as possible.

When engaging with a Cloud Service Provider customer organizations should get visibility into how security has been built into the Software Development Lifecycle (SDLC). It should seek assurances from the provider that their development team has regular training in developing secure code. The provider should also be conducting secure code reviews of their software to identify any potential security bugs in their code. Another area to be examined by the customer organization is to see how often the provider conducts threat tree analysis against their systems. Finally, the customer organization should determine from the Cloud Service Provider what the provider's policies are regarding identifying vulnerabilities in its code, patching those vulnerabilities, and how it keeps customers abreast of these issues.

The customer organization should also discover what secure coding principles the Cloud Service Provider is using. There are a number of guides that are easily available for organizations to incorporate into their SDLC such as

- The Open Web Application Security Project (OWASP) Top 10 Project[37];
- The Open Web Application Security Project (OWASP) Cloud Top 10 Security Risks[38];
- SANs Top 25 Most Dangerous Software Errors[39]; and
- SafeCODE's Practices for Secure Development of Cloud Applications.[40]

Data Encryption

One of the most effective security controls when engaged with the cloud is to implement encryption both when the data is at rest and when in transit. Customer organizations need to ensure that any data transmitted to and from the Cloud Service Provider is encrypted. This could be either by employing SSL to encrypt traffic as it traverses the Internet or by using a VPN to connect to the provider.

When data is stored (at rest) on the Cloud Service Provider's systems it should also be encrypted. It is important to understand what encryption algorithms the Cloud Service Provider employs for this. Ideally the encryption algorithms should be industry standard and peer reviewed. Should the Cloud Service Provider offer its own in-house developed solution then this should be a cause of concern.

Encrypting data is not just about the algorithms used but also how the keys to encrypt and decrypt that data are managed. In a cloud environment, it is important that the customer organization considers whether they need to retain all access to the keys and that the provider cannot access them. It is important to note that if the cloud provider does not have access to keys (i.e., plain text data), it is going to be limited in what functionality (value) it can deliver (except when using homomorphism encryption in certain use cases).

Should the provider have access to the keys then it is possible the provider can also then use these keys to decrypt the data. Ideally any encryption solution should only be managed by the customer organization with the provider having no ability to generate its own keys or modify those of others.

Denial of Service Attack Mitigation

In recent years we have seen an increase in the use of Denial of Service (DOS) and Distributed Denial of Service attacks against various organizations. DOS attack is where attackers send some traffic to the targeted systems that they can no longer provide the service to legitimate users. Customer organizations should determine what mitigation tools and services the Cloud Service

Provider has in place, not just to protect the provider's own service, but also the instances of the service for the customer.

Security Monitoring

Recognizing that there is suspicious activity occurring against systems is key to being able to respond quickly and effectively. Logs provide security teams with the ability to identify potential attacks, be alerted to ongoing attacks, and help investigate an attack. In a tradition IT environment, it is possible to implement monitoring of security and other relevant logs. However, it is not as straightforward in a cloud environment. To determine how effective a customer organization's incident detection and response will be in the cloud the organization needs to determine what visibility it will have to logs.

It may be a case that the organization will not have direct access to the logs and will have to rely on the Cloud Service Provider's security team to monitor the services and report any suspicious activity to the customer. In this case, it is important the customer organization ensures this activity is included and managed within the SLA.

Should the Cloud Service Provider allow access to the logs for the customer then the customer needs to determine

- The level of access they can have to the logs. Will it be direct access or via an API?
- How the customer's log data is isolated from another customer's log data.
- How the customer will monitor those logs.
- The devices, such as firewalls, routers, servers, and switches, which should be configured to record events.
- The events that should be recorded for each type of system or component on the service.
- Where events should be stored. Will they be stored on system within the provider's environment or will the customer store the events on their own premises?
- The retention policy for event logs and their details.
- How alerts are created in certain events, event patterns, or combination of events.
- What tools and utilities are implemented to monitor for these events.

Firewalls

Firewalls are security devices used to manage network traffic between two networks. In most cases firewalls are configured to only allow certain traffic through and to deny all other traffic. While it would be expected that a Cloud Service Provider would have firewalls in place, the customer organization should familiarize itself with the types of firewalls the provider employs and whether or not they satisfy the risk profile of the customer organization. Areas to consider are

- Whether or not the firewall is dedicated to the customer or shared among other clients?
- How often are the firewall rules reviewed regularly to ensure they are still applicable and required?
- Are changes to the firewall rules reviewed to ensure they do not conflict with other rules for the customer or indeed with other customers' rules?
- How often are the latest software patches and security updates installed on the firewall?
- Are they regularly tested to ensure that they provide the level of security required?
- How often are the firewall configurations reviewed to ensure they are still applicable and appropriate?
- Are the firewalls monitored for security alerts?
- Are Web Application Firewalls in place or available for use by the customer?

Intrusion Detection Systems

While the Cloud Service Provider should have mechanisms in place to detect threats such as computer viruses, it should also have mechanisms in place to detect malicious or suspicious network traffic, such as an IDS or Intrusion Prevent System (IPS). An IDS can monitor network traffic for suspicious activity that may indicate an attack is taking place and raise an alert should it do so. An IPS is similar to an IDS system with the additional ability to automatically launch a number of prescribed actions to react and prevent the attack.

Customer organizations should determine if the risk profile requires the Cloud Service Provider to have an IDS or IPS in place.

Personnel Controls

The people who will be working with the systems and data are a key element in maintaining the security of those systems and data. Good security requires that all staff are properly trained in how they use and interact with the systems they are using to prevent untrained people corrupting any data. Good security training should enable staff to better understand the risks involved in working with such systems and data and how they can help minimize those risks. It also requires that those charged with securing the systems and/or data are properly trained, skilled, and experienced in the technologies and the disciplines required for their role.

While an organization can manage the above responsibilities with its own staff, it does not have the same direct control with the staff of the Cloud Service

Provider. The customer organization in that case should determine from the provider how the following areas are dealt with:

- Background checking

What background checking does the Cloud Service Provider conduct when hiring new staff, be they permanent, temporary, or contractors? It is important to know how in-depth those background checks are to determine and verify (where possible) the following:

- Employment history
- Educational qualifications
- Criminal background checks, in particular those that may be most relevant for the role such as convictions relating to fraud and computer crime. Note that in some countries it is not possible for companies to conduct criminal background checks unless their business is in certain areas such as access to children, access to vulnerable people, or working on data related to certain government or financial institutions.
- Credit history, in particular to determine if the individual has a poor credit rating or that they may be in financial difficulty. If this is the case then that individual could be at a higher risk of committing fraud. As with criminal background checks, it should be noted that running credit history checks on employees may not be legal.

Insider Threat
People working within a company, be that the customer organization or the Cloud Service Provider, have trusted access to key systems and data. This access could be either accidentally or deliberately abused and the security of those systems and data undermined.

When engaging with a Cloud Service Provider a customer organization needs to realize that the insider threat not only comes from within their own organization but now extends to the staff of the Cloud Service Provider, and indeed any supplier or subcontractor the provider engages with.

It is important therefore that customer organization gets assurances from the Cloud Service Provider that it is monitoring the insider threat and has controls in place to reduce the risk. These controls could be ensuring access controls are properly in place and maintained, there is segregation of duties clearly outlined and managed, that privileged access is granted only on a need to know basis, that access to systems is closely monitored, and that regular reviews of access rights are conducted.

The CERT Insider Threat Center[41] run by CERT/CC,[42] which is part of Carnegie Mellon University, has a lot of additional research available in this area.

- Security Awareness

Making staff aware of the security threats that face an organization and how they can manage those threats is a key element in maintaining security of key data and systems. Customer organizations should get visibility and be satisfied that the Cloud Service Provider is running an effective security awareness program. In particular the provider should ensure that staff at different levels and from different parts of the business receive security awareness training appropriate to their role.

Securing the cloud is not a task that organizations should leave to the Cloud Service Providers to do alone. The customer organization is responsible for its data and its services and therefore needs to work with the Cloud Service Provider to ensure that the appropriate security controls are in place to protect those data and systems. Securing the cloud is a shared responsibility and can only be properly achieved by a collaborative effort by all parties.

This chapter has highlighted some of the areas that customer organizations should consider when migrating data to the cloud. More comprehensive details and recommendations can be found in the Cloud Security Alliance's "Security Guidance for Critical Areas of Cloud Computing."[43] In addition, the ENISA provides excellent advise in its "Procure Secure—A Guide to Monitoring of Security Levels in Cloud Contracts"[44] to ensure those controls are performing and working as expected.

END NOTES

1. M. Whitman and H. Mattord, *Management of information security* – (January 19, 2010), ISBN-10: 1435488435488849.

2. ISO 31000:2009 – *Principles and guidelines on implementation*, http://www.iso.org/iso/catalogue_detail.htm?csnumber=43170.

3. *Cyber Insurance: The next big thing for businesses – entrepreneur magazine*, (July 6, 2014), http://www.entrepreneur.com/article/235355.

4. *Cloud Computing Risk Assessment* https://www.enisa.europa.eu/activities/risk-management/files/deliverables/cloud-computing-risk-assessment.

5. http://www.cert.org/octave/osig.html.

6. http://www.cramm.com/.

7. http://csrc.nist.gov/groups/SMA/fisma/framework.html.

8. http://www.iso.org/iso/home/store/catalogue_ics/catalogue_detail_ics.htm?csnumber=56742.

9. http://www.enisa.europa.eu/activities/risk-management/current-risk/risk-management-inventory/inventory-of-risk-management-risk-assessment-methods-and-tools.

10. https://cloudsecurityalliance.org/download/security-guidance-for-critical-areas-of-focus-in-cloud-computing-v3/.

11. https://cloudsecurityalliance.org/download/security-guidance-for-critical-areas-of-focus-in-cloud-computing-v3/.

12. https://cloudsecurityalliance.org/download/security-guidance-for-critical-areas-of-focus-in-cloud-computing-v3/.

13. http://cloud.cio.gov/action/secure-your-cloud#fedramp.

14. http://www.nist.gov/manuscript-publication-search.cfm?pub_id=909494.

15. http://www.enisa.europa.eu/activities/Resilience-and-CIIP/cloud-computing/procure-secure-a-guide-to-monitoring-of-security-service-levels-in-cloud-contracts.

16. https://cloudsecurityalliance.org/download/security-guidance-for-critical-areas-of-focus-in-cloud-computing-v3/.

17. https://cloudsecurityalliance.org/download/security-guidance-for-critical-areas-of-focus-in-cloud-computing-v3/.

18. http://cloud.cio.gov/action/secure-your-cloud#fedramp.

19. http://cloud.cio.gov/action/secure-your-cloud#fedramp.

20. http://www.nist.gov/manuscript-publication-search.cfm?pub_id=909494.

21. http://www.nist.gov/manuscript-publication-search.cfm?pub_id=909494.

22. See note 15 above.

23. See note 15 above.

24. https://cloudsecurityalliance.org/research/cdg/.

25. http://eur-ex.europa.eu/LexUriServ/LexUriServ.do?uri=CELEX:31995L0046:en:HTML.

26. http://www.gpo.gov/fdsys/search/pagedetails.action?granuleId=CRPT-104hrpt736&package-Id=CRPT-104hrpt736.

27. http://www.efta.int/eea.

28. http://www.export.gov/safeharbor/.

29. *Model contracts for the transfer of personal data to third countries* http://ec.europa.eu/justice/data-protection/document/international-transfers/transfer/index_en.htm.

30. https://cloudsecurityalliance.org/star/.

31. http://www.bbc.com/news/technology-27191500.

32. See note 15 above.

33. UK Information Commissioner's Office Guide to Privacy by Design http://ico.org.uk/for_organisations/data_protection/topic_guides/privacy_by_design.

34. http://ico.org.uk/for_organisations/data_protection/topic_guides/~/media/documents/library/Data_Protection/Practical_application/pia-code-of-practice-final-draft.pdf.

35. Association of Chief Police Officers Good Practise Guide for Digital Evidence http://www.acpo.police.uk/documents/crime/2011/201110-cba-digital-evidence-v5.pdf.

36. https://cloudsecurityalliance.org/research/imf/.

37. https://www.owasp.org/index.php/Category:OWASP_Top_Ten_Project.

38. https://www.owasp.org/index.php/Category:OWASP_Cloud_%E2%80%90_10_Project.

39. http://www.sans.org/top25-software-errors/.

40. http://www.safecode.org/publications.php.

41. http://www.cert.org/insider-threat/.

42. http://www.cert.org/about/.

43. https://cloudsecurityalliance.org/research/security-guidance/.

44. See note 15 above.

Certification for Cloud Service Providers

For end customers of cloud computing, the chapter that discussed the security for cloud providers would have made interesting reading but the reality is that this level of visibility is rarely available. In the majority of cases, the use of certifications is the primary vehicle for providing assurance to customers, both current and potential. The role of certifications can therefore be used to provide a degree of trust into the security deployed by the provider, but may also be a mandatory requirement for customers within specific geographies or industry verticals.

The purpose of this chapter is to review the various cloud security certifications available. As expected, a multitude of standards each with their varying strengths is available. Also detailed within this chapter are Cloud Security Alliance (CSA) certifications that were briefly referenced in Chapter 2, which includes the Cloud Controls Matrix (CCM) as well as the Consensus Assessments Initiative Questionnaire (CAIQ).

CERTIFICATION FOR CLOUD SERVICE PROVIDERS

The title for this particular section is a little misleading; this is because although a number of information security-related certifications exist specifically for cloud computing, there exist considerably more that are used for traditional IT environments, and that have been adopted by Cloud Service Providers (CSP). There have also been many books dedicated to these individual standards (for example, the excellent book by co-author Brian Honan entitled "ISO 27001 in a Windows environment"[1]). Subsequently, the intention is not to detail how to apply the various standards, but rather provide the reader with an understanding of what is available, and the relative merits of each standard. In particular where and why a standard would be used as opposed to another? For a broader assessment of the various certification schemes (beyond security), please refer to the November 2013 publication by ETSI entitled "Cloud standards coordination."[2] The following are some of the common security frameworks used by CSP; this list is certainly not exhaustive and therefore the reader is encouraged to review the ETSI document as well as guidance developed by ENISA.[3]

CSA Open Certification Framework

Introduced in Chapter 2, the open certification framework (OCF) "is an industry initiative to allow global, accredited, trusted certification of cloud providers."[4] Based on the research conducted by the CSA Governance Risk and Compliance (GRC) stack, the OCF supports a number of assurance tiers ranging from self-certification to continuous monitoring as defined within Chapter 2 (under STAR). The structure of OCF is graphically illustrated in Figure 6.1.

Detailed in Chapter 2, this open framework is particularly helpful to potential customers in achieving transparency into the security controls deployed by service providers. The foundation for the framework is based upon the outputs from the GRC stack and in particular the CCM and CAIQ.

CSA GRC Stack – CCM

The CCM provides the core security principles for CSP which can be used to articulate their security maturity to potential end customers. Originally released as version 1.0 in April 2010, the latest revision is currency at v.3.0 that was released in March 2013. Version 3 of the matrix itself is comprised of a total of 16 domains each containing a varying number of controls that are organized into subdomains. These domains are as follows:

- Domain 1: Application and interface security
- Domain 2: Audit assurance and compliance

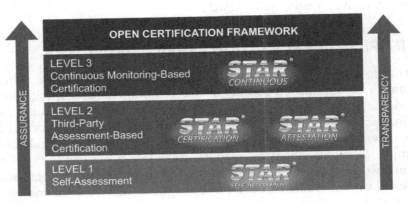

FIGURE 6.1

Open certification framework (OCF).

- Domain 3: Business continuity management and operational resilience
- Domain 4: Change control and configuration management
- Domain 5: Data security and information lifecycle management
- Domain 6: Datacenter security
- Domain 7: Encryption and key management
- Domain 8: Governance and risk management
- Domain 9: Human resources
- Domain 10: Identity and access management
- Domain 11: Infrastructure and virtualization security
- Domain 12: Interoperability and portability
- Domain 13: Mobile security
- Domain 14: Security incident management, E-discovery, and cloud forensics
- Domain 15: Supply chain management, transparency, and accountability
- Domain 16: Threat and vulnerability management

This latest revision introduces three new domains from previous versions, namely, interoperability and portability (domain 12), mobile security (domain 13), as well as supply chain management (domain 14). Subsequently, the total numbers of controls have increased from 98, to now 138. As detailed in Chapter 2, the opportunity for potential end customers is to leverage STAR to identify providers that have adopted the CCM and have self-certified or utilized an independent third party. Having gone through over a year in review, according to Sean Cordero Co-Chair of the CCM Working Group: "CCM adoption gives cloud providers a manageable set of implementation ready controls that are mapped to global security standards. For customers, it acts a catalyst for dialogue about the security posture of their service providers, something that before the CCM existed was impossible. Keeping this balance in CCM v3 was a significant undertaking that could not have happened without the dedication of CSA member companies such as Microsoft, Salesforce, PwC, and the 120+ individual members who participated in the worldwide peer review. For their efforts and dedication we are grateful."[5]

Consensus Assessments Initiative Questionnaire

Like the CCM, the CAIQ is also part of the CSA GRC stack. Initially released in October 2010, the assessment questionnaire was updated and released as version 1.1 in September 2011. Available in spreadsheet format, the questionnaire provides a series of questions in which the respondent can answer Yes or No, across multiple control groups that a cloud customer or auditor would likely ask of a provider. The control groups are as follows:

- Compliance
- Data governance

- Facility security
- Human resources security
- Information security
- Legal
- Operations management
- Risk management
- Release management
- Resiliency
- Security architecture.

Like the CCM, the CAIQ can be used by the providers as part of a self-assessment submission. Intended to be a companion to CSA Guidance and the CCM, the questionnaire allows potential end customers transparency and assurance as to the security posture of CSP.

External Certification Schemes/Standards

Many cloud providers are marketing the certifications and standards that their implementations have been certified or tested against. In addition to the CSA certification schemes, there are very many more that are used as a means to provide potential end customers assurance as to the security deployed by the provider. The following summarize many of these, however, the reader is reminded that this list is not exhaustive.

EuroCloud Star Audit

The EuroCloud Star Audit is governed by EuroCloud, an independent not-for-profit organization based out of Luxembourg. The certification process, however, does differ to alternate schemes with the manner in which certified companies demonstrate compliance. Many certification schemes support a binary response, for example, "we are certified" or "we are not certified." With EuroCloud, those organizations that undertake the audit can articulate certification through EuroCloud stars, ranging from 1 to 5.

Evaluation of the service provider is based against a checklist that includes the following categories:

- Profile
  - General information
  - Physical data location customer data
  - Service management
  - Extended company profile
  - Reference information about the cloud service
  - Certifications

- Contract and compliance
  - Adequate contract terms
  - Rules for data management
  - Contractual data privacy requirements
  - Service-level agreements
  - Terms in case of bankruptcy
  - Terms for pricing and cost allocation
- Security and data privacy
  - Security management
  - Technical security
  - Technical data privacy measures
  - Data integrity
  - Auditability
- Operations and infrastructure
  - General DC assessment
  - Access control
  - Area and environment assessment
  - Resilience
  - DC operations
- Operations processes
  - Customer support
  - Service management
  - Data backup processes
  - Quality assurance[6]

At present, the completed assessments can be disclosed by the service provider, with a Website under preparation. The certification itself will be applicable for a 2-year period, and according to ENISA has been deployed across the EU.[7]

ISO/IEC 27001

Governed by the International Organization for Standardization (ISO), and the International Electrotechnical Commission (IEC), the origins of ISO/IEC 27001 certification goes back almost two decades. The origins go as far back as 1995, under the BS 7799 standard. The first revision was undertaken in 1998 with the first part that contained best practices. The standard was later adopted by the ISO, and renamed as ISO/IEC 17799. In 2005, the standard was revised and incorporated into the ISO 27000 series as ISO/IEC 27002.

The second part of BS 7799 was adopted by ISO in 2005 as ISO/IEC 27001. In 2013, both ISO/IEC 27001 and ISO 27002 have been revised and updated.

The official title of ISO/IEC 27001 is "Information technology—Security techniques—Information security management systems (ISMS)—Requirements." The development of the standard(s) within the ISO as well as IEC includes technical committees that are comprised of national bodies, as well other public/private sector international organizations. The publication of international standards requires approval from at least 75% of the national bodies that cast a vote.

Unlike other standards documented within this chapter, ISO 27001 is not developed specifically for cloud computing; it provides "requirements for establishing, implementing, maintaining and continuously improving an ISMS."[8] The 2005 revision focused on the *Plan-Do-Check-Act* model. However, the 2013 revision focused on measuring the effectiveness of the information security management system (ISMS) and introduced a new section on outsourcing. Another change is that the latest revision has 114 controls across 14 groups as opposed to 133 controls in 11 groups:

- A.5: Information security policies (2 controls)
- A.6: Organization of information security (7 controls)
- A.7: Human resource security—6 controls that are applied before, during, or after employment
- A.8: Asset management (10 controls)
- A.9: Access control (14 controls)
- A.10: Cryptography (2 controls)
- A.11: Physical and environmental security (15 controls)
- A.12: Operations security (14 controls)
- A.13: Communications security (7 controls)
- A.14: System acquisition, development, and maintenance (13 controls)
- A.15: Supplier relationships (5 controls)
- A.16: Information security incident management (7 controls)
- A.17: Information security aspects of business continuity management (4 controls)
- A.18: Compliance with internal requirements, such as policies, and with external requirements, such as laws (8 controls).[9]

Organizations that are seeking to demonstrate compliance against the standard have the opportunity to use a certification body that would be responsible for conducting audits to assess the compliance against the standard. A list of accredited certification bodies is maintained by the National Accreditation body within each country. Upon successful completion of the audit, the certification body certifies the ISMS. A detailed overview of the process is as follows[10]:

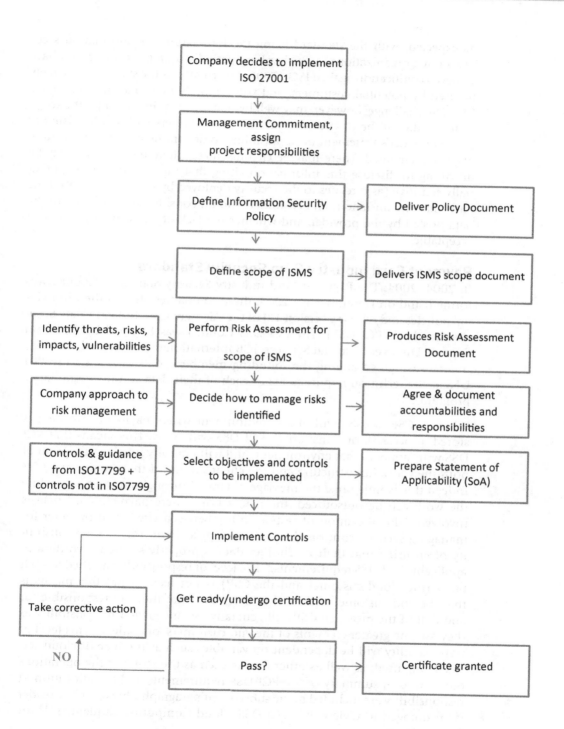

As expected, with the standard being the foundation for information security among organizations for such a long period, a number of providers have achieved certification against ISO 27001, particularly, as the standard will likely be used by potential customers, and will naturally be sought in prospective CSP. The challenge, however, may well be transparency, in particular the scope of the ISMS will be of critical concern. End customers will require visibility of the provider's Statement of Applicability to determine which controls have been implemented. There may be circumstances where the provider may be unwilling to disclose this information citing that the information is potentially sensitive (as it relates to the security deployed by the provider). In these particular circumstances, end customers should consider the sensitivity of the data hosted by the provider, and whether the lack of transparency is indeed acceptable.

Payment Card Industry Data Security Standard

In 2004, 2004: The Payment Card Industry Security Standards Council was formed, and on December 15, 2004, these companies aligned their individual policies and released version 1.0 of the Payment Card Industry Data Security Standard (PCI DSS). The PCI DSS Council was founded by American Express, Discover Financial Services, JCB International, MasterCard, and Visa Inc. It was agreed among the founding members to "incorporate the PCI DSS as the technical requirements of each of their data security compliance programs."[11]

Where a CSP is used within an environment where payment card data is stored, processed, or transmitted, PCI DSS will apply. This means that PCI DSS will "apply to that environment, and will typically involve validation of both the CSP's infrastructure and the client's usage of that environment."[12] Indeed this is much like the message reiterated throughout the book; while the work can be outsourced, the risk is not. Where payment card data is involved, "the allocation of responsibility between client and provider for managing security controls does not exempt a client from the responsibility of ensuring that their cardholder data is properly secured according to applicable PCI DSS requirements." The level of responsibility applied to each party (the cloud customer and the CSP) is not fixed. What this means is that the end customer will need to ascertain what they are responsible for and that of the provider. CSP will generally assume greater responsibility as they assume greater elements of the end customers' operations. This level of responsibility will be dependent on variables such as the type of cloud service being used, as well as other factors such as the scope of the operations outsourced. A summary of the PCI DSS requirements and the allocation of responsibility are included in the subsequent paragraphs, however, the reader is encouraged to review the "PCI DSS Cloud Computing Guidelines"[13] for further details.

Requirement 1: Install and Maintain a Firewall Configuration to Protect Cardholder Data

Unlike the other cloud models, within a SaaS implementation, the responsibility of the network is entirely the responsibility of the CSP. In other models, the responsibility of the network is *generally* a shared responsibility; there will, however, be exceptions. For example, within PaaS implementations, the provider may assume responsibility.

Requirement 2: Do Not Use Vendor-Supplied Defaults for System Passwords and Other Security Parameters

Within the PaaS and IaaS environments, there will be an element of shared responsibility, and as such it is important that during the contract negotiation phase that this delineation is clearly defined. For example, within an IaaS environment, everything from the operating system (OS) and above will be the responsibility of the end customer, whereas everything below the OS will be the responsibility of the CSP. For example, changing the default password for the network infrastructure (e.g., routers) will be the responsibility of the provider, but the end customer must ensure that the default administrator account for the Windows Server has been changed. Within a SaaS environment, all responsibility is assumed by the provider.

Requirement 3: Protect Stored Cardholder Data

Defining the method of encryption to use in order to protect cardholder data is generally the responsibility of the cloud customer within both IaaS and PaaS environments. In addition, determining what exactly to encrypt and where to store the keys is equally their responsibility. However, as has been discussed in earlier chapters, determining their physical location may be unknown and so therefore the responsibility will be shared. Unlike for SaaS where the responsibility is generally assumed by the CSP, there are instances where the cloud end customer can ensure the data is encrypted before entering the cloud.

Requirement 4: Encrypt Transmission of Cardholder Data across Open, Public Networks

While requirement 3 focused on the application of controls for protecting data at rest, requirement 4 turns its attention for the data that is transmitted across open networks (e.g., the internet). In a SaaS scenario, for example, the CSP is likely to define the mechanisms with which data is transmitted, and as such the provider will assume responsibilities. However, for the IaaS environment, a degree of control is provided to the customer and as such they will likely assume responsibility. For PaaS, this will likely be a shared responsibility.

Requirement 5: Use and Regularly Update Antivirus Software and Programs

Responsibility for the installation of antivirus (AV) updates will be that of whoever manages the OS. Within a PaaS and IaaS, this is generally the end customer, however, this may also be the CSP and will vary upon the terms of service. For SaaS implementations, the updating of AV will be the responsibility of the CSP.

Requirement 6: Develop and Maintain Secure Systems and Applications

There will be a multitude of devices within all three cloud implementations where responsibility of maintaining security will differ between the provider and end customer. For example, within an IaaS environment, the customer will maintain security for the OS and above, whereas underlying devices will likely be managed by the provider. Unlike previous requirements, the SaaS environment may seem to have some components that the end customer is responsible for maintaining security for. One such example may be the APIs that interacts with the service, these *may* be the responsibility of the end customer.

Requirement 7: Restrict Access to Cardholder Data by Business Need to Know

Across all three cloud implementations, the responsibility for defining logical access to cardholder data and enforcing the need to know principle will be the responsibility of the end customer. However, physical access will be the responsibility of the provider, and therefore the responsibility for meeting requirement 7 will be shared.

Requirement 8: Assign a Unique ID to Each Person with Computer Access

The end customers will likely have the opportunity to create unique login accounts for all three cloud models, and therefore the responsibility will rest with them and not the provider. Further, the ability to assign strong authentication for these accounts will also be the responsibility of the end customer. However, enforcing unique ID and strong authentication to each person accessing the underlying infrastructure will be the responsibility of the CSP. Furthermore, for both PaaS and SaaS models, the CSP is likely to have administrative access so will therefore hold a degree of responsibility. Note that there may be instances for SaaS models where the level of control afforded to the end customer is limited so the CSP will assume greater responsibilities for these instances.

Requirement 9: Restrict Physical Access to Cardholder Data

Responsibility for restricting physical access across cloud models is likely to rest with the CSP. As mentioned throughout the book, the right to audit is generally not afforded to end customers, and therefore the use of certifications/third-party assessments can be used to provide assurance but ultimately the control and responsibility rests with the provider.

Requirement 10: Track and Monitor All Access to Network Resources and Cardholder Data

Monitoring within a cloud environment will differ based not only on the model, but also different providers will offer varying degrees of granularity to the clients. Monitoring of the underlying infrastructure will likely be the responsibility of the provider across all models. Within a PaaS and IaaS environment, the end customer is likely to be responsible for monitoring the OS and applications. The SaaS environment likely offers less granularity to the end customer and therefore responsibility is likely to rest with the provider.

Requirement 11: Regularly Test Security Systems and Processes

The testing of security and processes will vary based on the individual provider. It is therefore recommended to determine with the individual provider whether the end customer is afforded the opportunity to conduct their own scans. Within a SaaS environment this is not likely to be an option, and the provider may well conduct the scans themselves while offering a service to their customers to meet this requirement.

Requirement 12: Maintain a Policy that Addresses Information Security for All Personnel

Access to cardholder data stored across any of the three cloud models will allow personnel within both the customer and provider the opportunity to access. Therefore meeting this requirement will be the responsibility of both parties, however, the end customer should ensure that the policies adopted by the provider are sufficient as part of any due diligence process.

What the preceding information clearly demonstrates is that responsibility for meeting the requirements of PCI DSS will vary not only in terms of the model used, but also vary across providers. It is therefore imperative for the end customer to clearly define the various roles and responsibilities and ensure that these are not only included within formal contracts (e.g., using service-level agreements (SLAs)), but appropriate monitoring is in place to ensure the responsibilities owned by the provider are met.

Federal Information Security Management Act

In 2002, the U.S. President signed the E-Government Act recognizing the importance of Information Security "to the economic and national security interests of the United States."[14] This meant that every federal agency were required to "develop, document, and implement an agency-wide program to provide information security for the information and information systems that support the operations and assets of the agency, including those provided or managed by another agency, contractor, or other source."[15] The Act itself sets out a series of high-level requirements with compliance mandatory for federal agencies within the United States. The "high-level security requirements" mandated by Federal Information Security Management Act (FISMA) are further specialized through Federal Information Processing & Standards (FIPS) and other more detailed standards, such as the National Institute of Standards and Technology (NIST) SCAP[16]; this is graphically depicted in Figure 6.2.[9]

"The National Institute of Standards and Technology (NIST) outlines nine steps toward compliance with FISMA:

1. Categorize the information to be protected.
2. Select minimum baseline controls.
3. Refine controls using a risk assessment procedure.
4. Document the controls in the system security plan.
5. Implement security controls in appropriate information systems.
6. Assess the effectiveness of the security controls once they have been implemented.
7. Determine agency-level risk to the mission or business case.
8. Authorize the information system for processing.
9. Monitor the security controls on a continuous basis."[17]

From a cloud computing perspective, a number of providers have sought accreditation against FISMA which had already, for example, been "obtained by Google for its Apps service and by Microsoft for its cloud infrastructure and its BPOS-Federal service."[18] For potential cloud end customers that require FISMA compliance, they will need to pay particular attention to the designation applied to the provider; there are three allocated levels of threat: low, moderate, and high.

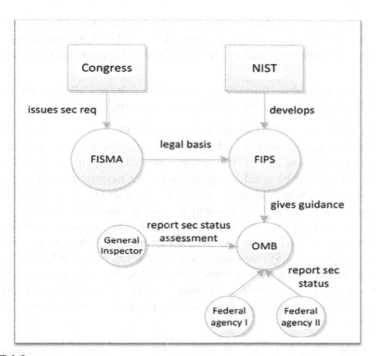

FIGURE 6.2
FISMA audit framework.

The Federal Risk and Authorization Management Program

Intended to provide a standardized approach for the assessment of CSP, the federal risk and authorization management program (FedRAMP) is a mandatory requirement for cloud deployments by U.S. federal agencies, as well as service models that operate at low and moderate risk impact. Introduced in 2011, the U.S. Federal Cloud Computing strategy implemented a "cloud first strategy": "This policy is intended to accelerate the pace at which the government will realize the value of cloud computing by requiring agencies to evaluate safe, secure cloud computing options before making any new investments."[19] Key to this strategy will be the implementation of FedRAMP, which according to a memo published by the Executive Office of the President[20]:

"Each Executive department or agency shall:

- Use FedRAMP when conducting risk assessments, security authorizations, and granting ATOs for all Executive department or agency use of cloud services;

- Use the FedRAMP PMO process and the JAB[a]-approved FedRAMP security authorization requirements as a baseline when initiating, reviewing, granting and revoking security authorizations for cloud services;
- Ensure applicable contracts appropriately require CSPs to comply with FedRAMP security authorization requirements."

A FedRAMP Program Management Office (PMO) has been established to create the process by which stakeholders will adhere to the requirements of the program. In addition, the office will also develop contractual documentation that can be used by agencies in the negotiation with potential service providers, which includes standard contract language and SLAs. The requirement is for every department to utilize FedRAMP contracts appropriately, requiring CSPs to comply with FedRAMP security authorization requirements, as well as its use when conducting risk assessments. As a result, a number of CSP are marketing their services as 'FedRAMP compliant' in an effort to garner customers from U.S. federal agencies. The controls within FedRAMP itself are based on NIST SP800-53 (R3), however, there are additional controls that have been included which vary based on the impact level[21]:

Impact Level	NIST Baseline Controls	Additional FedRAMP Controls	Total Controls Agreed by JAB for FedRAMP
Low	115	1	116
Moderate	252	45	297

The additional controls are across multiple areas; however, the majority reside within access control (6) and system and communications protection (11). The following lists the broader control areas that FedRAMP is comprised of:

- Access control
- Awareness and training
- Audit and accountability
- Security assessment and authorization
- Configuration management
- Contingency planning
- Identification and authentication
- Incident response
- Maintenance

---

[a]JAB: This refers to the Joint Authorisation Board; this board is comprised of Chief Information Officers from the Department of Defense, Department of Homeland Security, and U.S. General Services Administration, and supported by technical representatives from these organizations.

- Media protection
- Physical and environmental protection
- Planning
- Personnel security
- Risk assessment
- System and services acquisition
- Systems and communications protection and
- System and information integrity.

Once the CSP has made a FedRAMP application and the controls have been implemented, the next step in the process will be to work with an accredited Third-Party Assessment Organization (3PAO) to undertake an independent assessment. A list of accredited 3PAOs is available on the FedRAMP Website which also contains contact details, including a named individual nominated as Point of Contact. Becoming an accredited 3PAO requires an application to "meet both technical competence in security assessment of cloud systems and management requirements for organizations performing inspections."[22] The accreditation of 3PAOs is done through the American Association for Laboratory Accreditation which not only evaluates the technical competence of the applying organization, but also ensures their compliance against ISO/IEC 17020.

Federal agencies that are looking to leverage cloud services will have the opportunity to review the existing list of providers that have FedRAMP authorization at the following URL (correct at the time of writing): http://cloud.cio.gov/fedramp/cloud-systems.

Federal agencies will be expected to complete an inventory of CSP currently in use and identify those that are not FedRAMP compliant. The agency will then be expected to undertake a process to ensure that all providers achieve compliance. This may require noncompliant providers to undertake certification, in which case the agency will be expected to notify the FedRAMP PMO that the provider wishes to pursue the "Authority to Operate" with their agency. Further, if provisional authorization is required the agency is expected to track the application with the service provider's effort to achieve certification.

In January 2014, it was reported that "Eleven vendors – including Akamai, Amazon Web Services, AT&T, Hewlett–Packard, IBM, Lockheed Martin, and Microsoft – are now authorized to operate cloud services for all or some federal agencies. A dozen more services are moving through the application process and more are in the pipeline, says FedRAMP director Maria Roat."[23] Further, the process for service providers can be particularly onerous: "It can take providers six to nine months to put the needed management disciplines and technical controls in place. Then begins the continuous monitoring, reporting, and remediation work that FedRAMP requires. For vendors unused to working in the government IT environment, the cost of entry is stiff... it would take between $25 million and $35 million in engineering and staffing costs for a commercial cloud service provider to meet the government's demanding IT security standards."[24]

Cloud Industry Forum Code of Practice

Established in 2009, the Cloud Industry Forum aims "to provide transparency through certification to a Code of Practice for credible online Cloud service providers and to assist end users in determining core information necessary to enable them to adopt these services."[25] Compliance against The Code of Practice is achieved either through annual self-certification, or the provider can seek independent certification through a certification body that has been approved by the Cloud Industry Forum. Those organizations that adopt the self-certified process will be authorized to use a "Certification Mark," whereas those that have been certified via a certification body are authorized to use an "Independent Certification Mark."

Within the code of practice, there exist a number of declarations that relate to security, as well as to the GRC stack of the Cloud Security Alliance:

- A.1.6. Security Control Transparency with the Cloud Security Alliance: Requests the providers to state whether they have completed the CSA Consensus Assessments Initiative Questionnaire.
- A.1.9. Existing Certifications (Optional): Allows the providers to define whether they have any other relevant certifications.
- A.2.6. Provisions for Information Security: The provider will detail the measures implemented for information security.
- A.2.7. Data Protection Provisions: To detail the geographies where data will or may be held during the length of the contact. This will also include a summary of the relevant data protection legislation and measures used to achieve compliance.
- A.2.8. Provisions for Service Continuity: The measures used to maintain continuity of the service.
- A.2.9. Provisions for Audit: Details the ability to conduct independent audits.

Potential end customers have the opportunity to visit the following URL (correct at the time of writing) to find a provider that has undergone certification: https://selfcert.cloudindustryforum.org/certification/.

This search facility provides both providers that have completed certification and those that are undergoing the certification. In addition, those organizations that have completed the certification process will have the scope of services that are covered by the code as well as the expiration date of the certificate. The code of practice is an excellent source for potential customers when identifying and engaging with a potential service provider. The scope of the certification goes beyond security, however, it does cover key questions that are likely to be part of the broader due diligence process.

IT-Grundschutz Certification

The IT-Grundschutz is a certification scheme that was established by the national security agency of Germany, known as the Federal Office for Information Security (BSI). The "goal of the Federal Office for Information Security (BSI) is to promote IT security in Germany."[26] Originally published in 1994 and updated in 2005, the IT-Grundschutz provides a methodology for the management of information security for an organization's information assets. Certification will involve both an official ISO certificate against ISO 27001, but also an audit against the technical controls defined within IT-Grundschutz.

IT-Grundschutz is comprised of the following five parts:

- *BSI Standard 100-1 Information Security Management Systems (ISMS)*: Based on ISO 27001 and 27002, the 100-1 standard defines the requirements of an ISMS, and how it can be implemented.
- *BSI Standard 100-2 IT-Grundschutz Methodology*: Focuses on how the ISMS can be implemented in practice, this includes the development of a policy.
- *BSI Standard 100-3 Risk Analysis based on IT-Grundschutz*: Includes the steps required to carry out a risk assessment, as well as how to determine which assets should be included.
- *BSI-Standard 100-4: Business Continuity Management*: As the name implies, the 100-4 standards details how to establish and manage BCP within the organization.
- *IT-Grundschutz Catalogs*: includes an overview and for specific threats to be placed in specific categories.

Although the aforementioned standards are not cloud specific, the Federal Office for Information Security (BSI) published a white paper entitled 'Security Recommendations for Cloud Computing Providers'[27] intended "to provide a basis for discussion between CSPs and cloud customers." The paper is seen as the first step for the development of security within cloud computing environments, with further additions anticipated to be included in the IT-Grundschutz as modules. In particular, it is anticipated for BSI 100-2 to be "adjusted, particularly in the area of modeling complex, virtualised information networks." Security recommendations within the paper are defined into three categories:

1. Category B: Basic for all CSPs.
2. Category C+: Includes additional requirements where high confidentiality is required.
3. Category A+: Includes additional requirements where high availability is required.

The white paper presents a series of security recommendations that are classified as to whether they apply to public and/or private clouds and whether the threat level is average or elevated for each implementation. Finally the

Network Security	Private ⇨			Public ⬈		
	B	C+	A+	B	C+	A+
Security measures against malware (anti-virus, Trojan detection, anti-spam, etc.)	✓			✓		
Security measures against network-based attacks (IPS/IDS systems, firewall, Application Layer Gateway, etc.)		✓	✓	✓		
DDoS mitigation (protection against DDoS attacks)			✓	✓		

FIGURE 6.3
Security recommendations for network security.

recommendations are put into one of the three aforementioned categories (B, C+, or A+). An example of the security recommendations for network security is illustrated in Figure 6.3.

The white paper is a thoroughly comprehensive series of security recommendations, and the reader is encouraged to review the document particularly where high availability or confidentiality is required.

TUV Rheinland Certified

The TUV Rheinland certification allows CSP to demonstrate their security posture to potential customers through the Certified Cloud Service certificate. Certification is achieved through an audit that determines the implementation of the certificate requirements: stress testing against the architecture, check against the performance pledges within contracts/SLAs, as well as penetration testing for the technical detail checks. Upon successful completion of all of these measures, the provider is certified for a 3-year period which will be regularly checked.

According to ENISA; "TÜV Rheinland Certified Cloud Service is the most widely used and independent cloud service certification in Germany and becomes more and more relevant across Europe."[28] For end customers, a public site is available that supports searching for companies that have undergone the certification process and is available at (correct at the time of writing): http://www. certipedia.com/.

While every effort was made to provide as comprehensive a list of certification schemes as possible, what is clearly evident is that there are a multitude of additional available schemes that have not been detailed. This will include the likes of HIPAA, as well as other information security schemes. However, what the above demonstrates is that while end customers were previously forced to leverage schemes that were not developed specifically with cloud in mind, this is now changing. Equally while the number of schemes may be confusing, with overlap between most of the above, the good news is that all provide a degree of transparency which is imperative in furthering the adoption of 'secure' cloud computing. Also, as was inferred throughout this text, there exist many flavors of cloud computing with many providers certifying to win business in specific geographies and/or verticals. Therefore regardless of the industry the end customer is in, and the likely regulatory requirements they have to adhere to, chances are that a CSP meeting their needs will exist. Equally, many of these schemes also provide a central repository that allows potential customers to review and verify the certification status of providers in an easy and efficient manner.

END NOTES

1. Brian Honan, IT Governance 2nd edition, *ISO 27001 in a Windows Environment* (April 2010), [cited July 2014]. Available from: http://www.amazon.co.uk/ISO27001-Windows-Environment-2nd-Edition/dp/1849280495/ref=sr_1_2?ie=UTF8&qid=1403663814&sr=8-2&keywords=brian+honan.

2. ETSI, *Cloud Standards coordination* (November 2013), [cited July 2014]. Available from: http://www.etsi.org/news-events/news/734-2013-12-press-release-report-on-cloud-computing-standards.

3. ENISA, *Certification in the EU Cloud Strategy* (February 2014), [cited July 2014]. Available from: https://resilience.enisa.europa.eu/cloud-computing-certification.

4. Cloud Security Alliance, *Open Certification Framework: Vision Statement* (August 2013), [cited June 2014]. Available from: https://downloads.cloudsecurityalliance.org/initiatives/ocf/OCF_Vision_Statement_Final.pdf.

5. DarkReading.com, *CSA Releases expanded Cloud controls in new CCM v.3* (September 2013), [cited June 2014]. Available from: http://www.darkreading.com/csa-releases-expanded-cloud-controls-in-new-ccm-v3/d/d-id/1140701?.

6. EuroCloud, *Scope* [cited June 2014]. Available from: http://eurocloud-staraudit.eu/home/scope.html.

7. ENISA, *EuroCloud Star Audit* [cited June 2014]. Available from: https://resilience.enisa.europa.eu/cloud-computing-certification/list-of-cloud-certification-schemes/eurocloud-star-audit.

8. The ISO 27000 Directory, *An Introduction to ISO 27001 (ISO27001)* [cited July 2014]. Available from: http://www.27000.org/iso-27001.htm.

9. Wikipedia, *ISO/IEC 27001:2013* [cited July 2014]. Available from: http://en.wikipedia.org/wiki/ISO/IEC_27001:2013.

10. The ISO 27001 Directory, *The ISO 27001 Certification Process* [cited July 2014]. Available from: http://www.27000.org/ismsprocess.htm.

11. PCI Standards Council, *About Us* [cited June 2014]. Available from: https://www.pcisecuritystandards.org/organization_info/index.php.

12. Cloud Special Interest Group, PCI Security Standards Council, *Information Supplement: PCI DSS Cloud Computing Guidelines* (February 2013), [cited June 2014]. Available from: https://www.pcisecuritystandards.org/pdfs/PCI_DSS_v2_Cloud_Guidelines.pdf.

13. Cloud Special Interest Group, PCI Security Standards Council, *Information Supplement: PCI DSS Cloud Computing Guidelines*, (February 2013), [cited June 2014]. Available from: https://www.pcisecuritystandards.org/pdfs/PCI_DSS_v2_Cloud_Guidelines.pdf.

14. NIST, *Detailed Overview* [cited June 2014]. Available from: http://csrc.nist.gov/groups/SMA/fisma/overview.html.

15. NIST, *Detailed Overview* [cited June 2014]. Available from: http://csrc.nist.gov/groups/SMA/fisma/overview.html.

16. Dr Marnix Dekker, Christoffer Karsberg, Martina Lakka, Dimitra Livera and ENISA *Auditing Security Measures*, (September 2013), [June 2014]. Available from: http://blogs.computerworld.com/cloud-security/22474/will-fisma-fedramp-impact-cloud-security.

17. SearchSecurity TechTarget, *Federal Information Security Management Act* [cited June 2014]. Available from: http://searchsecurity.techtarget.com/definition/Federal-Information-Security-Management-Act.

18. John Brodkin, Arstechnica, *Amazon Cloud Earns Key FISMA Government Security Certification* (September 2011), [cited June 2014]. Available from: http://arstechnica.com/business/2011/09/amazon-cloud-earns-fisma-government-security-accreditation/.

19. Vivek Kundra, The White House, *Federal cloud computing strategy* (February 2011), [June 2014]. Available from: https://cio.gov/wp-content/uploads/downloads/2012/09/Federal-Cloud-Computing-Strategy.pdf.

20. Steven Van Roekel, Executive Office of the President, *Memorandum for Chief Information Officers* (December 2011), [cited June 2014]. Available from: http://cloud.cio.gov/sites/default/files/documents/files/fedrampmemo.pdf.

21. ISPAB Presentation, *Federal Risk and Authorisation Management Programme (FedRAMP)* (February 2012), [cited July 2014]. Available from: http://csrc.nist.gov/groups/SMA/ispab/documents/minutes/2012-02/feb3_fedramp_ispab.pdf.

22. FedRAMP—3PAO, *FedRAMP Overview* [cited July 2014]. Available from: http://cloud.cio.gov/fedramp/3pao.

23. Information Week Government, *Cloud providers align with FedRAMP security standards* (January 2014), [July 2014]. Available from: http://www.informationweek.com/government/cybersecurity/cloud-providers-align-with-fedramp-security-standards/d/d-id/1113499.

24. Information Week Government, *Cloud providers align with FedRAMP security standards* (January 2014), [July 2014]. Available from: http://www.informationweek.com/government/cybersecurity/cloud-providers-align-with-fedramp-security-standards/d/d-id/1113499.

25. Cloud Industry Forum, *About the Cloud Industry Forum* [cited June 2014]. Available from: http://cloudindustryforum.org/about-us.

26. Michael Hange, *Taking advantage of opportunities – avoiding risks* [cited June 2014]. Available from: https://www.bsi.bund.de/EN/TheBSI/thebsi_node.html.

27. Federal Office for Information Security, *Security recommendations for cloud computing providers* [cited June 2014]. Available from: https://www.bsi.bund.de/SharedDocs/Downloads/EN/BSI/Publications/Minimum_information/SecurityRecommendationsCloudComputingProviders.pdf?__blob=publicationFile.

28. ENISA, *Certified Cloud Service – TUV Rheinland* [cited June 2014]. Available from: https://resilience.enisa.europa.eu/cloud-computing-certification/list-of-cloud-certification-schemes/certified-cloud-service.

The Privacy Imperative

When we mention the term privacy and the cloud, you would be forgiven as the reader to question: "What exactly does this mean?" To be entirely honest, when we began the process of defining the individual chapters for the book, out of all the chapters, this one felt the least defined in terms of scope. We knew of course that no technology book, let alone cloud book, would be complete without at least one chapter on privacy (as the recent *Applied Cyber Security and the Smart Grid*, coauthored by Raj Samani would attest). However unlike other publications, when it comes to cloud computing, we can address the subject from a number of angles, for example:

- The recent allegations regarding government surveillance, the impact that this has on the privacy of customer data, and ergo the impact this has had on the willingness for end customers to utilize cloud computing services. Otherwise for many known as the Snowden effect!
- The use of cloud computing and the impact that this has upon national data protection/privacy regulations.

To summarize the above two points, does cloud computing make my data less private, or make myself less likely to achieve compliance with data protection legislation? The primary focus of this chapter is consider compliance against data protection legislation, however we will consider the first question due to the level of scrutiny the cloud, and in particular, U.S. providers have recently come under.

DOES CLOUD COMPUTING MAKE MY DATA ANY LESS PRIVATE?

The common (mis)perception on this question will of course be *yes*. After all, how else could we explain the recent survey conducted by the Cloud Security Alliance (CSA) of 500 respondents, which found that 56% of non-U.S.

residents were less likely to use U.S.-based cloud providers, in light of recent revelations about government access to customer information.[1] This infers that, in particular, non-U.S. customers feel that by using U.S. cloud providers, their data (or indeed their customer data) will be less private through the use of U.S. providers. Such sentiments would appear to be echoed by policy makers, and in particular, the European Parliament Committee on Civil Liberties, Justice and Home Affairs. The initial findings[2] from the investigation into the mass surveillance on the EU citizens:

- Note that trust in U.S. cloud computing and cloud providers has been negatively affected by the abovementioned practices; emphasize, therefore, the development of European clouds as an essential element for growth and employment and trust in cloud computing services and providers and for ensuring a high level of personal data[a] protection

However, while we consider this advice, the question quickly becomes: *Is using the cloud (at least certain clouds) by itself make the data any less private?* If we ask this particular question, the argument would be: *No it does not.* Consider that when two organizations are hosting customer data, one is using a traditional outsourcing model (or as many would argue a private cloud!) and the other is using a public cloud provider. Both implementations are being hosted out of U.S. data centers, the question is whether the cloud customers are more likely to have their data subpoenaed under say the Patriot Act solely because they are cloud customers. Addressing this particular point, according to a study undertaken by international law firm, Hogan Lovells, many other countries have "laws in place allowing them to obtain personal data stored on cloud computing services[3]"; these include (but not limited to) the U.K., Ireland, Germany, France, Japan, and Canada. Of course using this argument, the answer will be no. Simply by using a service marketed as the "cloud" does *not* increase the likelihood of data being accessed by any agency/department. Further, the ability to *lawfully* access data using mechanisms such as the Patriot Act is also afforded to many other countries globally. This is reinforced by a white paper[4] by A&L Goodbody entitled "No Cloud over the Patriot Act"; "the powers granted to specific US law enforcement authorities under the Patriot Act already existed prior to the enactment of the statute in 2001 and are no broader than equivalent powers granted to law enforcement authorities in Ireland, and in other European jurisdictions." The paper continues to provide a list of equivalent laws in Ireland as defined in Table 7.1.

---

[a]Personal data: "Personal data" or "data" shall mean any information relating to an identified or identifiable natural person. An identifiable person is one who can be identified, directly or indirectly, in particular by reference to an identification number, or to one or more factors specific to his physical, physiological, mental, economic, cultural, or social identity. (Source: Article 2.a Directive 95/46/EC.)

Table 7.1 Equivalent Legislation to Patriot Act in Ireland

Legislation	Application
Postal and Telecommunications Services Act 1983 ("the 1983 PTS Act") and the Interception of Postal Packets and Telecommunications Messages (Regulations) Act 1993 ("the 1993 PPTM Act")	Permits limited authorization for interception of postal packages and telecommunications messages (to include e-mails) for national security or criminal investigations. This is only applicable to certain licensed providers of telecommunications networks under Irish law.
The European Communities (Electronic Communications Networks and Services) (Privacy and Electronic Communications) Regulations 2011 ("the 2011 Regulations")	Provides that listening, tapping, storage, or other kinds of interception or surveillance of communications and the related traffic data by persons other than users, without the consent of the users concerned, is prohibited (unless authorized under the PPTM Act or other laws that would fall under Article 15 of Directive 2002/58 EC).
Criminal Justice (Surveillance) Act 2009 ("the 2009 CJ Act")	Permits ex parte orders for surveillance.
Criminal Justice Act 2011 ("the 2011 CJ Act")	Permits a court to make orders for delivery and/or making available of documents (to include electronic files and other formats) to the Garda in the context of a criminal investigation.
Data Protection Acts 1988–2003 ("the Data Protection Acts")	Provides for strict governance of data processing by controllers and processors of data. Data processing carried out by a Garda or a member of the Defense forces or by an order of a court will be excluded from the general rules under the Data Protection Acts.
Communications Retention of Data Act 2011 ("the 2011 Data Retention Act")	Data (to include call records and traffic data), which are retained by a person engaged in the provision of publicly available electronic communications service or public communications network under this Act may be requested by the Garda where it is required for the prevention, detection, investigation, or prosecution of a serious crime, the safeguarding of the security of the State, or the saving of human life.

Admittedly, we could have presented equivalent legislation from any number of countries; however, it is worth focusing attention to Ireland partly because of such a concentration among major providers to establish operations in the country. However, as the above table demonstrates the argument that the Patriot Act should act as the motivating factor to establish operations in Ireland, or any other geography is wide of the mark. According to Bryan Cunningham of Cunningham Levy LLP: "Why Ireland? Boosters cite the 'Patriot Act,' perhaps somewhat inaccurately, for the notion that "the Patriot Act" enabled the US Government to compel companies based in the United States to hand over any person's information, regardless of nationality, and that cloud companies with headquarters in Ireland somehow are immune from US Government or, presumably, other nations' surveillance.[5]" With this in mind, analysts at IDC advise: "Users need to ignore the Patriot Act scare stories.[6]"

In the same vain, there are some added complexities to this rather simple and crude argument; first, the lack of transparency means that as an end customer I may not know (1) where my data are physically located and (2) I may not even be told if my data are accessed either if the provider is notified, or indeed uncovers an incident.

Subsequently the simple answer provided earlier is further complicated. However with the appropriate due diligence, in terms of defining the physical location where data are stored, ensuring that incident response policies from the provider meet the organizational requirements, and so forth. The risk of such an issue should be mitigated, and indeed no greater than utilizing a traditional outsourcer, or in fact hosting internally. Moreover, customers storing data with third parties, or in fact even those stored on premise should certainly consider technical controls to mitigate the risk of unauthorized access, or access that may be lawful but not appreciated. This includes using technical controls to encrypt data stored at rest for example.

Of course, these preceding paragraphs will be debated, and you the reader may agree or in fact vehemently disagree with this position. However the intention here is to move away from the arguments that we all hear and question whether they are based in reality, for example, the Patriot Act argument. *Do not use a U.S. provider for cloud computing because of the Patriot Act*, is one such that appears in most social media discussions, but sadly many making arguments fail to recognize the similar legislation across other countries. Therefore, for an organization using cloud, it is important to understand the legal environment where the data will be physically located, and ensure that the worst-case scenarios align with your risk appetite, or whether it is possible to reduce the risk to a level so that it does not exceed the acceptable level.

If we step away from this rather contentious issue, let us focus on one of the biggest barriers to cloud adoption, the legality of using cloud computing with regards to data protection legislation.

PRIVACY LEVEL AGREEMENT

Transparency: This has been a recurring message throughout the book as it relates to cloud security. However there are particular implications for this not being achieved, particularly as it relates to the storage, or processing[b] of personal data with cloud computing. Where the cloud end customer is the data controller, there will exist a number of obligations to ensure that the cloud service provider (CSP) has appropriate controls in place to protect the personal data processed

---

[b]"Processing of personal data" ("processing") shall mean any operation or a set of operations that is performed upon personal data, whether or not by automatic means, such as collection, recording, organization, storage, adaptation or alteration, retrieval, consultation, use, disclosure by transmission, dissemination or otherwise making available, alignment or combination, blocking, erasure or destruction. (Source: Article 2.b Directive 95/46/EC.)

within the cloud (note: the term processing will also include storage). Examples of some of these obligations are detailed by the UK Information Commissioner's Office (ICO) in its report entitled "Guidance on the use of cloud computing[7]":

> The obligations of the cloud customer as a data controller will not end once a cloud provider is chosen. A continual cycle of monitoring, review and assessment are required to ensure that the cloud service is running in the manner expected and as the contractual agreement stipulates.

Taking this, and indeed some of the other many obligations, the data controller will have regarding the protection of personal data that a working group within the CSA was established for the development of a Privacy Level Agreement (PLA). The PLA is intended to allow the end customer to review the CSP's commitment to protect personal data, as well as provide protection should the CSP fall out of compliance or fail to adequately protect the said data.

The PLA produces a series of baselines for the provider to declare regarding the level of protection applied to personal data. Declaring this as an effective way to communicate the level of protection employed by the provider gives a level of transparency to the end customer regarding the baseline level of security deployed by the provider regarding protection of personal data. Consider the ease with which an end customer can ascertain the *baseline* of protection provided using the PLA, one simple question, and a binary response. Moreover, this assertion is intended to be included as an attachment to the service agreement and aligns with recommendations and guidance provided throughout 2012 by the Article 29 Working Party and several European data protection authorities.

PLA Outline

There are 16 sections within the PLA. There is no intention within the book to simply copy and paste what is included within the PLA, however we will try to summarize some of the key points within the sections, and in particular, their relevance to the end customer, but would recommend referring to the document for additional details.

Identity of the CSP

The provider will be expected to detail high-level information such as name, address, and any local representative. Within this section, however, there will be a question about the role of the provider from a data protection perspective. Typically the CSP is often seen as the data processor, in fact under the Article 29 Working Party Data Protection Working Party opinion on cloud computing it cites, "The cloud client determines the ultimate purpose of the processing and decides on the outsourcing of this processing and the delegation of all or part of the processing activities to an external organization. The cloud client therefore acts as a data controller.[8]"

This, of course, is not always the case. In addition to the information provided within the PLA, which focuses on guidance from both the ICO and the Commission nationale de l'informatique et des libertés, there is legal precedent whereby this assumption is proven (in certain circumstances to be incorrect). Documented in the book entitled "Cloud Computing: A practical introduction to the Legal Issues,[9]" a legal position that challenged the view that the service provider was always the data processor. While not a cloud provider per se, the case from 2006 involved a service provider who provided features that were cloudlike. In 2006, the Society for Worldwide Interbank Financial Telecommunication (SWIFT) was subpoenaed under the U.S. antiterror laws to provide agencies with personal data collected for money transfers. In the same year, the Belgian data protection authority provided an opinion that SWIFT were in breach of data protection rules, and later in 2006, the Article 29 Working[10] Party found SWIFT to not be a processor that it had originally considered itself to be but indeed a controller.

- "While SWIFT presents itself as a data processor, and some elements might suggest that SWIFT has acted in the past as a processor in certain cases on behalf of the financial institutions, the Working Party, having considered the effective margin of maneuver it possesses in the situations described above, is of the opinion that SWIFT is a controller as defined by Article 2 (d) of the Directive, for both the normal processing of personal data under its SWIFTNet service as well as for the further processing by onward transfer of personal data to the UST."

Part of the reason for this assertion included the fact that SWIFT determined the security standard, and location of its data standards, and itself complied with the U.S. subpoenas without informing the financial institutions. The reason for focusing so heavily on the distinction between the controller and processor is based on the obligations of each stakeholder. In particular, the data controller has "statutory responsibilities to data subjects and is subject to scrutiny of the regulatory regime and ultimately sanction through the courts; the processor has no such responsibility or real scrutiny.[11]"

It is for this very reason that the distinction by the CSP regarding its perceived role is very relevant, whereby if it is indeed a data processor then its responsibilities regarding data protection are greatly diminished. However, in the case of SWIFT, it is worth noting that despite their assertion, it is possible for this to be challenged should the provider undertake actions that may be deemed as behaving like a data controller.

Processing of Personal Data
In addition to the defining its role, the CSP will also be expected to define the physical location where personal data will be stored. Again, this becomes a critical point for the end customer who may store personal data within the

cloud where certain customers may not be allowed to store personal data in particular geographies due to data protection regulation. In the United Kingdom, for example, the eighth principle of Data Protection Act states that:

- "Personal data shall not be transferred to a country or territory outside the European Economic Area (EEA) unless that country or territory ensures an adequate level of protection for the rights and freedoms of data subjects in relation to the processing of personal data[12]"

While there are documented examples that do allow personal data to potentially be transferred outside of those listed countries, the level of effort required to maintain compliance can be onerous for the data controller/end customer. Latter sections (4) do request that the provider details whether data are transferred outside of the EEA, and if so on what legal basis this is done (for example, adequacy such as Safe Harbor). Being aware of such potential transfers is imperative for the end customer, and in particular, where they act as data controllers as transfers outside of the EEA could result in being breached of data protection regulation.

Data Security

Section 5 of the PLA demands the provider to specify "the technical, physical, and organizational measures in place to protect personal data against accidental or unlawful destruction or accidental loss, alteration, unauthorized use, modification, disclosure or access, and against all other unlawful forms of processing." This becomes important, particularly where the end customer acts as the data controller; this is because the controller must ensure that the processor has appropriate safeguards in place. Herein lies one the main challenges, we have often discussed the issues regarding the lack of transparency when it comes to cloud computing, and yet when it comes to data security, the controller must take reasonable steps to ensure compliance. With public cloud computing, the likelihood is that the right to audit will not be available; therefore, the controller will be required to seek alternate means to demonstrate "reasonable steps." One such option will be to leverage security standards and within the PLA the provider will be requested to define the security control frameworks that are used, and which controls apply. In addition, the provider will be requested to "describe which technical, physical, and organizational measures the CSP has in place to support transparency and to allow review by the customers."

In addition, under section 7, the provider will be required to define whether any third-party audits will be made available to the customer, with their scope and frequency also defined. This again becomes particularly relevant where the data controller will be required to demonstrate "reasonable steps" in terms of security deployed by the data processor. Furthermore, the use of independent third-party audits is seen as a suitable mechanism to assess the security deployed by the processor by the ICO. Also, the frequency of the audit becomes relevant, as the controller is expected to be provided with regular updates of the security controls deployed by the processor.

Of course the above paragraphs are only a small snapshot into the categories within the PLA, the below Table 7.2 is a full list with a short summary. However for further details, and in particular the references with guidance from the various data protection bodies, the reader is encouraged to review the entire document.

Table 7.2 Summary of the Cloud Security Alliance (CSA) Privacy Level Agreement

1. Identity of the CSP (and of representative in the EU as applicable), its role, and the contact information of the data protection officer and the information security officer.	This section requires the CSP to provide details about their business and contact details of relevant personnel. This includes the data protection officer, security officer, etc.
2. Categories of personal data that the customer is prohibited from sending to or processing in the cloud.	The CSP will define those categories of personal data that are explicitly prohibited from sending to the provider.
3. Ways in which the data will be processed.	The CSP will define how the end customer can issue instructions to the provider. Also, the providers will define those tasks that they will carry out on behalf of the customer and those that the customer will have to request.
4. Data transfer	We touched on this earlier in the chapter, but this section is where the provider will specify if there will be any transfers of data held by the provider. In particular, the provider will be requested to specify where the data will be transferred to, and under what grounds.
5. Data security measures	This section requires the provider to detail the controls in place to protect the personal data stored by the provider. In particular, this will not just be technical controls, but also physical and organizational measures in place. In addition, the provider can define the security standards/frameworks that are used to protect such information.
6. Monitoring	The provider will specify if the customer can monitor the controls deployed, and the mechanisms to achieve such visibility.
7. Third-party audits	If the provider authorizes independent third-party assessments, then this would be specified within this section. Moreover, the provider will elaborate the scope of the assessment, frequency, and the level of details the report will entail (and ultimately made available to the customer). In addition, the CSP will state the auditor chosen by the customer or chosen by both parties and who will pay for the cost of the audit.
8. Personal data breach notification	"Personal data breach" means a breach of security leading to the accidental or unlawful destruction; loss; alteration; unauthorized disclosure of, or access to, personal data transmitted, stored, or otherwise processed in connection with the provision of a service provided by a CSP. Specify whether and how the customer will be informed of personal data and data security breaches affecting the customer's data processed by the CSP and/or its subcontractors, within what time frame and how.

Table 7.2 Summary of the Cloud Security Alliance (CSA) Privacy Level Agreement *Continued*

9. Data portability, migration, and transfer back assistance	Specify the formats, the preservation of logical relations, and any costs associated to portability of data, applications, and services. Describe whether, how, and at what cost the CSP will assist customers in the possible migration of the data to another provider or back to an in-house IT environment.
10. Data retention, restitution, and deletion	This section requires the CSP to detail how they will keep and destroy data upon termination of the service. ■ How long the personal data will or may be retained. ■ Methods to delete data, and if the data are retained after the customer has deleted the data or terminated the contract. ■ How the provider meets the legal requirements concerning data retention that apply to the CSP and the cloud customer.
11. Accountability	How the provider will ensure and demonstrate will maintain compliance for itself and subcontractors.
12. Cooperation	How the provider will work with customers to ensure compliance with relevant data protection requirements.
13. Law enforcement access	The process the provider uses to deal with requests from law enforcement regarding the disclosure of personal data. In particular, the provider will be required to specify how (and if) they will notify the affected customer.
14. Remedies	Defines the actions available to the customer if the provider, or indeed any of their subcontractors, breaches the obligations set out within the PLA. These remedies may include compensation, service credits, etc.
15. Complaint, dispute resolution	Includes the contact details of the representative at the provider who can receive complaints regarding personal data handling practices. This will also include the contact details of the third party that may be contacted in order to assist in the resolution of a dispute with the CSP.
16. CSP insurance policy	Details whether the provider has any cyber insurance policy, and the scope of the policy.

CSP, cloud service provider.

At the time of writing, the launch of a working group for the development of the second version of the PLA has been announced. It is intended for version 2 of the PLA to produce three deliverables:

1. **"PLA—Compliance tool for EU market:** The first deliverable of the PLA Working Group was a transparency tool for the EU market; based on these initial results, the WG v2 will develop a compliance tool that will satisfy the requirements expressed by the Art 29 WP and in the Code of Conduct currently development by the EC.
2. **Feasibility Study on Certification/Seal based on PLA:** The group will create a document assessing the feasibility of a Privacy Certification Module in the context of the Open Certification Framework and establish a roadmap and guidance for its creation and implementation.
3. **PLA Outline for the Global Market:** CSA will extend the scope of the PLA v1 by considering relevant Privacy Legislation outside the EU.[13]"

The development of the second version of the PLA will be a welcome addition to end customers aiming to ensure compliance against data protection legislation outside of the EU. It is, however, worth noting that the PLA is not the only tool available for end customers to address privacy concerns, or rather will not be the only tool.

DATA PROTECTION CERTIFICATION

The Data Protection Certification is an emerging initiative that aims to address the manner in which the industry addresses data protection legislation particularly within public cloud environments. It intens to deliver a blueprint of controls in Web and PDF formats. It is intended for both the IT and Information Security teams within the end customer or those of the cloud provider to quickly identify and detail the controls that are deployed within a given cloud instance.

Problems the Data Protection Certification Aims to Address

Castles in the Cloud: The classic infrastructure approach of putting key controls on the end points and fortifying the perimeter is antiquated. Even if every cloud provider builds their "castle in the cloud" what protects users' data traveling between them?

Compliance does not Equal Trustworthiness: The long rote of compliance is taking its toll in the cloud. Providers are facing enormous staffing challenges with addressing assessments to satisfy compliance requirements. As part of the research conducted by the leadership team of the data protection certification team, one organization reported supporting 100 assessments to satisfy just three regulations. Another provider reported supporting 750 assessments, regardless of the level of resources dedicated compliance to standards and regulations will not guarantee the safety or trustworthiness of data in the cloud. It only implies that the provider or the consumer has a well-controlled environment.

How the Data Protection Certification Address the Problem(s)

The Cloud Data Protection Cert presents controls based on the sensitivity of the data, and the cloud model deployed. In addition to the standard list of controls, further customized guidance is provided following the outcomes of a built-in self-assessment. The way that data are classified and treated aligns to business usage and contexts. The focus is on making it easy for the business to protect their own data, and therefore allowing the subjective assessment to determine the value of the data to be undertaken by business owners. Cloud Data Protection Cert prescribes controls according to a tiered data sensitivity model. "Regulated Data" has the most rigorous set of controls, "Commercial Data" has a robust but less rigorous set of controls, and "Collaborative Data" has the most flexible and least number of controls. This data classification is key but missing from typical IT security frameworks and standards. It provides both cloud providers and consumers a standardized approach for ensuring that data protection controls are appropriately applied and thereby greatly diminishing the risk of data theft and exposure.

Simplifying Trust and Protection: Once data are classified, the appropriate level of protection can be applied to govern user access and data, and to protecting transactions and work streams.

At the time of writing, the Cloud Data Protection Cert is undertaking a formal review, and therefore is subject to change. While the individual detail may change the goal of the program is likely to remain, which is to integrate the cortication into data protection standards, and ultimately become the baseline for cloud security requirements.

For more information, please refer to the Cloud Data Protection Cert.

1. Visit http://clouddataprotection.org/cert/
2. Access your blueprint of controls after the following three selections:
   a. Your role: Cloud provider or cloud consuming organization
   b. Data type—Regulated, commercial, or collaborative
   c. Cloud Delivery Model—SaaS, IaaS.

The Cloud Data Protection Cert is an emerging body of work within the CSA, addressing a fundamental area of major global concern as it relates to not only cloud computing but the fabric of daily life. Therefore, like the PLA should act as the cornerstone for cloud customers and providers to provide the transparency so desperately sought to not only remain compliant but protect some of the most valuable data that the organizations have.

At the time of writing, there have been a number of remarkable developments associated with privacy considerations as they relate to cloud (and broader), and there will be many more to come. Most recently, for example, in April 2014, United States Magistrate Judge, James Francis ruled that the U.S. companies must turn over private information when served with a valid search warrant from U.S. law enforcement agencies. Within the ruling, the judge stated, "Even when applied to information that is stored in servers abroad, an SCA warrant does not violate the presumption against extraterritorial application of American law.[14]" The case involved Microsoft, which challenged the search warrant because the data were stored on a server located in Ireland and subsequently beyond the U.S. law enforcement jurisdiction. While Microsoft has appealed the ruling, the broader impact could be significant according to Caspar Bowden, an independent privacy researcher who preempted *Prism* in a report to the EU Parliament in October 2012, who stated, "If the US Cloud industry was worried before about lack of confidence of foreign customers, this judgment just upped the ante very considerably (subject of course to any appeals).[15]"

END NOTES

1. Cloud Security Alliance, *CloudBytes Town Hall: NSA/PRISM Lessons learned*, [cited March 2014]. Available from: https://cloudsecurityalliance.org/research/cloudbytes/nsa-prism-lessons-learned/.

2. European Parliament, *DRAFT REPORT: on the US NSA surveillance programme, surveillance bodies in various Member States and their impact on EU citizens fundamental rights and on transatlantic cooperation in Justice and Home Affairs* (December 2013), [cited March 2014]. Available from: http://www.europarl.europa.eu/sides/getDoc.do?pubRef=-//EP//NONSGML%2BCOMPARL%2BPE-526.085%2B02%2BDOC%2BPDF%2BV0//EN.

3. Grant Gross, ComputerWorld, *Study: Patriot Act doesn't give feds special access to cloud data* (May 2012), [cited March 2014]. Available from: https://www.computerworld.com/s/article/9227403/Study_Patriot_Act_doesn_t_give_feds_special_access_to_cloud_data.

4. A&L Goodbody, *No Cloud over Patriot Act* (March 2012), [cited July 2014]. Available from: http://www.irelandip.com/uploads/file/No%20Cloud%20over%20Patriot%20Act(1).pdf.

5. Bryan Cunningham, Safegov.org, *Is Ireland the first cloud haven?* (February 2014), [cited July 2014]. Available from: http://safegov.org/2014/2/27/is-ireland-the-first-"cloud-haven".

6. TechCentral.ie, *Ignore Patriot Act scare stories* (October 2012), [cited July 2014]. Available from: http://www.techcentral.ie/ignore-patriot-act-cloud-scare-stories/.

7. Information Commissioners Office (ICO), *Guidance on the use of cloud computing*, [cited March 2014]. Available from: http://ico.org.uk/for_organisations/guidance_index/~/media/documents/library/Data_Protection/Practical_application/cloud_computing_guidance_for_organisations.ashx.

8. Article 29 Working Party, *Opinion on cloud computing* (July 2012), [cited March 2014]. Available from: http://ec.europa.eu/justice/data-protection/article-29/documentation/opinion-recommendation/files/2012/wp196_en.pdf.

9. Renzo Marchini, *Cloud computing: a practical introduction to the legal issues* (July 2010), [cited March 2014].

10. Article 29 Working Party, *Opinion 10/2006 on the processing of personal data by the Society for Worldwide Interbank Financial Telecommunication (SWIFT)* (November 2006), [cited March 2014]. Available from: http://ec.europa.eu/justice/policies/privacy/docs/wpdocs/2006/wp128_en.pdf.

11. Ibid.

12. Information Commissioner's Office, *Data Protection Act*, [cited March 2014]. Available from: http://ico.org.uk/for_organisations/data_protection/the_guide/principle_8.

13. Cloud Security Alliance, *Cloud security alliance announces launch of privacy level agreement (PLA) V.2 working group* (April 2014), [cited April 2014]. Available from: https://cloudsecurityalliance.org/media/news/csa-announces-pla-v-2/.

14. Samuel Gibbs, *U.S. Court forces Microsoft to hand over personal data from Irish Server* (April 2014), [cited July 2014]. Available from: http://www.theguardian.com/technology/2014/apr/29/us-court-microsoft-personal-data-emails-irish-server.

15. Ibid.

Cloud Security Alliance Research

For those who have tracked the progress of this book, you may have noticed at least three different iterations regarding its content. These changes were caused by simply the desire to try and include as much of the excellent work that Cloud Security Alliance (CSA) volunteers and staff have contributed, and multiple iterations of the table of contents in the attempt to squeeze more in. Obviously, one thing that is very clear is that while every effort was made to include as much as we could, there is still a considerable amount of excellent work that has not been referenced thus far.

We (the authors) recognized very early on that if we attempted to dedicate a chapter to each of the CSA working groups, that the book would likely never be completed and would likely resemble the cloud version of the Encyclopedia Brittanica! Even if we were able to draw a line under the work, the likelihood is that the content would be so substantial that it would have to be released as volumes, just like those physical Encyclopedias gathering dust on our bookshelves today.

This, of course, is testimony to the dedicated support from the CSA family, the fact that so many wonderful and talented individuals have dedicated their time and expertise in the development of content that is making our digital world a safer place. Subsequently the purpose of this chapter is to incorporate areas of research that did not feature within the preceding text, and while every attempt was made to summarize *all* working groups and deliverables, we recognize that this was not possible. The readers are therefore strongly encouraged to not only see the following text as a reference guide, but also visit the CSA research site for a broader understanding of *all* areas currently being worked on, and where the readers can identify the area of research that aligns with their interest and expertise, and contribute to future deliverables.

BIG DATA WORKING GROUP

At the beginning of this book, it was stated that cloud computing is one of the hottest topics within the technology industry, it is however not alone and must surely be joined by the term "Big Data." This term, much like cloud computing, suffers from multiple sources offering varying definitions. We, the authors were then presented with a number of options in determining which definition to present within this text. According to analyst firm Gartner,

> "Big Data" is high-volume, -velocity, and -variety information asset that demands cost-effective, innovative forms of information processing for enhanced insight and decision-making[1].

An alternative definition was cited in the U.S. White House in their May 2014 publication entitled "Big Data: Seizing Opportunities Preserving values[2]"; *"data is now available faster, has greater coverage and scope, and includes new types of observations and measurements that previously were not available."* In practical terms, Big Data provides remarkable opportunities that are being realized by many organizations across both public and private sectors. One such example was realized by the Los Angeles and Santa Cruz police departments, who with a private sector organization used software to predict those crimes that are *likely* to occur. By providing crime data, the software was able to pinpoint the likelihood of a crime occurring within a 500-ft radius; this resulted in a 33% decrease in burglaries and 21% decrease in violent crimes where the software was used.[3] This particular approach is known as predictive policing, allowing policemen on the beat to focus on those areas that are likely to result in more crime.

Despite such positive benefits, there have been significant security and privacy concerns associated with Big Data. In the white paper by Robert H. Sloan and Richard Warner entitled "Big Data and the 'New' Privacy Tradeoff," they cite, "both the potential benefits and risks from Big Data analysis are so much larger than anything we have seen before." To understand some of these risks, the Big Data Working Group (BDWG) within the CSA was established in order to identify techniques that are scalable to address the security and privacy issues. The intent of the working group is to develop deliverables that can be used as best practice for security and privacy challenges for Big Data. Such deliverables also include development of relationships that can assist in the development of appropriate standards and appropriate research.

Before presenting the deliverables produced by the working group thus far, it is worth noting the role cloud computing plays within "Big Data." In the CSA research entitled "Top Ten Big Data Security and Privacy Challenges,[4]" "Big Data is cheaply and easily accessible to organizations large and small through public cloud infrastructure. Software infrastructures such as Hadoop enable developers to easily leverage thousands of computing nodes to perform data-parallel computing. Combined with the ability to buy computing power on-demand from public cloud providers, such developments greatly accelerate the adoption of Big Data mining methodologies." Cloud computing therefore can be seen as a great enabler for the broader adoption of Big Data, and "subsequently new security challenges have arisen from the coupling of Big Data with public cloud environments."

BDWG Research Deliverables

The preceding paragraphs cited the various security and privacy concerns associated with Big Data, these were presented as part of the deliverables from the BDWG through the Top Ten Big Data Security and Privacy Challenges.

Top Ten Big Data Security and Privacy Challenges

Published in 2013, the Top Ten Challenges present the following as the top 10 challenges to Big Data security and privacy:

1. Secure computations in distributed programming frameworks: Frameworks such as MapReduce are referred to as distributed computational frameworks because they allow the processing of large amounts of data across a distributed environment. It is comprised of two parts: (1) mapper, which distributes the work to the various nodes within the framework and (2) reducer, which combines the work collates and resolves the various results. Security and privacy risks arise with untrusted mappers that have the ability to impact confidentiality (by snooping on requests), but also integrity through altering scripts or the results. To address these risks, there exist two models to maintain trust between mappers: (1) authenticate each mapper to establish an initial trust relationship and repeat this process periodically and (2) mandatory access control to ensure that access to files only aligns with a predefined security policy.

2. Security best practices for nonrelational data stores: Data stores for nonrelational data may introduce security challenges due to their lack of capability. This includes the following scenarios:
   a. Transactional integrity: Nonrelational data stores such as NoSQL experience challenges in achieving transactional integrity; introducing such validation will result in degradation of performance

and scalability. To address these trade-offs, it is possible to leverage techniques such as Architectural Trade-off Analysis Method that can be used to evaluate the proposed integrity constraints without significantly impacting performance.

   b. Lax authentication mechanisms: Both the authentication and password storage mechanisms for NoSQL are not considered strong. Subsequently risks exist that would allow an attacker to carry out a replay attack, where legitimate authentication is captured and replayed (therefore allowing the attacker access to resources). Equally, the REST communication protocol, which is based on HTTP, is prone to cross-site scripting and injection attacks. Furthermore, there is no support from third-party modules that would support alternate authentication modules.

   c. Inefficient authorization mechanisms: There exist multiple authorization techniques across various NoSQL solutions. Many, however, only apply authorization to the higher layers and also do not support role-based access control.

   d. Susceptibility to injection attacks: NoSQL is susceptible to a number of injection attacks that would, for example, allow the attacker to inject columns into a database of their choosing. This not only impacts the integrity of the data, but also the potential of denial-of-service (DOS) attack impacting the availability of the database.

   e. Lack of consistency: Users are not provided with consistent results because each node may not be synchronized with the node holding the latest image.

   f. Insider attacks: The combination of the above, as well as the implementation of poor security mechanisms (e.g., security logging) would allow potential insider attacks to be conducted without detection.

3. Secure data storage and transactions logs: While the data and transaction logs can be stored and managed across various storage media manually, the volume of such data means that automated solutions are becoming more prevalent. Subsequently such automated solutions may not track where the data are actually stored introducing challenges in the application of security. An example would be where data that are not often used is stored on cheaper storage, however if this cheaper tier does not have the same security controls and the data are sensitive, then a risk is introduced. Subsequently organizations should ensure that their storage strategy not only considers the retrieval rate for such data, but also the sensitivity of data.

4. End-point input validation/filtering: A Big Data implementation will likely collect data from a multitude of sources but the challenge will be attributing the level of trust associated with the data provided from such

sources. To illustrate the multitude sources, consider the following from the U.S. White House publication cited earlier, "The advent of the more Internet-enabled devices and sensors expands the capacity to collect data from physical entities, including sensors and radio-frequency identification (RFID) chips. Personal location data can come from GPS chips, cell-tower triangulation of mobile devices, mapping of wireless networks, and in-person payments." A threat exists where a malicious attacker is able to manipulate the data provided by the sensor(s), impersonate a legitimate sensor, manipulate the input sources of the sensed data (for example, if a sensor collects data about temperature, it will be possible to artificially change the temperature within the vicinity of the sensor, and that is ultimately submitted), or manipulate the data transmitted by a sensor.

5. Real-time security monitoring: A key use case for Big Data is its ability to assist in the security of other systems. This particular example includes both the monitoring of the Big Data infrastructure as well as using this same infrastructure for security monitoring; for example, a cloud service provider could leverage Big Data to analyze security alerts in real time and subsequently reduce the number of false positives within its environment. The challenge, however, is that the sheer volume of alerts go beyond the capacity for human analysis. With Big Data, these alerts will likely increase even further, and place greater pressure on already overstretched security teams. In the White Paper published by security firm RSA entitled "RSA-Pivotal Security Big Data Reference architecture[5]," the use of Big Data for security monitoring can address the following requirements:

   a. Better visibility from networks to servers, and applications to end points

   b. More contextual analysis to help prioritize issues more effectively

   c. Actionable intelligence from diverse sources, both internal and external, to tell the system what to look for in an automated way, and respond quicker

   If a public cloud is used to support Big Data security monitoring, it is important to consider the risks that include the security of the public cloud, the monitoring applications itself, and the security of the input sources. It is worth noting the recent publication by the CSA BDWG entitled "Big Data Analytics for security intelligence[6]" for further information.

6. Scalable and composable privacy-preserving data mining and analytics: The use of Big Data can lead to privacy risks being realized. These risks can be either through data leakage, where, for example, an insider may intentionally release the data, or indeed through an authorized third party. Alternatively, another consideration is the release of data for research purposes. Where large data volumes are concerned, there is a

risk that even if the data are anonymized, it may be possible to infer the data subject. For example, consider a health care example; while the name, house number, and zip code are obfuscated, it is possible for a medical professional to identify the data subject within a given town because only one person has a particular combination of medical conditions. To mitigate these risks, organizations should consider the use of security controls such as encryption, access controls, and separation of duties. Another approach is the use of pseudonymization, where identifying fields are replaced with artificial fields (pseudonyms). According to Neelie Kroes, the EU Commissioner responsible for the Digital Agenda, using pseudonymization means that "Companies would be able to process the data on grounds of legitimate interest, rather than consent. That could make all the positive difference to Big Data: without endangering privacy. Of course, in those cases, companies still (need) to minimize privacy risks. Their internal processes and risk assessments must show how they comply with the guiding principles of data protection law. And—if something does go wrong—the company remains accountable.[7]"

Further details on the privacy considerations are published in the research entitled "Big Data and the future of Privacy,[8]" which considers five fundamental questions regarding the role of privacy, and the measures to mitigate privacy risks as it pertains to Big Data:

a. What are the public policy implications of the collection, storage, analysis, and use of Big Data? For example, do the current U.S. policy framework and privacy proposals for protecting consumer privacy and government use of data adequately address issues raised by Big Data analytics?

b. What types of uses of Big Data could measurably improve outcomes or productivity with further government action, funding, or research?

c. What technological trends or key technologies will affect the collection, storage, analysis, and use of Big Data?

d. How should the policy frameworks or regulations for handling Big Data differ between the government and the private sector?

e. What issues are raised by the use of Big Data across jurisdictions such as the adequacy of current international laws, regulations, or norms?

7. Cryptographically enforced data-centric security: Protecting access to data has invariably involved the application of security to the systems in which the data are stored. This approach has, however, a large number of attacks that can circumvent the security and allow the attacker access to the data. An alternate approach is to use strong cryptography, which while does have threats such as covert side-channel attacks and are more difficult to carry out.

While there are challenges in using cryptography within Big Data environments, these are discussed within the BDWG research entitled "Top Ten Challenges in Cryptography for Big Data.[9]" It summarizes that cryptography should be seen as an enabling technology critical for the adoption of cloud computing and Big Data. This is because it provides "mathematical assurance" about the level of trust that can be attributed to the use of third parties when handing over critical/personal data to a third party.

8. Granular access control: Enforcing the need-to-know principle is an important foundation in achieving confidentiality in the data. One of the measures that can be leveraged to achieve this principle is the use of mandatory access control, with appropriately strong authentication. It should be feasible for end customers to understand the access control methodologies deployed by the cloud provider and determine if they are appropriate.

9. Granular audits: Although security monitoring will provide a feed of security events as they occur, there is a potential that an attack may have been missed. Subsequently, regular audits are an important measure to identify intrusions that may have been missed. Although this is not a new area, the scope, granularity, as well as the number of inputs will likely differ.

10. Data provenance: The provenance, in other words, the source of the data will likely be of importance. The provenance will determine the level of trust associated with the data, for example, when investigating a security incident, it may be important to know how the data were created, particularly if the security incident could end up in a court/disciplinary situation.

The Top Ten Challenges as they relate to the Big Data ecosystem are graphically depicted in Figure 8.1.

The role of Big Data in the growth of cloud computing, and in particular, the public cloud is significant; "Big Data analytics are driving rapid growth for public cloud computing vendors with revenues of the top 50 public cloud providers shooting up 47% in the fourth quarter of the last year to $6.2 billion, according to Technology Business Review Inc.[10]" With stories of Big Data being able to predict pregnancy of a teen even before her own father,[11] and these larger data stores not only increasing the number of persons who have access to the data (and therefore increasing the risk) but also becoming more attractive to attackers; the need for security and privacy for Big Data, and particularly Big Data in cloud computing (where the level of transparency and flexibility in determining controls will be as great as those internally hosted environments), has never been so important. It is for this reason the readers are encouraged to track the research and deliverables produced by the BDWG.

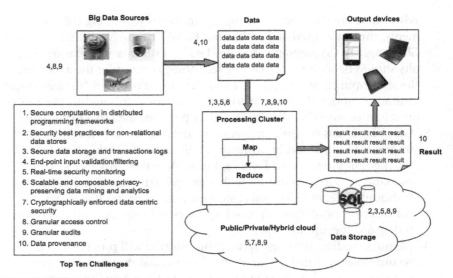

FIGURE 8.1

Top 10 security and privacy challenges in the Big Data ecosystem.

CLOUD DATA GOVERNANCE

With the transition to cloud computing, end customer organizations hand over the management of systems that host their data to third parties. The level of control will depend on the cloud model itself, which will vary based on the as-a-service model used. Such a transition will invariably mean that the level of transparency provided to end customers will decrease particularly in those areas that cannot be technically measured (for example, an update of antivirus software). As such the governance employed by the provider, which involves the processes, roles, and technologies for managing governing data in cloud computing environments will likely raise concerns, particularly as these are more difficult to measure in real time. It is for this reason that the Working Group entitled on Cloud data governance was established to:

- Understand the requirements of the various stakeholders in governing and operating data in the cloud.
- Provide a series of recommendations on the best practices to address the issues raised in the earlier phase.

CSA Research Deliverables

At present, the deliverables available from the working group provide the survey results from the "Cloud Consumer Advocacy Questionnaire and Information

Survey Results (CCAQIS).[12]" The following summarize some of the key findings under version 1.0 of the survey:

Data Discovery

Does the CSP Provide a Capability to Locate and Search All of a Customer's Data?	
Yes	59%
No	41%

Location of Data

Does the CSP Allow a Customer to Select a Specific Location for Use and/or Storage of the Customer's Data?	
Yes	82%
No	18%

Data Aggregation and Inference

Does the CSP Provide Customers with Controls Over Its Data to Ensure That Data can or cannot be Aggregated According to Customer Needs and/or Restrictions?	
Yes	58%
No	42%

Does the CSP Provide the Ability to Mask Data from Selected Customer Personnel, as Determined by a Customer, to Prevent Data Aggregation or Inference Problems for a Customer?	
Yes	65%
No	35%

Encryption and Key Management Practices

Does the CSP Provide End-to-End Encryption for Data in Transit?	
Yes	84%
No	16%

Data Backup and Recovery Schemes

Does the CSP Offer Data Backup and Recovery Services to Customers?	
Yes	88%
No	12%

If Yes, is the Specific Location for Such Selectable by the Customer?	
Yes	53%
No	47%

No two clouds are alike. This statement was inferred in Chapter 1, and the above is evidence of that particular statement with clear evidence as to the lack of standardization across cloud service providers in the area of governance. However, there are some trends that are of interest:

CSP's Areas of Strength and Weakness as it Relates to Cloud Governance	
Mature Areas	**Immature Areas**
■ Control over aggregation of data ■ Vetting of encryption algorithms ■ Define access to their data ■ Technical enforcements of multitenancy	■ Timeliness of removal of data ■ Cryptographic key management scalable to cloud ■ Methods for handling data remanence ■ Data remanence and methods used to ensure data are removed ■ Mechanisms for customers to determine which columns are encrypted and to prevent inference from nonencrypted column

Following the results of the survey, the second phase of the Cloud Data Governance Group can focus on efforts defining those best practice recommendations. However, what is clearly evident that with such variance among providers regarding the level of governance, the due diligence process has never been so important.

CLOUDCERT

In Chapter 1, there was a discussion regarding the advent of EU regulation that would class cloud computing as "critical infrastructure." This classification is understandable with the concentration of computing resources, whereby a cloud incident can have a greater detrimental impact to multiple organizations than if the resources were internally hosted. As a result of this greater impact, which cloud computing represents, the CSA launched the CloudCERT initiative. Comprised of subject matter experts across cloud service providers, telecommunications providers, national CERTs, as well as industry representation, the mission for CloudCERT is to:

> Enhance the capability of the cloud community to prepare for and respond to vulnerabilities, threats, and incidents in order to preserve trust in cloud computing.

CLOUDTRUST PROTOCOL

Introduced in Chapter 2, the CloudTrust Protocol (CTP) is intended to provide cloud end customers with the ability to query the security controls deployed by the provider. One of the many challenges that we have discussed throughout this book is the lack of transparency within cloud computing, the CTP intends to address this issue. In certain circumstances, particularly where regulated data are being hosted by third-party providers (such as CSPs), the end customer will be responsible for ensuring that third parties have the appropriate controls in place, and failure to ensure these places will leave the end customer (or data controller) liable for potential fines. Subsequently, utilizing certification and as such annual attestation regarding the controls deployed by the provider may not provide the level of requisite confidence.

The original developer is CSC, who in their white paper entitled "Digital Trust in the Cloud[13]" sees CTP as an asynchronous "question and response" protocol that is presented to all providers and is ultimately controlled by the clients themselves. This allows the end customer to query the configuration, operating status, and other key questions of the provider that the end customer is interested in identifying about the provider. The provider, when receiving the information request can decline responding, however should recognize that they will have the opportunity to respond and deliver information "in the best possible way for them." Within the CSC publication entitled "Digital Trust in the Cloud: A précis for CTP 2.0,[14]" a ratio is presented to explain the number of elements of transparency a provider is able to support. This is referred to as the CloudTrust Index (CTI), which can be used by end customers to determine how transparent a provider is with regards to the security, privacy, and compliance. It is however worth noting that not every cloud implementation will require CTI of 1 (being the highest level of assurance). The level of assurance sought will be dependent on the sensitivity of data/services that are externally hosted. This is depicted in Figure 8.2;

Implementing CTP is not restricted to one particular operating model, although "the design intention has always been to create fully automated

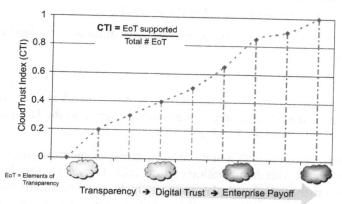

FIGURE 8.2
CTI used as a transparency indicator.

implementations of the CTP as an end-to-end RESTful Web service, such complete automation is not strictly necessary to achieve the ultimate objective, i.e., reclaiming important elements of transparency in the cloud.[14]" Although an automated approach may be considered the intention, alternate out-of-band communications are also available such as the use of e-mail. Even though the latter may be inefficient, it is anticipated for providers to adopt more in-band communications for CTP queries such as the publication of APIs. In terms of the elements of transparency, the second revision of CTP has 23 elements across multiple families, for example, under the family audit log, the following elements are included:

- Provide log of policy violations {in last "n" hours} (e.g., malware elimination, unauthorized access attempts, etc.)

What does this mean?

Would allow the end customer to see those events that are in violation (or indeed attempted violation) of the client policies. For example, this may be any attempt to access specific files that are hosted by the provider.

- Provide audit/event log {for last "n" hours}

What does this mean?

This log request asks the provider to send all log files from the date ("n" hours) back to the customer regardless of whether a violation occurred or not.

- Provide a list of currently authorized users/subjects and their permissions

What does this mean?

This request requests a log that will detail those entities that have authorized access to those items that are assets owned by the end customer. This will also include the permissions allocated to those entities.

- Provide incident declaration and response summary {for last "n" hours}

What does this mean?

Requests log data of those events that the service provider determines to be incidents as well as description of the actions taken, and the latest update on the status of the identified incident.

The above are only a snapshot of those transparency elements within version 2 of the CTP; however, with the migration of more critical services to the cloud there is no question that the CTP will play an increasingly more important role with the selection of a service provider, as well as the ongoing management of CSPs.

ENTERPRISE ARCHITECTURE WORKING GROUP

The Enterprise Architecture Working Group has produced a number of deliverables. Most recently, version 2 of the Enterprise Architecture is both a methodology and a set of tools enabling security architects, enterprise architects, and risk management professionals to leverage a common set of solutions that fulfill their common needs to be able to assess, where their internal IT and their cloud providers are in terms of security capabilities and to plan a road map to meet the security needs of their business.[15]"

It is anticipated the architecture to be used in any number of design phases; these range from assessing opportunities for improvement, creating road maps for technology adoption, defining reusable security patterns, and during the assessment phase of potential cloud providers/security vendors against common capabilities.

INCIDENT MANAGEMENT AND FORENSICS

Even though the area of incident management is covered in detail, it is worthwhile detailing the output of the CSA working group focusing on incident management and forensics to understand the particular areas of research. As will be detailed in Chapter 9, the introduction of cloud computing adds additional complexity to the management of security incidents, not least compounded with the fact that the data are managed by a third party. The intention of the working group is to develop best practices in the management of security incidents within the cloud. The scope of the group will address the following topics (note this list is not exhaustive):

- Incident management (IncM) in cloud environments: This will include the life cycle of IncM, legal considerations, locations of available evidence, etc.
- Cloud forensics: To include CSP capabilities, mapping against ISO 27037, the process for conducting cloud forensic investigations, etc.
- eDiscovery
- Legal and technical issues related to cloud forensics: To include best practices for SLAs required for forensics support, the management of personally identifiable data, etc.

Available research from the working group includes a document entitled "Mapping the Forensic Standard ISO/IEC 27037 to Cloud Computing.[16]" The purpose of ISO 27037 is to establish a baseline within the sphere of digital forensics. The research maps the components of the ISO standard and considers the requirements in the context of cloud; these particular requirements focus on the areas of identification, collection, acquisition, and preservation of digital evidence. In particular, the analysis considers the complexities that end customers of cloud services face as they relate to the requirements defined by the ISO standard, for example; it will be necessary to collect (5.4.3) digital evidence such that they are "removed from their original location to a laboratory or another controlled environment for later acquisition and analysis." However for cloud environments, this will likely prove challenging and as such is "acquisition should usually be preferred over collection to avoid impacts to parties not involved in the matter and the gathering of irrelevant information that must be excluded during analysis." Subsequently for end customers, it is important to ascertain the level of forensic support provided by the CSP, as not all currently provide complete support. Further, as detailed within the research, the area of cloud forensics still has specific challenges that are generally easier to manage for internally provisioned services. The customer is therefore strongly encouraged to incorporate this as part of any due diligence process.

INNOVATION INITIATIVE

According to the charter[17] of the innovation initiative within the CSA II, its mission is:

- Identify specific issues relating to trust and security that would inhibit the adoption of next generation information technology
- Articulate the guiding principles and objectives that IT innovators must address.
- Help innovators incubate technology solutions that align with our principles and address the systemic gaps we have identified.

It is intended for the working group to introduce innovators into the CSA community, and refer them into the CSA II subcommittee or to external partners. This subcommittee will be comprised of capital partners and technologists, and will allow innovators to get feedback on their products/services to become actively supported. The deliverables of the initiative "may come in the form of a report on an annual basis to the CSA from the working group providing the key metrics of performance and the measurable outcomes."

SECURITY AS A SERVICE

The Security as a service working group focuses its research to define the term security-as-a-service as well as the various categories within this definition. In addition, there are multiple research deliverables that focus on the implantation practices for the defined security service categories.

With end customers leveraging various security-as-a-service offerings from different providers, they will ultimately lose control over not only the data, but also functionality and the operations. This naturally means that the provider will be required to provide the requisite transparency to customers; the level of transparency will be entirely dependent on the level of assurance required. The risks to an end customer using such a service that are compounded by the lack of transparency include (but not limited to): vendor lock-in, identity theft, and unauthorized access. Organizations either considering or leveraging any of the following services in the cloud should consider the guidance provided by the working group:

Category 1: Identity and Access Management (IAM)

"Identity management includes the creation, management, and removal (deletion) of a digital identity. Access management includes the authorization of access to only the data an entity needs to access to perform required duties efficiently and effectively.[18]" The purpose of the guidance is "to define the requirements of secure identity and access management, and the tools in use to provide IAM security in the cloud."

Category 2: Data Loss Prevention

Data loss prevention (DLP) technologies are used to ensure that data, both in transit or at rest, adhere to the policies as defined by the organization. For example, this may be to ensure that data which contain the word CONFIDENTIAL are sent outside of the organization. This policy could also be applied to alternate storage devices, such as USB drives. The opportunity exists for end customers to utilize DLP-as-a-service whereby functionalities such as encryption, or identifying data (e.g., keyword searching) can be used to mitigate threats such as data leakage, regulatory compliance, etc.

Category 3: Web Security

Customers have the opportunity to leverage Web security as a service; this ensures that all traffic can be diverted through a cloud service for inspection before entering the enterprise, or indeed inspecting all outbound traffic. Within this category, there are additional areas of functionality such as Web filtering, where all outbound Web requests from users can be checked against the internal policy to determine if users are allowed to access the requested resources. For example, is a user allowed to check his/her social media accounts during working hours? For inbound traffic, these services can be used to ensure that incoming requests are not malicious. This, of course, is only a small snapshot of the types of services offered through Web security as a service.

Category 4: E-mail Security

Applying e-mail security controls within a cloud-based service ensures that all (inbound and outbound) e-mails into an organization are scanned for malicious content, or indeed content that deviates from policy. Some of the features include scanning e-mails to determine if they are classed as spam, phishing, contain malware, or should be encrypted as defined by the end customer policy.

Category 5: Security Assessment
The use of cloud computing to deliver security assessments has been in use for some time, with early trailblazers sitting comfortably within this category. Customers benefit from the quick setup time, pay-per-use payment models that exist (although alternate models will exist, such as subscription services), and elasticity. These services can be used to identify vulnerabilities within both hosts inside the enterprise and externally facing systems, security assessments can also be used for compliance purposes.

Category 6: Intrusion Management
A growing service category is the use of dedicated cloud providers to review relatively large data sets to identify evidence of intrusion. This can be done in-line, whereby traffic is routed through a security service provider, or indeed a hybrid deployment with sensors deployed within the end customer's environment. These services would leverage deep packet inspection technology that would include signatures, behavioral analysis as well as other methods to identify anomalies that would indicate potential intrusions.

Category 7: Security Information and Event Management
The role of security information and event management (SIEM) systems is to collect log and event data to provide an overall view of security within a given environment. By transitioning an SIEM service to the cloud, the end customer has the opportunity to transition the management and storage of logs to the cloud, as well as the event correlation in order to identify potential intrusions into the monitored environment.

Category 8: Encryption
The role of encryption-as-a-service (EaaS) simplifies the key management process; "You throw data at it and it does all the key management and key backups. It's all done centrally. All the user needs to know is what data to protect and who needs to be given access. People have been afraid of encryption for a very long time, so the 'as a service' model makes it easier for them to consume[19]" according to Tsion Gonen of Safenet. Key management is the only one element that falls into the EaaS category; other offerings include various Virtual Private Network (VPN) services, as well as the encryption of data both at rest and in transit.

Category 9: Business Continuity and Disaster Recovery
Recovery in the event of a disaster would seem best placed within a cloud environment. For example, many organizations would want to have a "hot site," a

fully functioning facility ready in case their primary environment fails. This could prove costly, however within a cloud based environment "a tenant could make use of low-specification guest machines to replicate applications and data to the cloud, but with the provision to quickly ramp up the CPU, RAM, etc., of these machines in a business continuity/disaster recovery scenario.[20]"

Category 10: Network Security

The provision of network security will likely include both virtual and physical devices that demand integration to ensure that the virtual network environment has visibility of all applicable traffic. Services within this category will include not only firewall services, but also DDoS (distributed denial of service) protection, intrusion detection, and intrusion protection services.

SECURITY GUIDANCE FOR CRITICAL AREAS OF FOCUS IN CLOUD COMPUTING

Now in its third revision,[21] the guidance provided by the CSA was originally published in 2009 under v1.0. It was updated later in 2009; the third and current version was published in 2011, building upon previous versions. The intention of this third version was to provide recommendations that could be measured and therefore audited. The guidance makes numerous recommendations to help reduce risk when adopting cloud computing, and should be seen as a method to determine the level of tolerance during the migration of an asset to the cloud.

The guidance is comprised of a number of domains highlighting the cloud computing areas of concern, which are divided into broad policy areas (governance) and tactical security considerations (operational). The domain areas are as follows:

1. Cloud computing architectural framework
2. Governance and enterprise risk management
3. Legal issues: Contracts and electronic discovery
4. Compliance and audit
5. Information management and data security
6. Portability and interoperability
7. Traditional security, business continuity, and disaster recovery
8. Data center operations
9. Incident response, notification, and remediation
10. Application security
11. Encryption and key management
12. Identity and access management
13. Virtualization
14. Security as a service

The "guidance contains extensive lists of security recommendations. Not all cloud deployments need every possible security and risk control." Therefore organizations are encouraged to spend "time up front evaluating your risk tolerance, and potential exposures will provide the context you need to pick and choose the best options for your organization and deployment.[21]"

SOFTWARE DEFINED PERIMETER

The traditional approach toward protecting an organization would leverage a perimeter that supported separation between the trusted environment and the external untrusted world. However, multiple pressures has meant that according to Paul Simmonds (speaking in 2007 as board member for the Jericho forum) said of firewalls, "In a large corporate network, it's good as a quality-of-service boundary but not as a security service.[22]"

To address the challenges associated with the fixed traditional perimeters, the role of software-defined perimeters (SDPs) is seen as the solution in implementing perimeters, while being afforded the flexibility of being deployed anywhere. In "its simplest form, the architecture of the SDP consists of two components: SDP hosts and SDP controllers.[23]" The SDP host will be able to initiate a connection, or alternatively accept a connection, all of which are managed through interaction with SDP controllers. The controller will manage the hosts that are able to communicate with one another, and whether any external authentication service will be used. The workflow is graphically depicted in Figure 8.3; this illustrates that once the hosts and controllers are brought online (and gone through the authentication phase), the controller will provide the host with a list of those hosts that it can accept connections from (accepting hosts) with additional policies (e.g., to use encryption). Once

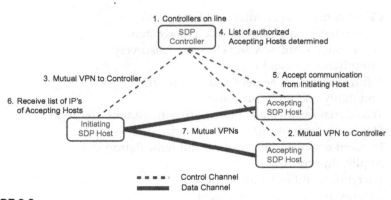

FIGURE 8.3

Software-Defined Perimeter (SDP) workflow. *Software Defined Perimeter Working Group.*[23]

completed, the initiating SDP hosts would initiate a connection to authorized accepting hosts, as defined by the list received from the controller.

Beyond the mechanics of the SDP, there exists a multitude of use cases where an SDP can be used to improve the security of a given environment:

- Enterprise application isolation: John Kindervag of Forrester wrote, "There's an old saying in information security, we want our network to be like an M&M, with a hard crunchy outside and soft chewy center.[24]" This "old saying" uses the M&M to explain that once an attacker has breached the external perimeter of its intended target, it effectively has free reign over the internal environment, or the soft chewy center! To address this issue, organizations may wish to isolate those assets that are considered high value. Using SDP to isolate these high-value assets from *normal* assets, the organization has the opportunity to mitigate the risk of the attacker laterally moving across the entire infrastructure.
- SDP within cloud environments: SDP has the opportunity to be deployed across all cloud models and architectures. For example, end customers have the opportunity to use SDP in order to hide and secure all public cloud instances that are used. Alternately for Infrastructure-as-a-service environments, SDP can be used as a "protected on-ramp" for customers.
- Cloud-based virtual-desktop infrastructure (VDI): A VDI environment uses virtualization to present a desktop to the end user. The use of such an infrastructure could well benefit from being hosted in a cloud environment, not least because of the payment model (e.g., by the hour), but also the accessibility of the service. However, this approach could result in issues because the VDI will likely require access to internal services (e.g., file access, internal applications, etc.). In these instances, it is expected that an SDP can assist by allowing the end organization to limit access at a granular level.
- Internet of Things (IoT): The IoT landscape will be comprised of a multitude of devices, many that will host particularly sensitive data, and that may not be able to support the installation of security software. An SDP will allow organizations to hide and secure such services.

Such use cases clearly articulate the importance and role of SDPs in the provision of security in a world where traditional perimeters are no longer suitable. The intention of the Software-Defined Working Group will be to build up on other work within this environment the inclusion of all stakeholders. The document entitled SDP Specification v1.0[25] released on April 2014 defines the SDP protocol; this includes the authorization protocol, and the authentication used between hosts. Also included are the logs that will be included, which at a minimum will include the following fields:

- Time: When the log was created
- Name: Of the event
- Severity: Ranging from debug to critical
- Device address: IP address of the machine that generates the record

It is recommended that all logs to be passed to an SIEM system to provide an overall view of security within the environment.

As has been articulated throughout this chapter, and indeed the preceding chapters within the book, the CSA is an inclusive organization that allows experts to contribute to the deliverables documented within this text (as well as those that are not included). Therefore if you, the reader, have a particular interest, or indeed disagree with any of the deliverables detailed, please get involved with the appropriate Working Group, your inputs will be greatly welcomed.

END NOTES

1. Svetlana Sicular. Forbes.com. *Gartner's Big Data Definition Consists of Three Parts, Not to Be Confused with the Three V's.* (March 2013), [cited July 2014]. Available from: http://www.forbes.com/sites/gartnergroup/2013/03/27/gartners-big-data-definition-consists-of-three-parts-not-to-be-confused-with-three-vs/.

2. U.S. White House. *Big Data: Seizing opportunities preserving values* (May 2014), [cited July 2014]. Available from: http://www.whitehouse.gov/sites/default/files/docs/big_data_privacy_report_may_1_2014.pdf.

3. Nicole Laskowski. TechTarget.com. *Ten big data case studies in a nutshell*, [cited July 2014]. Available from: http://searchcio.techtarget.com/opinion/Ten-big-data-case-studies-in-a-nutshell.

4. Big Data Working Group. Cloud Security Alliance. *Top Ten Big Data Security and Privacy Challenges* (June 2013), [cited July 2014]. Available from: https://cloudsecurityalliance.org/research/big-data/#_downloads.

5. RSA. *RSA-Pivotal Security Big Data Reference Architecture,* [cited July 2014]. Available from: http://www.emc.com/collateral/white-paper/h12878-rsa-pivotal-security-big-data-reference-architecture-wp.pdf.

6. Big Data Working Group. *Big Data Analytics for Security Intelligence* (September 2013), [cited July 2014]. Available from: https://cloudsecurityalliance.org/download/big-data-analytics-for-security-intelligence/.

7. Out-Law.com. *Kroes backs plan to enable pseudonymised data to be processed without consent* (December 2013), [cited July 2014]. Available from: http://www.out-law.com/en/articles/2013/december/kroes-backs-plans-to-enable-pseudonymised-data-to-be-processed-without-consent/.

8. Big Data Working Group. Cloud Security Alliance. *Big Data and the future of privacy* (March 2014), [cited July 2014]. Available from: https://downloads.cloudsecurityalliance.org/initiatives/bdwg/Comment_on_Big_Data_Future_of_Privacy.pdf.

9. Big Data Working Group. Cloud Security Alliance. *Top Ten challenges in cryptography for Big Data* (March 2014), [cited July 2014]. Available from: https://cloudsecurityalliance.org/download/top-ten-challenges-in-cryptography-for-big-data/.

10. Brandon Butler. *Big data drives 47% growth for top 50 public cloud companies* (April 2014), [July 2014]. Available from: http://www.networkworld.com/article/2176086/cloud-computing/big-data-drives-47–growth-for-top-50-public-cloud-companies.html.

11. Kashmir Hill. Forbes. *How Target figured out a teen girl was pregnant before her father did* (February 2012), [July 2014]. Available from: http://www.forbes.com/sites/kashmirhill/2012/02/16/how-target-figured-out-a-teen-girl-was-pregnant-before-her-father-did/.

12. Cloud Data Governance. Cloud Security Alliance. *Cloud Consumer Advocacy Questionnaire and Information Survey Results* (August 2011), [cited July 2014]. Available from: https://cloudsecurityalliance.org/research/cdg/#_downloads.

13. Ronald B. Knode. CSC. *Digital Trust in the Cloud* (August 2009), [cited July 2014]. Available from: www.csc.com/cloud/insights/57785-into_the_cloud_with_ctp.

14. CSC. *Digital Trust in the Cloud: A précis for CTP 2.0* (July 2010), [cited July 2014]. Available from: www.csc.com/cloud/insights/57785-into_the_cloud_with_ctp.

15. Enterprise Architecture Working Group. Cloud Security Alliance. *Enterprise Architecture v2.0* (February 2013), [cited July 2014]. Available from: https://cloudsecurityalliance.org/research/eawg/#_downloads.

16. Incident Management and Forensics Working Group. Cloud Security Alliance. *Mapping the Forensic Standard ISO/IEC 27037 to Cloud Computing* (June 2013), [cited July 2014]. Available from: https://cloudsecurityalliance.org/download/mapping-the-forensic-standard-isoiec-27037-to-cloud-computing/.

17. CSA Innovation Initiative. Cloud Security Alliance. *Cloud Security Alliance Innovation Initiative (CSAII) Working Group Proposal* (February 2012), [cited July 2014]. Available from: https://downloads.cloudsecurityalliance.org/initiatives/innovate/Innovation_Initative_Charter.docx.

18. Security as a Service Working Group. Cloud Security Alliance. *Identity and Access Management* (September 2012), [cited July 2014]. Available from: https://downloads.cloudsecurityalliance.org/initiatives/secaas/SecaaS_Cat_1_IAM_Implementation_Guidance.pdf.

19. Elizabeth Harrin. Enterprise Networking Planet. *Cloud Storage vendors offering encryption as a service* (February 2012), [cited July 2014]. Available from: http://www.enterprisenetworkingplanet.com/netsecur/cloud-storage-vendors-offering-encryption-as-a-service.html.

20. Cloud Security Alliance. *Security-as-a-Service specification*, [cited July 2014]. Available from: https://downloads.cloudsecurityalliance.org/initiatives/secaas/SecaaS_V1_0.pdf.

21. Cloud Security Alliance. *Security Guidance for critical areas of focus in cloud computing v3.0* (November 2011), [cited July 2014]. Available from: https://cloudsecurityalliance.org/download/security-guidance-for-critical-areas-of-focus-in-cloud-computing-v3/.

22. Ellen Messmer. NetworkWorld. *E-commerce, security issues challenge network firewall role* (September 2007), [cited July 2014]. Available from: http://www.networkworld.com/article/2285569/lan-wan/e-commerce-security-issues-challenge-network-firewall-role.html.

23. Software Defined Perimeter Working Group. Cloud Security Alliance. *Software Defined Perimeter* (December 2013), [cited July 2014]. Available from: https://downloads.cloudsecurityalliance.org/initiatives/sdp/Software_Defined_Perimeter.pdf.

24. John Kindervag. Forrester. *No more chewy centres: Introducing the zero trust model of information security* (November 2012), [cited July 2014]. Available from: http://www.forrester.com/No+More+Chewy+Centers+Introducing+The+Zero+Trust+Model+Of+Information+Security/fulltext/-/E-RES56682.

25. Software Defined Perimeter Working Group. Cloud Security Alliance. *SDP Specification v1.0* (April 2014), [cited July 2014]. Available from: https://downloads.cloudsecurityalliance.org/initiatives/sdp/SDP_Specification_1.0.pdf.

CHAPTER 9

Dark Clouds, What to Do In The Event of a Security Incident

DEATH AND TAXES

- Building a security incident response team
- Incident response challenges in the cloud
- The future
- Security breach

It is said that in life there are two certainties that we all have to deal with. These are death and taxes. Those of us who work in information security have a third certainty that we must also factor in, and that is at some stage we will be involved in a security breach. As with death and taxes, preparation is critical when dealing with a security breach. This is particularly true when dealing with cloud computing.

As we know, the cloud offers businesses many advantages and benefits. However, with these benefits the cloud also introduces new risks. If these risks are realized, they can result in a security breach that must be dealt with effectively to minimize the impact of such a breach. An ineffective response can lead to prolonged outages, loss of data, negative impact on the organization's reputation and the attackers getting away with it, and more than likely coming back for more.

Over the years, the information security industry has developed and matured a large number of processes, tools, techniques, and procedures for dealing with security incidents. Many companies have adopted these principles into their own incident response framework. They have been built on guidelines such as the "Computer Security Incident Handling Guide (NIST Special Publication 800-61, Rev. 2[1])," the "Handbook for Computer Security Incident Response Teams (CSIRTs)"[2] by Carnegie Mellon Software Engineering Institute, and the "Step by Step Guide for Setting up CERTs"[3] from the European Network and Information Security Agency to name but a few.

BUILDING A SECURITY INCIDENT RESPONSE TEAM

Under these traditional guidelines, the incident response team has been developed to enshroud many different disciplines across the business to ensure a complete approach when managing the fallout resulting from a security breach. The composition of a security incident team can take many forms, one of the common approaches is depicted in Figure 9.1.

The incident response team should be led by the information security manager as they are often the people with the most experience and expertise in dealing with computer security incidents. The remaining members of the team should be made up from competent and experienced representatives from each of the various departments within the business. These individuals should also have the relevant autonomy and authority to make decisions that could impact the business. A computer security incident can happen at any time day or night and the incident response team needs to be able to respond to evolving situations without having the additional burden of seeking approval from management who may not be available at the time of the incident. However, please note that not all members will be required for every incident. The key skills and inputs required from each of the departments, as well as the information security manager, are presented below, as well as the circumstances their participation is not required.

Skills Required of the Security Incident Response Team

- Information security team: Those from the information security team should compose the core of the incident response team, as it is assumed they will have requisite training, skills, and experience to be able to deal with the security incidents as they occur. Typically, they would have the skills and training to forensically capture and analyze information as

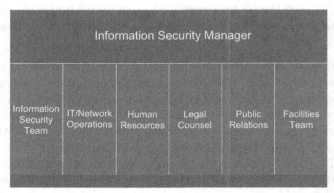

FIGURE 9.1
Computer security incident response team.

required. They should also have the knowledge and skills to understand and recognize the various types of attack methodologies used by criminals and how to counter them. Where they may not have the specific technical skills, it is assumed they will have access to suitably skilled third parties that they can oversee and verify the quality of their work.

- Information technology (IT)/network operations department: The IT/network operations team is a critical element in the incident response team. It is typically the team that will be the first line of defense, and of detection, of any security incidents. The team could become aware of suspicious behavior from the monitoring tools used by the team to manage and support the infrastructure. Alternatively, a user reporting strange behavior to the support desk may also indicate an attack. This team is also familiar with the normal day-to-day usage of systems and the company's networks; as such any deviations from normal traffic or system behavior could indicate a compromise is underway or has already happened. When dealing with an incident, the IT/network operations team will be best placed to understand the impact of the attack, or indeed any suggested remediation actions on key systems.

- Human resources (HR): Many studies show that a significant number of security incidents are due to insiders within the company either deliberately or accidentally causing a breach. A user could be duped into clicking on a malicious link in an e-mail, which could allow the attacker gain access to core systems. On the other hand, a staff member could deliberately compromise a system either as a result of being bribed or coerced into such action, or he or she may simply be disgruntled and seek to get revenge on the company by compromising key systems. Should a security breach involve a member of staff it is important that the HR team is engaged with the incident response team to ensure that the proper processes and procedures are followed to comply with good HR practice and not to impinge on the rights of staff or on the ability of the company to pursue a disciplinary matter. Therefore, the participation from HR may not always be required (e.g., where no internal employee is involved), however, because the incident may involve long working hours in a highly stressful and demanding environment. It is essential that HR where not actively involved are briefed to ensure those on the team are receiving the right support from the company in doing their jobs and that they are compensated, if necessary, in the appropriate manner. It is important, therefore, that the HR department is consulted during the development of any incident response processes to ensure they are in line with good HR management. They should also be consulted during any responses to security incidents.

- Legal: As with HR, it is essential that the information security manager seeks sound legal advice in the development of the incident response processes and procedures. Should an incident occur, the legal members of the team will be essential in ensuring the company, and by extension the incident response team, respond to the incident in line with any legal and regulatory requirements that may be imposed on the company. It is also important that the legal team is consulted during the incident to ensure that any information disclosures do not jeopardize the investigation or subsequent court cases, or indeed expose the organization to any legal liabilities. Moreover, the legal team may require expert support or training regarding legal processes related to potential incidents (e.g., specific country legislative frameworks for gathering evidence). This will need to be identified well in advance.
- Public relations: An often overlooked, but an equally important, element in managing a response to a security incident is how information is communicated to key stakeholders such as customers, senior management, the media, the public, staff, and suppliers. For each of those groups how the message is delivered may vary and indeed the details communicated in those messages may need to differ for each group. During an incident, it is essential that the organization can maintain control of the information being discussed in public. This is to ensure that key details are not leaked that may alert the attackers their attack has been detected, or that may prejudice any subsequent legal case, or indeed may cause unnecessary worry and concern in groups such as customers, staff, or the general republic. Communicating in an open and honest way that does not undermine the investigation or expose the organization to any potential legal liabilities is a skill that is best left to those with expertise in this area. There have been a number of recent examples where the companies involved have received negative headlines regarding the manner in which they handled the communication of a particular incident. On the flip side, recently Twitter was commended for the
- Facilities team: In traditional incident response to computer security breaches there may be elements of the breach that involve the physical world. Should the incident involve a physical element, such as a break-in at a facility or a member of staff, there may be a requirement to involve the facilities management team so evidence can be extracted from systems such as closed-circuit television cameras, or access logs to secure areas. Subsequently, the facilities team is unlikely to be part of the core team.
- External expertise: Depending on the nature of the computer security incident there may be the requirement to get external expertise to help with the investigation. For example, the incident may involve systems for which there is no internal expertise, such as forensic investigations of a non-IT device, and therefore need external help.

Depending on the seriousness and impact of an information security incident it may be necessary to mobilize and involve all members of the information security incident response team, or simply only involve a subset of the team.

How the team responds and manages the computer security incident will be determined by their policies and procedures. In most cases, these will follow the seven main stages of incident response as outlined in the above publications. The different stages relating to traditional incident response are as follows:

1. Detection/notification: To respond to a security breach, we first have to be made aware that it has happened. There are a number of ways that we can become aware of a breach. Our security systems, such as intrusion detection systems or firewall monitoring, may alert us to a potential breach. Alternatively, unusual network behavior, such as strange network traffic patterns or unusual log-in activity, could also indicate an ongoing breach. Another source could be from our users who notice something amiss. Organizations should ensure the process to report a security incident, and be easy to use for employees. It is also advisable to test the process, for example, reporting an incident to determine the time taken to reach the security team is used by many organizations. It is also not unusual for an external party, such as law enforcement, partner organizations, customers, the media, or even the attacker, to notify the affected organization aware of the breach (e.g., blackmail). No matter how the breach is detected, the key point is the incident response process cannot begin until the organization is aware it has a problem. It makes sense that the earlier a breach can be detected, the sooner it can be responded to, and thereby minimize the impact it can have on the organization.

2. Containment: Having identified that a security breach has occurred, the next step is to ensure the impact of the breach is restricted to as few systems as possible and that the attack cannot progress any further within the organization. This phase also involves identifying how the breach occurred in the first place, the root cause of the breach. This is an essential step in the process so as to ensure the breach does not reoccur once the systems are back online. Not identifying which vulnerability or weakness was exploited can enable the breach to occur again by allowing the attacker to exploit that vulnerability again.

3. Eradication: Once the root cause for the breach has been eliminated, it is essential to review the compromised systems to ensure the attacker has made no alterations to the affected systems or installed any additional software that could allow them to compromise the systems again. Any suspicious changes to systems or accounts should be investigated to ensure there were not made by an attacker.

4. Remediation: With the breach contained and the intrusion eradicated, the next phase in the process is to eliminate the cause of the breach and remove any possible malicious software the attacker may have installed onto the compromised systems. This may involve patching the compromised systems with the latest software updates, modifying configuration and/or system settings, or reconfiguring rules on a firewall.

5. Recovery: Once the breach has been remediated, it is time to recover the systems back to the state they were in before the breach occurred. This involves recovering system files and data from backup media, making sure that anything that is restored is secure and will not enable the breach to happen again.

6. Review: Once the breach has been dealt with and all systems are recovered and back online, one of the most important phases in incident response begins. This is reviewing how the incident was actually handled and managed. The purpose of the review is to identify what was done well during the incident and what areas need improvement. These improvements may be alterations to processes and procedures, additional training for staff, investing in new tools, or reconfiguring systems to be more secure to prevent a breach occurring in the first place. It is important to hold this review as soon as possible to ensure all lessons learned are captured and not forgotten over time.

7. Communication: Throughout the whole innocent response process, it is important to have effective communications happening at all times. During the incident, it is important to ensure that interested parties are kept abreast of what is happening. These parties may be senior management, stakeholders, shareholders, regulators, staff, and of course media. For each of those parties it is important to ensure the right message is communicated to each group in the appropriate manner. For example, information given to the media may be different than that given to senior management. Communications is important, as it keeps everyone abreast of what is happening during the incident and ensures the right information is getting to the right people at the right time.

INCIDENT RESPONSE CHALLENGES IN THE CLOUD

While the above processes have been tried and tested over time in traditional IT environments, the challenge we face now is how to apply and adapt these processes to cloud computing.

During a traditional computer security incident, all the systems can be physically accessed by the incident response team. Where necessary, logs can be securely gathered from servers, routers, firewalls, and other devices. Disks can be forensically captured to enable examination of any evidence that may be held on them. Containing an incident can be relatively straight forward as the network is fully under the control of the affected organization that can shut down servers or cut off network segments if required.

When it comes to the cloud though, the traditional incident response process becomes more difficult to achieve or may not be possible at all. Due to the nature of cloud computing, the customer data, services, or systems may be located across many virtual machines (VMs), running across many physical systems, which may be in many different data centers, located in different sites and jurisdictions around the world.

What type of cloud platform you use will also determine how the incident response plans will be developed. For example, how an incident is dealt with in an Software as a Service (SaaS) environment will be different to how an incident is dealt with in a Platform as a Service (PaaS) environment, which in turn will be different from managing an incident in an Infrastructure as a Service (IaaS) environment.

While it is possible for the customer to be able to access the key networking, system, and application logs within their own local environment, access to key security and system logs within a cloud platform will be dependent on the cooperation and capabilities of the cloud service provider.

The nature of cloud computing not only introduces ambiguity over where data are located brings a lot of privacy and regulatory compliance issues, for example, the European Data Protection Directive, but also has implications on how a security breach should be handled.

Developing a Framework for Incident Response in the Cloud

The challenges that cloud computing presents to those responsible for incident response unfortunately cannot be overcome with a simple solution. What may be suitable for one organization may not suit another organization. For this reason, we need to look at developing a framework for incident response that each organization should use as a foundation to build its cloud incident response capabilities upon. All of the elements of a framework for incident response in the cloud as outlined in the remainder of this chapter may be suitable for some organizations; for others, only certain elements may be suitable. This may be due to the capabilities of the organization itself, the capabilities of the cloud service provider they are engaged with, or indeed there may be constraints due to legal, regulatory, or contractual issues.

The following framework should be considered when the decision to engage with a cloud service provider has been made by the business. At this stage, when the business requirements are being gathered, the customer should include their cloud security requirements, including their requirements around incident response.

Fail to Prepare, Prepare to Fail

The key to successfully managing a security incident in the cloud is preparation. This preparation must happen well before any security incident and indeed it should be happen well before even engaging with the cloud provider.

To ensure proper preparation, it is essential that the individual responsible for information security within their organization and managing incident response of potential breaches engages with other key business areas to understand what their requirements are with regards to cloud computing. They will need to ensure they are involved in the process of selecting the preferred cloud service provider and that all information security requirements are considered from the very outset, including the requirements with regards to incident response. In many cases, this will introduce the challenge of marrying the business requirements for a cloud service provider against the requirements for strong incident response capabilities. In particular, this could become a major area of contention should the cloud service provider satisfy all the business needs but not the requirements in relation to incident response.

Should this conflict in requirements arise, it is important to ensure this is communicated clearly to the business and senior management within the organization the impact moving to such a cloud service provider will have on the organizations' capabilities to meet its ethical, legal, and/or regulatory obligations should a security breach occur. Getting involved as early as possible in the project should reduce the risk of this happening or at the very least ensure that all parties are fully aware of the deficiencies in the solution being proposed and accept those deficiencies.

To ensure the most appropriate solution is found, the cloud service provider should be engaged with and involved in the planning of your incident response process as early as possible. In essence, the cloud service provider will likely become a core part of the incident response team. Therefore, it is important that the provider(s) are fully engaged to determine and agree the roles and responsibilities in relation to incident response (as depicted in Figure 9.2). Note, there may be more than one provider, so this will involve engagement with potentially multiple providers.

Engaging the Cloud Service Provider

One of the key players previously identified within the incident response team is the legal counsel. In the traditional incident response process, their role comes into the fore during a security incident. Legal counsel can also play a key role in helping to engage with a cloud service provider. The Information security team should work with their legal counsel to ensure that all incident response requirements are included within any contractual and service level agreements. The following items are key elements to include within any contractual agreements with a cloud service provider to increase the capability of the incident response plan:

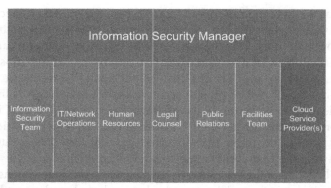

FIGURE 9.2
Incident response roles/responsibilities.

- Key contacts: It is important to ensure the response plan has the appropriate contact details, including emergency contact details, of key security personnel within the cloud service provider who have the skills, knowledge, capability, and authority in assisting and supporting a potential security incident. During a security incident, time will be of essence and therefore it is important to avoid having to work through multiple support levels within the provider's help desk to speak to the right members of the team. These contact details should also be regularly updated and maintained for that person(s) and their role as they may change roles over time.
- Communication tools: Efficient, secure, and regular communications during a security incident is essential. This can be a challenge within the end customer alone, not to mention when including the added complexity of working with an external third party. During a security incident it is important to be able to communicate with all key members of the incident response team in a secure manner. In some cases, this may be face to face meetings, but at times it will be important to communicate electronically. However, communicating over a network that may be compromised can expose activities to the attackers. To protect communications it is important to employ secure channels such as encrypted e-mail, encrypted instant messaging, and secure chat channels on systems isolated from the compromised network. Whichever solutions are chosen, it is imperative that the security team within the cloud security provider can communicate with these same secure systems. This will entail agreeing shared communication mechanisms and exchanging information such as public keys to enable such communication. Remember when looking at secure communication channels, particularly when communicating with external parties, it is important to have the capability to retain details of the communications

such as the time messages were sent and who the sender and recipient were. Other details that are useful to retain include headers of the message and indeed the message itself. This is to ensure an accurate log and timeline of what was discussed, by whom, and any subsequent actions that may arise. Should the incident result in a court case, it is important to be able to present accurate records as to how the incident was dealt with. Be aware though that when retaining such data, it is important to ensure that there is infringing on any data protection or other rights of the individuals involved and that such data are stored in a secure manner to prevent tampering or indeed disclosure to the attackers.

- Visibility: One of the key elements used by many incident response teams to identify how an attack happened, what has been breached, and who they attackers are, is log files. Log files are ubiquitous across all our systems. Every network device, computer, server, and application all produce log data in some way, shape, or form. This information when collated and analyzed properly can prove invaluable in dealing with a computer security incident. However, in a cloud environment the end customer may not have access to the log data required. Depending on the type of cloud platform used, the network infrastructure, the operating systems and even the application logs may only be accessible to the cloud service provider. The end customer may not have any direct visibility into those systems and it will be very dependent on the capabilities of the cloud service provider to interpret the logs in relation to the particular instance or system. Depending on the type of cloud platform used, it may be possible to build some form of monitoring. In an IaaS platform, for example, the end customer will be able to gain access to the logs of the systems that they have implemented and run within the environment. However, they will not have access to the raw log files of the underlying infrastructure that supports the IaaS platform. For this the customer will need to follow the steps above to gain access to such data. In a PaaS environment, the customer can look at including their own log files within the application or service that is being implemented. However, similar to the IaaS platform they will not have visibility into the log files for the underlying infrastructure or platform. In addition, the customer will have little or no visibility into the log files of the servers that their application will run on. Again, liaising with the cloud service provider for such access is a key step before signing any contracts. Within an SaaS, there is even less visibility into the log files. At best the customer may have the ability to view an audit trail of which users access the service and when, but more detailed log data may not be possible. In the move to the cloud it is important not to overlook the log file of the internal infrastructure. The internal infrastructure (of the customer) will have log files from firewalls, routers, servers, and other core systems. These log data could be extremely useful during an investigation into an incident within the cloud service provider, in particular, if the incident involves an insider within the customer's own organization. That insider may be a malicious user looking to commit fraud or disrupt operations, he or she could be someone who accidentally creates a security breach as a result of being badly trained and not being unfamiliar with the system, or the user could have been coerced or duped into creating a security incident by an external attacker. The log files on customer systems can help in identifying who was accessing their systems and when. This can help to either eliminate or include them in investigations. Within a PaaS platform, it may be possible to use the data from Application Program Interface (API) calls and interactions with the cloud to investigate the incident. Engaging with the cloud service provider early in the negotiation process can give leverage to get access to the log files and to what level. For privacy and other reasons, both the customer and provider need to ensure that access is provided only to the log data relevant to the customer and does not include any data belonging to any other clients. A corollary to that is customers want to ensure their log data are not released to any other third parties or clients of the cloud service provider.

The type of access to the log data is also important. Can the cloud service provider provide a real-time feed so the customer can integrate the feed from the cloud service provider into their own log monitoring and/Security Information and Event Management (SIEM) solution so that they can have real-time alerts to potential issues? Or will that feed be delayed by a certain amount of time before they can analyze it? If so, this could widen the window of opportunity for an attacker as they may go undetected. It may be the case the cloud service provider will simply give copies of the log files upon request. Such a solution typically involves a time delay as the logs are analyzed for data relating to the customer, data isolated from other data for other clients, and then forensically captured and extracted before being sent. This time delay will impact on the ability to respond quickly to events and is something that should be built into incident response processes.

Alternatively, if cloud service providers have their own log monitoring and management solution, they may be able to provide access to that system. While not providing direct access to the raw log data, it may provide a view into the key data required to manage any security incidents. This visibility may be provided by using a VM within the cloud service provider's environment. Alternatively, the provider may provide a browser-based solution to access their system. Whatever level of access provided, it is important to ensure that both customer and provider ensure the security and integrity of that log data are maintained. If collating all log data into one central system, it is important to ensure all communications from the log sources to the central log repository are encrypted and secure. Any log data stored in the central repository should also be stored on secure media that is encrypted and secured with access restricted only to those security personnel involved in analyzing that data.

A key point to remember when configuring a monitoring and collection solution is to standardize all clocks on each of the devices being monitored to the same time source. Typically in most organizations this would involve using the UTC (Coordinated Universal Time) time zone as the time zone for all devices to synchronize with. Each monitored device, system, or application should also use the Network Time Protocol (NTP) to ensure its own system clock is synchronized to an Internet time server. Alternatively, internal server synchronization may be used (e.g., with radio and/ or satellite). This is because NTP is based over the UDP protocol, which can easily be spoofed. It is recommended to leverage more than one time source, which is key for managing potential slight time differences. Another consideration with monitoring and gathering log data is to ensure the volume of such traffic does not cause performance or capacity issues with the customer's own network or indeed with the servers the data will be stored and processed on. Remember the log data from the cloud service provider in most cases will be traversing the Internet connection into the internal network. Should there not be enough bandwidth on that connection or the firewalls are incapable of dealing with large throughputs, they could inadvertently impact the customer's own access to the Internet. Should more than one cloud service provider be used, then the demands on the various systems will increase accordingly.

- Notification: If access to the raw log data is provided, then these data should be integrated into the customer's own monitoring solutions so that in the event of a security breach within the cloud service, early notification will be provided. However, access to the data may not be continuous, and only provided at agreed time intervals. If this is the case, the data should still be fed into the monitoring solution to help parse events within the log data and identify potential security breaches. Where the provider does not support, direct real time, or even intermittent access, to the log data, it is important to evaluate the capability of the provider to monitor, as well as the number of assets transferred to them. In this situation the key questions to ask the provider are
  - What tools does the cloud service provider use to monitor the systems for security incidents?
  - Does the cloud service provider monitor all elements of the infrastructure or only certain elements? If the latter, what are these elements?

- How does the cloud service provider monitor the systems that support the services offered? In particular, if that cloud service is spread across different servers, different VMs, different data centers, in different countries?
- Does the cloud service provider provide 24 × 7 × 365 monitoring or is it only local business hours for the cloud service provider's head office?
- How competent are the staff responsible for monitoring these systems? What training and experience do they have?

If the cloud service provider will be the sole party monitoring the security logs for the offered services, then it is important to ensure they notify the customer in event of a security breach impacting the service. Clear guidelines should be established to determine whom the provider should contact for specific security issues and also how the cloud security provider can contact those parties.

Not only should the cloud service provider notify in the event of a security breach impacting systems in their platform, but customers may also wish to be alerted of security incidents they experience that do not impact the service directly. Many cloud service providers may be reluctant to provide this level of information but it is a useful metric that can be used to determine how secure or resilient their service is. If they are suffering a high number of breaches, this may indicate a failure to implement appropriate security. Alternatively, if they have suffered few or no security incidents, then this can provide confidence that their security controls are effective. Of course, it may also indicate their security controls are not effective and they simply have not detected the breaches.

It is important to consider the reciprocal notification process; this focuses on where a security incident occurs on the own customer's environment that may negatively impact the systems provided by the provider. An example of this may be a computer virus or worm that has infected systems on the customer's own environment, and that could traverse the network into that owned by the cloud service provider.

- Roles and responsibilities: A framework for incident response in the cloud will include more than one party. There will be at least the end customer; in addition, there will be at least one cloud service provider (and possibly many more). Depending on the cloud model used there will also likely be other parties involved that need to be identified, as well as their roles and responsibilities clearly defined. If the model used is a public cloud offering, then the role of the Internet service provider (ISP) needs to be considered. In addition, the ISP of the cloud service provider may also play an important role in the Cloud Security Incident Response Framework. Even a private cloud model where the cloud service provider provides for all connectivity and delivery of the cloud service will require identifying clear demarcation lines and responsibilities. (The above is used for illustrative purposes, it is recognized that public and private clouds are not defined by the type of connectivity offered to customers. It is recognized that a private cloud service provider may (and often does) deliver services over the Internet). For example, who is responsible for gathering evidence and logs from the router on the various premises? In other words, where does the boundaries of one network end and where do they begin for another (e.g., cloud service provider)?

It is also important to clearly define the responsibilities for the various elements of the incident response process. This will be to determine who leads the response to an incident should it occur within the cloud service provider. Logic would dictate that is the sole responsibility of the cloud service provider and that the customer should have no input into their incident response process. However, there may exist legal, regulatory, or contractual obligations that demand the incident is dealt in a certain manner. As a result, the customer needs to ensure that they are a key stakeholder within the incident response process for the provider. Indeed, they should look to ensure there is a degree of authority to determine how the incident is managed. For example, the customer may be obligated by certain laws and regulations to handle a computer security breach in a certain manner. Alternatively the cloud service provider may be located within a different jurisdiction or may not be obligated to the same regulations as the customer. As a result, their standard response to the breach may not include the requirements that their customers' needs be adhered to. Should those requirements not be adhered to, it is the customer that will invariably fall foul of any subsequent enforcement notices and judgments. Ensuring the customer is an integral part of the provider's incident response process will enable them to make sure their requirements are met during the life cycle of the incident.

- Tools: Clear and concise policies, processes, procedures, responsibilities, and properly trained staff are all key components in an effective Cloud Security Incident Response Framework. However, these could all be undermined if the customer or provider does not have the appropriate tools and resources to support the framework. There is little or no point in developing ironclad agreements with a cloud security provider that obliges them to provide their raw log data if they do not have the appropriate tools to interpret and analyze that data. When developing a Cloud Security Incident Response Framework, it is important to determine what tools and capabilities are available. Some of the issues the customer needs to consider are
  - Do they have the tools capable of monitoring the log data the cloud service provider may be providing?

- Have they got the capabilities to integrate their incident response management system with those of the provider?
- Will there be a central system accessible to the customer and the cloud service provider where all actions during the incident are recorded? Will this be one system cohosted and funded or will it involve integrating the customer's incident response system and that of the cloud service provider?
- If there are more than one cloud service provider, can they be isolated incidents on a per provider basis within the system deployed by the customer to prevent providers discovering issues relating to other providers?

In addition to the tools and capabilities to manage an incident and integrate with those of the provider, the customer needs to make sure the provider has the right tools, and necessary training and skills in those tools, to manage an incident for the environment.

A key tool to consider in this review process is the computer forensics capability of the provider. The end customer will need to determine whether the cloud service provider has the appropriate forensic tools capable of capturing relevant data relating to the particular incident. This will need to consider how effective the forensic tools the cloud service provider has. The customer may wish to determine from the provider whether the forensic tools they use are commercially available tools, open source-based tools, or proprietary tools the cloud service provider developed themselves. Or indeed is it a mixture of tools from each of the various categories. Whatever tools the cloud service provider employs, it is important to ensure they are compatible with the systems employed by the customers and their own incident response processes.

Cloud Forensics

Cloud forensics is a topic that is still in its infancy and there is still a lot of research to be conducted in this area. Due to the nature of the cloud traditional digital forensic techniques may not be possible to capture evidence or other data.

> In an increasingly cloud-oriented society, the ability to identify, obtain, preserve, and analyze potential digital evidence is a critical business capability. Whether responding to a security incident, data breach, or in support of litigation, the ill-prepared organization will find itself at a severe (and potentially costly) disadvantage.
>
> **Cloud Security Alliance. (2013). Mapping The Forensic Standard ISO/IEC 27037 to Cloud Computing.[4]**

Many of the traditional tools, processes, and procedures that have been developed over the years are not relevant in a cloud environment. Traditional computer forensics focuses on the ability to physically attach to a device, be that a computer, a disk, or a phone, and to then take an image of that device, which can then be investigated and examined. However, the challenge we face with cloud computing is how to capture a cloud? The data, logs, and evidence we need to capture may be stored on separate systems located in separate data centers, which in turn could be located in different parts of the world. In other words, there is no one device that can be connected to and all the required evidence and logs gathered from. VMs offer the ability to capture the image, which can then be forensically copied and examined. However, capturing an image of a VM fails to capture the volatile data that may be in the memory of that machine, which in turn could lead to the loss of critical evidence that was stored in memory. There is also the issue of forensically capturing such images from multitenanted environments, in particular how to isolate a compromised system from other "clean" systems.

Another issue to consider is how to give the cloud service provider access to customer data for them to forensically capture information from compromised systems. Good practice is to secure data within the cloud through implementing appropriate security controls, or to use a cloud service provider that encrypts customer data in the cloud and where the customer retains control of all the keys. In order for the cloud service provider to access such data, they need to be able to decrypt it. This introduces the challenge of providing the cloud security provider with access to customer data and then revoking that access once the investigation is over.

Traditional forensic tools also look to capture all the data, which can then be investigated and examined. Capturing all the data from a cloud-based system may also include data and information belonging not just to one customer, but also to other customers of the cloud service provider. The provider will therefore need to capture the appropriate data only, while still preserving the evidence.

During an incident it may be necessary for the provider and customer to exchange forensics data. In order to preserve the integrity of such data, appropriate processes will need to be in place to support the use of digital signatures to pass evidence from one team to the other. Also, whatever systems are used to maintain a chain of custody for whatever evidence or artifacts are passed from one party to another. In many traditional incidents, the passing of such artifacts would be done face to face and the chain of custody would be managed by using a physical form to track who holds the evidence, from whom they received the evidence, and the date and time such evidence was handed over. In a cloud-based security incident, the cloud security provider may not be physically located in the same country as the customer. It is therefore imperative appropriate mechanisms are put in place whereby such evidence and artifacts can be transferred in a secure manner with a legally sound chain of custody record in place.

Jurisdictional Issues

Another key element in the development of a Cloud Security Incident Response Framework is to determine which jurisdiction applies in the event of a security breach. The customer may be located in a different country to that of the provider, while the data center(s) upon which the cloud service operates could be located across one or many other jurisdictions.

Many countries have cybercrime laws that determine how a computer security breach should be handled. Some of these laws are applied depending on whether the victim, perpetrator, or crime has been committed within that specific jurisdiction. It is possible that a security breach occurring in the cloud could be subject to cybercrime laws from various jurisdictions. For example, the laws applicable to the jurisdiction of the end customer may apply, similarly the cloud service provider may be located in a separate jurisdiction and be subject to local laws there, and the jurisdiction(s) where the data centers physically storing the data may also apply. It is important to understand what obligations parties are under the various criminal laws and whether they are applicable (the privacy chapter, and recent legal ruling applied to Microsoft), and to who they are applicable to (e.g., the cloud service provider, the data center provider, or a combination of any of the above). How to comply with the requirements of these laws will play an important role in the development of the Cloud Incident Respond Framework.

In addition to cybercrime laws, there may also be breach notification laws in place within the various jurisdictions that impact on the cloud service. The provider or customer may have to comply with breach notification laws depending on the laws and regulations within their geographic location or even industry. It is important therefore that an agreement between customer and the cloud service provider exists to determine if any security breach may trigger a breach notification obligation. The customer needs to ensure they do not want to fall foul of any breach notification laws simply because the provider failed to notify a security breach.

Similarly, the cloud service provider may be obligated to disclose a security breach under the laws and regulations within its jurisdiction. The customer needs to ensure they are notified of any such obligations and the prior notice period given in order to be prepared for any inquiries from the media or public regarding the impact.

Knowing the obligations, and those of the cloud service provider, are in relation to cybercrime and breach notification laws is critical in ensuring the Cloud Security Incident Response Framework is best positioned to manage certain types of incidents. How an incident should be responded to and who is responsible for managing the incidents and coordinating disclosures will depend on the obligations under these laws.

Supply Chain

The cloud service provider may use a number of suppliers to help it provide its service. These may be third-party apps that are integrated into the cloud service provider's service. Alternatively, they may provide services such as hosting, networking, or outsourced managed services. Should any of these parties suffer a security breach, it could impact on the cloud security provider, which in turn could impact customers. When developing the Cloud Security Incident Response Framework, it is important to ensure the provider identified any such third parties and has obligated them to the same incident response requirements.

Agree Processes and Procedures

A critical element in the Cloud Security Incident Response Framework is to ensure there are clearly documented processes and procedures to support the framework. The customer should look at the various types of incidents that they may encounter and agree with their cloud service provider who is responsible for which tasks, the contact details for the relevant parties, and what evidential requirements there may be to support the process to manage each of type of incident. Having these processes and procedures agreed to and documented as part of the framework can help ensure the most effective response happens in the event of a security breach.

Some of the types of incidents that should be considered include

- Dealing with a distributed denial of service attack
- Dealing with an intrusion
- Dealing with a malware infection
- Dealing with information leakage
- Dealing with insider abuse (this should include insiders at the end customer or those of the cloud provider)
- Dealing with a social engineering attack (this should include dealing with such an attack against both organizations)
- Dealing with extortion-based attacks

Practice and Drills

As with all skills and particularly those involving teams, practice makes perfect. Therefore, it is important that regular exercises are conducted to test the effectiveness of the Cloud Security Incident Response Framework. The midst of a critical incident is not the time to identify a rudimentary issue with how the customer and the cloud service provider will manage such an incident. It is always better to identify these problems during an exercise and then to apply any lessons learned to improve the framework.

These exercises could be simply desktop exercises whereby a walk-through of various scenarios are carried out with the relevant parties to identify if the processes, procedures, and other details work as expected. A desktop exercise can be an effective tool to ensure processes and procedures are workable with the added advantage of not requiring a lot of time and input from the various stakeholders. However, a desktop exercise is not effective in identifying any problems when the processes and tools are applied in a real-life scenario.

This is where drills can be quite effective in ensuring that all the tools, processes, procedures, and training of staff work as expected.

For example, do key members of the incident response team have access to the right software and the right encryption keys for their role? Are there the appropriate licenses for all the software planned for use as part of the incident response? Are there any items missing from the list of tools that identified as being part of the Cloud Security Incident Response Framework? Indeed, are there any tools missing not thought about when developing the framework?

It is of course important to include the cloud service provider's team in any drill conducted. An opportune time to run such drills would be during any penetration or vulnerability testing against the cloud service. This type of test could help in identifying how good the monitoring and detection tools are, how robust the log management process is, and how effective the digital forensics processes are. However, it should be noted that this level of engagement and commitment may depend on the cloud service provider. Some of them may not provide such a service.

THE FUTURE

The evolution of technology, or the introduction of new technology, brings with it many opportunities and benefits. As with any of these developments, how we secure presents many challenges, none more so than how to deal with a security incident that impacts that technology. As we have noted, the current techniques, tools, and skills that we have for traditional IT systems leave a lot of gaps when it comes to dealing with security incidents in the cloud.

However, that is not to say there is no hope or the future is bleak. On the contrary, there is a lot of work being done to address these gaps. Developing a Cloud Security Incident Response Framework is the first step in addressing those gaps. With such a framework in place, it is possible for the customer to identify ways to manage computer security incidents and just as importantly where the deficiencies are. This information is a big step along the road to being better prepared to keep the systems and data secure.

There are also a number of initiatives that are trying to address these gaps to and which you should be aware of. The Cloud Security Alliance is conducting a lot of research in this area. For example, there is the Incident Management and Forensics Group which is "seek to develop best practices that consider the legal, technical, and procedural elements involved in responding in a forensically sound way to security incidents in the cloud." The Cloud Security Alliance is also developing the incident response capabilities in the cloud with Cloud-CERT with the mission to "Enhance the capability of the cloud community to prepare for and respond to vulnerabilities, threats, and incidents in order to preserve trust in cloud computing."

As in many aspects of life "Failing to prepare, is preparing to fail," which is why it is so important that you develop a Cloud Security Incident Response Framework for your organization to manage any potential incidents that will impact on the cloud service providers your organization engages with.

END NOTES

1. NIST, *Computer security incident handling guide*, [cited July 2014]. Available from: http://www.nist.gov/customcf/get_pdf.cfm?pub_id=911736.
2. Carnegie Mellon Engineering Software Institute, *Handbook for computer security incident response teams (CSIRTs)*. [cited July 2014]. Available from: http://resources.sei.cmu.edu/library/asset-view.cfm?assetID=6305.
3. European Network Information Security Agency, *Step-by-step guide for setting up CERTs*. [cited July 2014]. Available from: http://www.enisa.europa.eu/activities/cert/support/guide.
4. Cloud Security Alliance, *Mapping the forensic standard ISO/IEC 27037 to cloud computing*. [cited July 2014]. Available from: https://downloads.cloudsecurityalliance.org/initiatives/imf/Mapping-the-Forensic-Standard-ISO-IEC-27037-to-Cloud-Computing.pdf.

CHAPTER 10

The Future Cloud

- Cloud computing for critical infrastructure
- Defining the security requirements for tomorrow's cloud

There is a sense of trepidation when trying to forecast anything technology related, there have been many great names that have tried and failed spectacularly when attempting to predict the future of the technology industry. There are, however, some emerging trends that even we would feel comfortable in predicting their direction; as follows:

- In the future there will be more users connected to the Internet.
- In the future there will be *more devices* connected to the Internet.
- In the future there will be *more data*, all of which will need to be stored, processed, and of course secured.

These three statements are hardly going to surprise anybody, they would certainly be classed as the safest predictions we can make, and unlikely to result in our entry into the multiple Web sites highlighting failed but rather amusing technology predictions. However, with these emerging trends beginning to be realized, we have to ask ourselves what role the cloud will play. To answer this question, we need to understand the scale of the emerging trends.

MORE, MORE, AND MORE

Regardless of the source, all evidence points to more data, users, and devices:

- IDC predicts the installed base of things connected will be 212 billion by the end of 2020, including 30 billion connected autonomous things.[1]
- Cisco predicts that the number of network-connected devices will be more than 15 billion, twice the world's population, by 2015.[2]

- Today's Internet has 2.09 billion users [cited Oct 2011]; by 2020, global Internet access will probably have risen to nearly 5 billion users.[3]
- The global big data market will show a 26% compound annual growth rate from 2013 to 2018.[4]

The above predictions are of course only a small snapshot of forecasts reinforcing the belief that we will witness more devices, data, and connected users in the future. However, it was not entirely necessary to reference external sources to reinforce the predictions; a simple look into our homes would likely have been sufficient. Once the home consisted of a single desktop and a dial-up modem to connect to the Internet; now it is not uncommon for the average home to have at least 3–5 devices. Perhaps more telling are the types of devices that are now being connected; these go beyond the traditional information technology (IT) devices such as laptops, tablets, and smartphones.

This is illustrated by the results of Project SHINE (SHodan INtelligence Extraction), which clearly demonstrate the types of devices and their functions are clearly evolving, and fall well outside of the traditional IT devices. Designed to understand the supervisory control and data acquisition (SCADA) and industrial control system (ICS) that are accessible from the Internet, it was reported as of September 2013 that "The average number of **new** SCADA/ICS devices found every day is typically between 2000 and 8000. So far we have collected over 1,000,000 unique IP addresses that appear to belong to either SCADA and control systems devices or related software products."[5] When we consider the types of devices that are being discovered, these include

- medical devices
- traffic management systems
- automotive control
- traffic light control (includes red-light and speeding cameras)
- heating, ventilation, and air conditioning/environment control
- power regulators/uninterruptible power supplies
- security/access control (includes closed-circuit television and webcams)
- serial port servers (many of which include Allen-Bradley DF1 capable protocols)
- data radios (point-to-point 2.4/5.8/7.8 GHz direct-connected radios)

As we can clearly see these are outside the general sphere of traditional IT, but the question now becomes, what role will cloud computing play in the future? According to an iView[6] published by analyst firm IDC entitled the Digital Universe in 2020, the type of information that will be stored in this future cloud will include considerably more than personal computers, phones, and consumer electronics, as depicted in Figure 10.1. According to IDC, it is predicted that the digital universe in 2020 will consist of 40 trillion gigabytes of data, with cloud computing forecasted to touch approximately

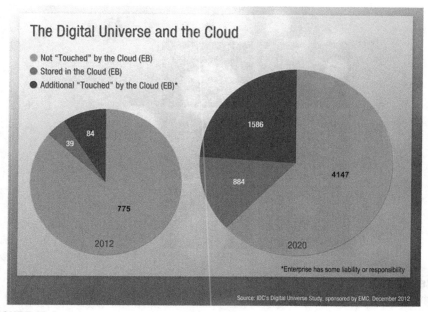

FIGURE 10.1
Growing role of cloud computing. EB, Exabyte.

40% of information within this universe, with 15% stored/maintained within the cloud.

With cloud computing therefore touching 1 in 2 information assets, and extending into processing, storage, and in some cases the management of devices within a critical infrastructure perspective, the need for cloud security has never been greater.

CLOUD COMPUTING FOR CRITICAL INFRASTRUCTURE

Broadly speaking, for many organizations, particularly those that operate within a critical infrastructure environment, there are three distinct zones. We can of course argue the definition of the term critical infrastructure but by and large these are those organizations that operate within industries that are critical to society.

Figure 10.2 provides a graphical illustration of the three zones, these are defined as Corporate IT, Command and Control (that includes those SCADA and ICS devices), and the Device network. Cloud computing has typically operated within the Corporate IT network, which experiences challenges we all read about from Bring Your Own Device to integration of cloud computing.

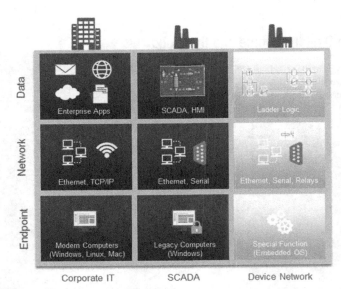

FIGURE 10.2
Zonal approach to critical infrastructure.

The question of course is the role of cloud computing when connecting and enabling the Command and Control, and Device zones. Particularly as these zones involve assets that are critical not only to the organization, but also to the society with which it serves. That is not to say that IT assets are not important, but in this particular context not critical.

Historically, and still in operation by many organizations today, is the belief that an air gap between the IT and Command and Control zones is all that is required to protect the critical assets. Without delving into the merits of this approach, there is an emerging trend to enable connectivity between these zones for business purposes. For example, within the Oil and Gas sector, the migration to smart oil fields allows the remote management of drilling operations that can and is leading to increased productivity through more oil production. What this means is that the risks the IT network has been facing for over the last 10–15 years are going to manifest themselves into critical zones. Of course, in the same vein there will also be opportunities that can hugely lead to efficiency gains such as the smart oil field, and of course cloud computing.

We have focused on the many benefits the cloud can provide to businesses, and there is nothing to suggest that these same benefits can be realized for ICS and SCADA environments (or commonly the Command and Control zone). Many of these benefits were detailed by Trend Micro, in the report entitled "SCADA in the Cloud: A security conundrum?"[7] Within the paper

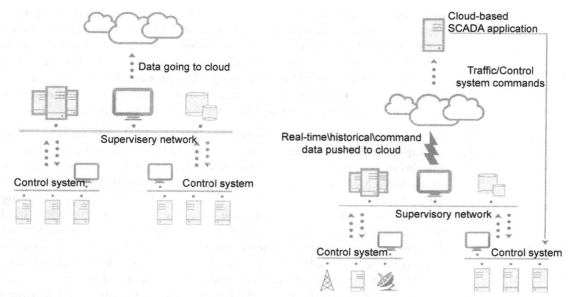

FIGURE 10.3
SCADA in the cloud. SCADA, supervisory control and data acquisition.

it detailed benefits of using the cloud within SCADA/ICS environments as the following:

- Redundancy and flexibility benefits: Cloud environments allow the ability to establish infrastructures considerably quicker than internally hosted systems, making the redundancy easier to resolve.
- Disaster recovery and automated updates: The ability to resolve issues quicker within cloud environments as opposed to organizations in noncloud environments. Indeed, cloud-enabled businesses are able to resolve issues within 2.1 h as opposed to 8 h.

Within the whitepaper, two architectures were proposed and graphically depicted in Figure 10.3. On the left-hand side of the graphic, SCADA applications are deployed on premise with data pushed to the cloud for analytics, and further access. The right-hand graphic has the SCADA applications hosted entirely within the cloud. Of course, each scenario has its own advantages and security risks. In the first scenario, there is the risk of data being compromised (confidentiality) within the cloud. These risks can either be for the data stored, or the data in transit (while being transferred between the application and cloud). The command and control element remains on premise, so the existing risks associated with securing an SCADA/ICS environment remains. In the latter example, however, there are additional risks that include data interception, but the implications are more significant than the first example. While of course confidentiality is a concern, there is also the risk of data being intercepted, modified, and replayed. This of course introduces integrity risks and the prospect of devices accepting unauthorized commands. The implications of such an incident occurring are of course significant, and while the earlier examples of MegaUpload becoming a significant inconvenience for its customers can be significant, there is no question that a major cyber event detrimentally impacting critical assets will be considerably more significant.

While this particular section is written into the final chapter, and indeed a chapter entitled the Future Cloud, it would lead one to believe that this migration is something we can experience in the future. However, there are many service providers already offering cloud-based SCADA solutions for critical infrastructure environments. Moreover, the cost savings can be significant. For example a "typical new in-house SCADA system for a small water treatment facility can have an upfront capital cost of about $11,500 for software, computer, telemetry, programming and setup. Compared to the initial approximate $1,600 cost of getting started with a cloud-based SCADA system, users can achieve about 90 percent reduction in costs."[8] This example is just the tip of the iceberg, with many automation companies expanding their portfolio for critical infrastructure customers to leverage cloud computing. In May 2013, for example, it was announced that automation vendor ABB and GlobaLogix partnered[9] to offer a Software-as-a-Service solution for the Oil and Gas sector. According to Sandy Taylor, Head of ABB's Oil, Gas and Petrochemical business unit, the "cloud-based SCADA infrastructure can save companies money and time by eliminating the need to build and maintain their own dedicated server rooms, while reducing SCADA administration costs and overall risks...The overall return on investment time can be reduced by 25–30% or more."

Indeed, the benefits that cloud computing can bring to critical infrastructure operators extend beyond simply monetary savings. According to Hitachi Data Systems, in their 2012 Whitepaper entitled "How to improve Healthcare with Cloud Computing"[10] the future of health care will be greatly aided by cloud computing: "electronic medical records, digital medical imaging, pharmacy records and doctor's notes are all consolidated and accessible. The ability of researchers to run analytics, better treatment options, optimal insurance programs and the possibilities of truly personalized healthcare have become a reality. Data drives the new healthcare world and access is greater than ever before. Big data becomes better managed due to cloud technology, as storage, compute power and consolidation reach levels never before achieved. Portability of data delivers information where it is needed, when it is needed."

While of course the benefits are very obvious and indeed for IT professionals have been realized for many years, they are now being commercially realized by Critical National Infrastructure (CNI) organizations. However, according to the European Network Information Security Agency (ENISA), in their report entitled "Critical Cloud Computing; A CIIP perspective on cloud computing services,"[11] dated December 2012, this is in fact a double-edged sword: "On the one hand, large cloud providers can deploy state of the art security and business continuity measures and spread the associated costs across the customers. On the other hand, if an outage or a security breach occurs then the consequences could be big, affecting many citizens, many organizations, at once." Moreover, we must also consider the impact of a major outage; within an IT environment the implications can be significant, for example, as was experienced by MegaUpload customers or indeed Amazon.com who were reported to have rejected US and Canadian customers when Amazon Web Services experienced an outage within its US-EAST data center for 59 min.[12]

Recognizing the role that cloud computing plays with regard to critical infrastructure has also been clearly identified by lawmakers. More specifically within Europe, and under the Network and Information Security (NIS) Directive, the scope has been defined as including cloud computing providers that support critical infrastructure operations. The inclusion of cloud computing within the scope of the NIS Directive is due to the risks to critical infrastructure, which according to ENISA are magnified due to the concentration of Information and Communications Technology (ICT) resources. In the event of a large-scale disruption, the consequences could be significant and impact many citizens and organization alike. Indeed, the impact is likely to be considerably greater due to the concentration of services, although it is worth noting that the likelihood will decrease.

DEFINING THE SECURITY REQUIREMENTS FOR TOMORROW'S CLOUD

What the preceding paragraphs clearly highlight is that cloud computing is beginning to find its way into sectors that traditionally were not under the control of the IT department. However, while there are many benefits, the impact should incidents occur can be more significant than what we have witnessed thus far.

Dynamic Attestation

With considerably more at stake, should there be not be a different approach regarding assurance of third-party services than what is being used today? In other words, is it acceptable to rely on annual assurance statements from third-party auditors (or even self-certification) when something as important as the energy network is reliant on maintaining service?

The answer of course is probably not, and this is partly why so many regulators and lawmakers globally are placing greater scrutiny on technology that supporting critical infrastructure.

Defining the specific assurance requirements will not be easy, mainly because different environments will require differing levels of assurance. However, one thing is clear that in the first instance greater transparency is necessary than simply relying on annual attestations. It is often cited that the use of cloud computing is like managing any other third party; there are, however, some challenges with this particular statement. Figure 10.4 graphically depicts a simple illustration of the supply chain related to a smart grid environment.

Within this environment you have the end customer sitting within ring 0, and as we extend out into further rings 1, 2, and so on, we can add multiple stakeholders within the broader supply chain. Within ring 0, however, the greatest level of transparency exists, roughly translated as those assets within my own control afford me the greatest transparency. As we begin to extend out into further rings, the level of transparency falls.

Within a cloud environment, however, the level of transparency is *likely* to be lower than a traditional outsourced contract (for the many reasons detailed earlier in the book, but effectively as the volume of customers and right to audit is generally removed). Subsequently, there will be a need to not only provide assurance but also to do so in a manner that is real time. The need for *dynamic attestation* will be driven largely due to the potential impact and prospect of regulatory requirements and their associated penalties (not only financial, with mandatory breach notification). This requirement can be translated as providing a mechanism that can give transparency and assurance on demand, and more importantly provide the necessary intelligence to proactively anticipate potential threats.

Third-Party Access

We are of course not proposing that the current cloud does not provide a mechanism for third-party access; however, it is suggested that the volume and

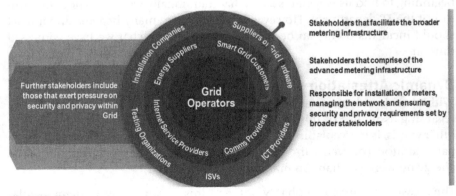

FIGURE 10.4

Growing supply chain. ISVs, Information security vendors.

subsequently likely sought granularity regarding permissions will be vastly different to today. Let us take one simple use case and combine one of the previous predictions, namely, the likely growth in data.

The use case to illustrate this requirement, why the smart grid of course (note that this particular use case is entirely due to its relevance and has nothing to do with the fact that coauthor Raj Samani's efforts in his previous book is conveniently titled "Applied Cyber Security and the Smart Grid" written with Eric D. Knapp)!

When people consider the smart grid, the default response is the smart meter. While there is considerably more to the grid than simply just meters, for the purposes of the example the default position is appropriate. With many governments around the world committing to deploying a meter in every home within the next 5–10 years (e.g., in Denmark the Minister for Climate has announced an act requiring utilities to install meters in every household[13]), the number of meters collecting data in every home will be expected to grow. According to Pike Research, the number of meters will grow to 535 million units by 2015, reaching a total number of installations of 963 million by the year 2020.[14] Combine the total number of meters, and the fact that these meters will be collecting data of energy consumption in every installation (known as the polling interval, which in some cases is as low as every 2 s), then we can see why with the earlier prediction of more data is looking a fairly safe bet.

With utilities collecting such a wealth of valuable data, there is absolutely no question that these data would be of enormous value for third parties; for example, consider a retailer looking to sell a washing machine; knowing what model of machines people use within the homes would be of great commercial interest. Putting aside the privacy considerations for one moment (this is covered in detail within the previously mentioned book, which covers the legal and regulatory requirements), and that many utilities are vowing not to share,[15] where transparency and explicit consent is gained we will witness huge demands for access to data gathered by these meters. Furthermore, the level of granularity and access control will have to contend with complex privacy rules so that data that uniquely identifies an individual are obfuscated, for example, and where an end customer wishes to, for example, purchase a new washing machine based on a communication from the retailer, then deanonymize their details.

With cloud computing seen as an integral part of the smart meter implementation demonstrated by utilities confirming migration of systems within their smart grid implementations to be hosted by Cloud Service Providers (CSPs), this particular use case is a good example of not only the requirements but also the direction of the future cloud. In this example, one of the key requirements for the future cloud will be to manage an enormous volume of third-party access requirements; this extends the current access requirements both in terms of volume as well as complexity. Other examples outside of the smart grid include the role of cloud computing within health care. According to research firms, the cloud computing market for health care purposes is predicted to reach $5.4 billion by 2017.[16] One particular use of cloud computing for health-related purposes will be for the storage of electronic health records (EHRs), which are likely to increase due to the requirements set out by the Patient Protection and Affordable Care Act. The act requires all US citizens to sign up for health insurance, which in itself will dramatically increase the number of medical records that facilities will have to support. Moreover, with a greater number of records, the medical facilities will need to ensure accessibility of the data by multiple third parties, including health insurance providers, medical researchers, and clinical staff. While there is quite rightly considerable interest in the use of cloud computing, particularly for research purposes, there exist privacy considerations when such data become accessible by third parties. Therefore, much like the smart grid example, the need to pseudonymize/anonymize data before providing access to third parties is necessary. This may include any number of stakeholders, and can include stakeholders undertaking the following roles (taken from the National Health Service (NHS) Care Record Guarantee[17]):

- check the quality of care (such as a clinical audit);
- protect the health of the general public;
- keep track of NHS spending;
- manage the health service;
- help investigate any concerns or complaints you or your family
- have about your health care;
- teach health care professionals; and
- help with research.

Dependent on the role of the individual, access to the EHR may need to obfuscate particular fields. For example, the Health Insurance Portability and Accountability Act (HIPAA) requires explicit consent from the data subject where the data are not used for treatment purposes:

> The Privacy Rule protects all personally identifiable health information, known as protected health information (PHI), created or received by a covered entity. Personally identifiable health information is defined as information, including demographic information, that "relates to past, present, or future physical or mental health or condition of an individual, the provision of health care to an individual, or the past, present, or future payment for the provision of health care for the individual" that either identifies the individual or with respect to which there is a reasonable basis to believe the information can be used to identify the individual.
>
> **45 C.F.R. § 160.103**

Restrictions on Use and Disclosure

> Covered entities may not use or disclose PHI except as permitted or required
> by the Privacy Rule13. A covered entity may disclose PHI without the
> individual's permission for treatment, payment, and health care operations
> purposes. For other uses and disclosures, the Privacy Rule generally
> requires the individual's written permission, which is an "authorization" that
> must meet specific content requirements.[18]

Within this scenario, access to third parties may require explicit consent from
the data subject. However, there are additional complications to this principle,
where the Privacy Principle permits the disclosure of Personal Health Information to specific stakeholders without consent under specific circumstances.
Subsequently, when we consider the level of granularity associated with data
access to EHRs that will be stored within a cloud environment, effectively
dependent on the role of the requesting party, the data may need to be obfuscated to remove personal identifiers. However, under specific circumstances,
any obfuscation will not be conducted where the stakeholder meets the specific conditions not requiring authorization (e.g., for research purposes this is
covered under 45 C.F.R. § 164.512). Alternatively, where explicit authorization
is granted then any controls to obfuscate PHI are equally not applied.

All sounds rather simple, does it not?

While there is no intention of delving into the details of HIPAA, or indeed any
other industry vertical regulation, it does demonstrate that as cloud computing becomes more ubiquitous and indeed used more within highly regulated
industries, there will be a need to add considerably more granular controls for
third-party access. Moreover, the volume of requests or rather the disparate
nature of those requesting access will only increase. Therefore, the future cloud
will need to consider the context behind specific requests for data, and ideally
dynamically obfuscate specific fields dependent on this context. In addition,
the likelihood is that the future cloud will have to support stronger authentication methods than the simple password. This of course is not a future cloud
consideration with multiple providers already offering such services, but certainly will likely be a requirement to support sensitive data.

Real-Time Assurance

We briefly touched on the real-time dependency of future cloud customers
to support critical operations. This was used to illustrate the requirement of
dynamic attestation, wherein an end customer can automatically verify the
security posture of assets hosted within a cloud environment. Another critical requirement related to real-time assurance is to proactively verify security
maturity, leveraging hardware to guarantee the integrity of assurance provided.

In many instances, assurance for the end customer is derived through service level agreements (SLAs) but according to research firm Heavy Reading, "The key for Cloud Service Providers is to find a service assurance solution that can monitor the cloud infrastructure at all levels while preemptively managing subscriber experience at the application level."[19] While for particular assets hosted in the cloud, there may not be a need for real-time quality of service attestation that the SLAs are met, when we consider the critical infrastructure environment discussed earlier it is likely the risk appetite for the end customer will demand real-time attestation.

Examples of such technologies are now becoming available in the market. Without wishing to appear as an endorsement, one such example is that provided by Intel through the trusted execution technology (TXT) capability.

Intel TXT

Available from 2007, Intel TXT[20] was released with the intention of providing a verified launch, utilizing a measured launch environment (MLE) that refers to a known good launch configuration. Any changes to this verified launch environment can be detected via cryptographic verification (hash or signed). Also, there is the ability to leverage the hardware to remove any residual data when the MLE is not correctly shutdown. Figure 10.5 shows how TXT works to protect a virtual server environment.

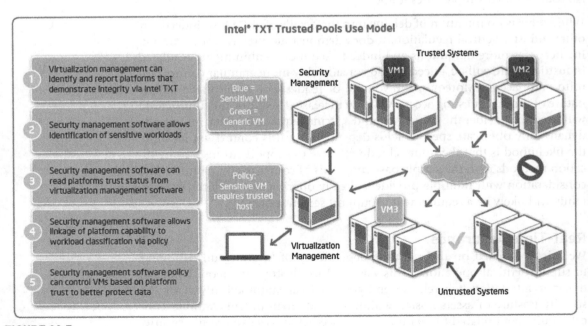

FIGURE 10.5
TXT trusted pools.

For a cloud-related environment, there are many advantages to the deployment of such a hardware-assisted approach to validate integrity. For example, the end customer can receive validation that a trusted hypervisor has been launched. Achieving this level of integrity may seem excessive for virtual machines supporting nonsensitive data/services but for highly critical environments is likely necessary. One such example of where such an environment is appropriate is under the concept known as "trusted pools," where only trusted hosts can participate within such pools. Polices can then be used to prevent unverified hosts access to the pool; this ensures that any potential compromised hosts are not allowed access to the trusted pool and negatively impact the trusted hosts.

End to End Validation

One of the earlier predictions centered on the increase in devices we are witnessing and will further witness within the Internet of tomorrow. Emerging challenges for end customers within this new world is the need for absolute validation that an incoming request has not been tampered with, and the integrity of the request is maintained. This is particularly important within a critical infrastructure environment, where the likelihood is that interactions will be undertaken between devices without any interaction with a human. This of course provides an opportunity to utilize the hardware between the machines (both within the cloud and communicating with the cloud), and to do so without the uncertainty of utilizing a user who could be manipulated, tricked, or bribed.

Establishing this hardware root of trust can be achieved with the use of solutions provided through the advent of technology being introduced into the market. Of course, there is no intention within this publication to endorse any commercial offerings; however, the following solution is significant and warrants further analysis.

CSP Future Requirements

Summarizing the requirements defined in preceding paragraphs, the future cloud will likely demand the following:

- Dynamic attestation: The ability to automatically query security maturity/compliance with agreed SLAs.
- Third-party access: Supporting high volumes of third-party requests, with granular access control models. In addition to the granularity of the access control, the ability to consider the context behind the request will be paramount in achieving compliance within highly regulated industries.
- Real-time assurance: Proactive attestation of security compliance undertaken in real time.
- End-to-end validation: Achieving a greater degree of assurance of the integrity behind the request to access cloud provisioned services.

While the above requirements for the future cloud are important, and indeed becoming more of an emerging series of requests from end customers, they by no means cover the entirety of the requirements for the future cloud. This is because there are many requirements emerging that are broader than just those within the control of the Cloud Service Provider (CSP).

Cloud Ecosystem Requirements

As we covered in the preceding chapter, some of the evolutions required for the future cloud involve technological innovation and adoption by CSPs. However, this is only the tip of the iceberg (and indeed the reader may have some recommendations that we may have omitted), with many requirements considerably broader than those within the control of the provider. One such example is achieving greater clarity regarding the complicated standards landscape when it comes to cloud computing.

Cloud Computing Standards Complexity

In November 2013, the European Commission on the European Cloud strategy published a final report entitled "Cloud Standards Coordination."[21] The purpose of the report was to review major aspects of cloud computing providing analysis into the standards landscape, which was perceived as a jungle of standards. The conclusion, however, was that the "cloud standards is large but not chaotic and by no means a jungle." Analysis undertaken summarized "20 relevant organizations in cloud computing Standardization and a selection of around 150 associated documents" to support the claim.

There are, however, a number of gaps identified within the cloud standards landscape; these are as follows.

Interoperability

The report concludes a lack of standards related to management specifications related to Platform as a Service (PaaS) and Software as a Service (SaaS). In particular, the report concludes that while proprietary solutions do exist, the implications are that this would generate vendor lock-in situations, which have been identified as a major concern for end customers of cloud. In addition, the report concludes a lack of standards associated with service metrics, and standards to provide monitoring data.

Security and Privacy

Security is recognized as integral for the wide-scale adoption of cloud computing; however, the assessment across multiple standards identified a lack of a common vocabulary to allow the end customer to express specific requirements as well as understanding the service offerings across multiple providers. Furthermore, there is a need for further metrics related to cloud computing.

Specific standards associated with accountability and cloud incident management citing the example of SLA infringement have been identified as areas that demand further standardization efforts.

Service Level Agreements

A main gap associated with cloud computing standards is the requirement for standardization relating to SLAs. In particular,

- Agreed terminology and definitions for service level objectives
- Metrics for each service level objective.

Regulation, Legal and Governance Aspects

Relating to the legal landscape, the report concludes the need for an international framework and governance, with associated global standards. The current landscape is built on national, and panregional (e.g., European Union) requirements; however, the global nature of cloud computing demands broader interoperable requirements.

The above activities undertaken by European Telecommunications Standards Institute (ETSI) are only a small snapshot into activities being undertaken in Europe, and indeed a smaller snapshot of global activities to establish the appropriate frameworks and tools necessary for the future cloud. Additional examples include

- Code of conduct for data protection: agreed a code of conduct for cloud computing providers to support a uniform application of data-protection rules.
- SLAs: Work to define a skeleton structure for cloud SLAs, identifying the components commonly found in cloud contracts and the most important elements for cloud SLAs, and propose a subset of these elements to focus on.
- Cloud computing contracts: identification of safe and fair contract terms and conditions for cloud computing services for consumers and small firms.

The above are related to the efforts within Europe, and specifically within efforts undertaken by the European Commission. Within the Cloud Security Alliance there are a number of research initiatives underway to address the above issues, as well as those raised within preceding chapters. A full list of these is available from within the Cloud Security Alliance Web site, with a summary included in Chapter 8 (https://cloudsecurityalliance.org/research/).

Cloud Broker Services

It is, however, worth drawing attention to an area of the cloud ecosystem that is an emerging area of focus, namely, cloud broker services. Within the CSA, a new working group is being established to define security best practices to brokers, as well as provide life cycle management for cloud brokerage services. According to National Institute of Standards and Technology (NIST) (SP 500-292), a cloud broker is "an entity that manages the use, performance and delivery of cloud services, and negotiates relationships between cloud Providers and cloud Consumers." It is anticipated the cloud broker market will see significant growth as awareness of its benefits permeate across potential customers. The many benefits of cloud brokers, is that they have the potential to eliminate many of the concerns end customers have with cloud computing as well as simplifying the overall process by which multiple CSPs are managed. For example, a policy may exist to ensure that all data leaving the internal network and being sent to the public cloud providers must not contain credit card numbers. The broker should not only be able to leverage some form of data loss prevention to inspect data, but also apply policy rules (e.g., do not allow these data to leave the enterprise, or allow but encrypt). The role of the broker is extended with announcements from CSPs that allow end customers the ability to provide their own keys to encrypt data on the cloud service. If we use Amazon S3 as an illustration, "In between, it is up to you to manage your encryption keys and to make sure that you know which keys were used to encrypt each object. You can store your keys on-premises or you can use AWS Cloud HSM, which uses dedicated hardware to help you to meet corporate, contractual and regulatory compliance requirements for data security."[22] Where multiple providers are being used, and specific regulatory requirements addressing the geographic location of keys (e.g., RIPA Part III), customers may look to leverage brokers for simplified key management. Such an approach will mean that for the end customer, the complexity required to assure cloud-provisioned services can be handled by the broker. In fact, this should eliminate or at least reduce the risk of vendor lock-in, and if handled appropriately ensure that regulated data are not transferred to locations that do not meet policy or applicable laws. Of course, if the broker is provided as-a-service, then this only pushes these concerns further downstream; in other words, it will be a broker lock-in and not a CSP lock-in. Regardless, this may be a risk that is accepted or alternatively an on-premise broker may be used.

According to Gartner Cloud Service, brokers can be divided into three categories:

- Cloud service intermediation: Intermediary that adds value to a service through the provision of additional capabilities. Examples will include services such as identity and access management where the end customer could acquire such capabilities to enhance the currently provisioned cloud services. The broker, however, will remain independent of the provisioned service provider.
- Aggregation: A brokerage service that combines multiple services into one, or new services. An example of this may be a broker that combines all of the offerings from the multiple cloud offerings that are being used, and offers a simple interface to manage the resources across all of the providers.
- Cloud service arbitrage: Although the aggregation service is likely to be fixed, the arbitrage category would automatically provide flexible aggregate

choices to the end customer. What this means is that the broker would automatically select the most appropriate CSP on behalf of the customer, migrate the workload, and allow the customer to benefit financially.

It is predicted for cloud service brokers as an industry to double in size, reaching $141bn by the year 2017.[23] For this reason, the CSA is establishing the Cloud Broker Working Group to address these challenges, and to establish cloud governance best practices, documenting use cases, identifying security standards requirements (for example, integration into the Cloud Controls Matrix (CCM) or Consensus Assessments Initiative Questionnaire (CAIQ)), as well as other areas for potential research as it applies to brokers. Cloud computing will continue to evolve, and introduce considerably more key stakeholders, which will likely demand further development of security standards, and guidance to ensure they do not become the weakest link.

This and other CSA research initiatives are open to volunteers wishing to provide their expertise into the various deliverables. Therefore, the reader is encouraged to get involved, and participate time permitting of course.

Cloud computing is evolving, and the number of use cases are growing exponentially. In certain cases, these use cases involve critical operations, to the hosting and management of systems keeping the lights on to treating the water delivered to consumer's homes. The need for a safe and secure cloud has therefore never been so important. Therefore, your support and expertise is greatly appreciated.

END NOTES

1. Larry Dignan, ZDNet, *Internet of Things: $8.9 Trillion Market in 2020, 212 billion connected things*, (October 2013), [cited December 2013]. Available from: http://www.zdnet.com/internet-of-things-8-9-trillion-market-in-2020-212-billion-connected-things-7000021516/.

2. Cisco, *Global Internet Traffic Projected to Quadruple by 2015*, (June 2011), [cited December 2013]. Available from: http://newsroom.cisco.com/press-release-content;jsessionid=9F2A5677FAC-60C600EFC7966A7A89550?type=webcontent&articleId=324003.

3. IoD Big Picture, *The future of the Internet, you ain't seen nothing yet*, (October 2011), [cited December 2013]. Available from: http://www.iod.com/MainWebSite/Resources/Document/Q3-The-future-of-the-Internet-you-aint-seen-nothin-yet.pdf.

4. Darryl Taft, eWeek, *Big Data Market to Reach $46.34 Billion by 2018*, (September 2013), [cited December 2013]. Available from: http://www.eweek.com/database/big-data-market-to-reach-46.34-billion-by-2018.html.

5. Eric Byers and Tofino, *Project SHINE: 1,000,000 Internet-Connected SCADA and ICS Systems and Counting*, (September 2013), [cited December 2013]. Available from: http://www.tofinosecurity.com/blog/project-shine-1000000-internet-connected-scada-and-ics-systems-and-counting.

6. John Gantz and David Reinsel, *Digital Universe in 2020: Big Data, Bigger Digital Shadows, and Biggest Growth in the Far East*, (IDC, December 2012), [cited January 2014]. Available from: http://www.emc.com/leadership/digital-universe/iview/cloud-computing-in-2020.htm.

7. Kyle Wilhoit, Trend Micro, *SCADA in the Cloud; A security conundrum?*, published 2013, [cited December 2013]. Available from: http://www.trendmicro.com/cloud-content/us/pdfs/security-intelligence/white-papers/wp-scada-in-the-cloud.pdf.

8. Waterworld, *Cloud-Based SCADA Offers Alternatives to Traditional Systems*, [cited December 2013]. Available from: http://www.waterworld.com/articles/print/volume-28/issue-10/editorial-features/cloud-based-scada-alternatives-traditional-systems.html.

9. ABB, *ABB and GlobaLogix partner to provide SCADAvantage in the cloud for oil and gas companies*, (May 2013), [December 2013]. Available from: http://www.abb.com/cawp/seitp202/5e226590a23709f8c1257b790031ccb8.aspx.

10. Hitachi Data Systems, *How to improve Healthcare with Cloud Computing*, (May 2012), [cited December 2013]. Available from: http://docs.media.bitpipe.com/io_10x/io_108673/item_650544/cloud%20computing%20wp.pdf.

11. European Network Information Security Agency (ENISA), *Critical Cloud Computing; A CIIP perspective on cloud computing services*. (December 2012), [cited December 2013]. Available from http://www.enisa.europa.eu/activities/Resilience-and-CIIP/cloud-computing/critical-cloud-computing/.

12. Zack Whittaker. ZDNet, *Amazon Web Services suffers outage, takes down Vine*, (August 2013), [cited December 2013]. Available from: http://www.zdnet.com/amazon-web-services-suffers-outage-takes-down-vine-instagram-flipboard-with-it-7000019842/.

13. Smart Grid Insights, *Danish growth companies are ready with enhanced smart meter features*, (September 2013), [cited December 2013]. Available from: http://smartgridresearch.org/news/danish-growth-companies-ready-enhanced-smart-meter-features/.

14. Business Green Staff, *Smart meter installations to near one billion by 2020*, (August 2011), [cited December 2013]. Available from: http://www.espncricinfo.com/south-africa-v-india-2013-14/engine/current/match/648667.html.

15. Utility Week, *CGI will 'definitely not' sell smart data to third parties*, (August 2013), [cited December 2013]. Available from: http://www.utilityweek.co.uk/news/CGI-will-definitely-not-sell-smart-data-to-third-parties/907122.

16. Florence de Borja, CloudTimes. *Cloud Computing Health care market worth $5bn by 2017*, (July 2012), [cited January 2014]. Available from: http://cloudtimes.org/2012/07/18/cloud-health-care-market/.

17. *NHS Care Record Guarantee*, [cited January 2014]. Available from: http://webarchive.nationalarchives.gov.uk/20130513181011/http://www.nigb.nhs.uk/pubs/nhscrg.pdf.

18. Institute of Medicine (US) Committee on Health Research and the Privacy of Health Information: The HIPAA Privacy Rule; Nass SJ, Levit LA, Gostin LO, editors. Washington (DC): http://www.nap.edu/, National Academies Press (US); 2009 "Beyond the HIPAA Privacy Rule: Enhancing Privacy, Improving Health Through Research" Available from: http://www.ncbi.nlm.nih.gov/books/NBK9573/.

19. Banerjee and Wallace Heavy Reading, *Service Assurance in SDN & Cloud*, (July 2013), [cited January 2014]. Available from: http://www.heavyreading.com/details.asp?sku_id=3049&skuitem_itemid=1499.

20. James Greene, Intel Corporation, *Intel Trusted Execution Technology (TXT)*, [cited January 2014]. Available from: http://www.intel.com/content/dam/www/public/us/en/documents/whitepapers/trusted-execution-technology-security-paper.pdf.

21. *ETSI Cloud Standards Coordination*, (November 2013). [cited January 2014]. Available from: http://ec.europa.eu/digital-agenda/en/news/cloud-standards-coordination-final-report.

22. Jeff Barr, Amazon Web Services, *Use your own Encryption Keys with S3's Server-side encryption*, (June 2014) [cited July 2014]. Available from: http://aws.amazon.com/blogs/aws/s3-encryption-with-your-keys/.

23. Gartner.com, *Forecast: Public Cloud Services Brokerage 3Q2103*, (December 2013), [cited July 2014]. Available from: https://www.gartner.com/doc/2638220/forecast-public-cloud-services-brokerage.

Appendix

Taken from Security Guidance for Critical Areas of Mobile Computing, V1.0

The following are countermeasures to mitigate major authentication threats as described in the attack trees below. The threat is followed by the countermeasures. Some are security policy elements, which can be implemented by device administrators, some can only be addressed by app developers, and some can only be addressed by OS developers.

AUTHENTICATION BYPASS

The most common methods of authentication bypass are all possible because of developer errors. However, an enterprise information technology department can test software for vulnerabilities.

- SQL Injection—Implement escaping of reserved SQL words and characters such as ', =, OR, etc.
- Direct URL request—Access control system not applied beyond gateway resources. Access control should be applied to all resources.
- Session-ID prediction—Insufficient session-ID unpredictability; session-IDs should be randomly selected from a large space.
- Buffer overflow—Errors in memory management and address space predictability. Techniques such as ASLR (Address Space Layout Randomization) can be used to mitigate.
- Open-device—Always enforce use of device lock.

Valid credentials from device not owned by user – relevant attacks and countermeasures include:

- Password brute force
  - Enforce password rules
  - Throttle authentication attempts (limited failed authentication attempts). Throttling should be cloud based, not device based (otherwise physical access can defeat it).
  - Use context/behavioral anomaly detection (location, language, who-you-know, voice, etc.), where possible

- Username space brute force
  - Enforce password rules
  - Use context/behavioral anomaly detection (location, language, who-you-know, voice, etc.), where possible
- Phishing
  - User awareness, contextual authentication support, 2-factor authentication
- Man in the Middle (MITM), replay, and network compromise
  - Use unpredictable one-time session tokens or time-stamps to prevent replay.
  - Verify public key infrastructure certificates of web services
  - Always transmit credentials using secure socket layer/secure shell

Valid credentials from user-trusted device—relevant attacks and countermeasures include:

- Physical access to storage (allows attacker to circumvent PIN throttling)
  - Use secure, tamper-proof hardware (e.g., secure micro-SD) to store credentials. Always ensure credentials are encrypted using a private key, which is password protected by a high entropy password (this should usually be the device unlock PIN to ensure minimum usability cost).
  - Always use disk encryption for all sensitive data on mobile memory.
  - Enforce password rules for unlock PINs (use ASCII, entropy, more than 6 digit, dictionary resistant). Bear in mind that unlock pins often also give access to (decrypt) encryption keys, such as disk encryption keys and other credentials stored on the device. User-to-device authentication is therefore especially important.
  - Do not use insecure biometric device unlock mechanisms without liveness detection, such as face recognition, for sensitive applications.
  - Never store passwords in plain text—use salted hash
  - Decommissioning/loss/theft procedures should be in place (e.g., remote-kill, locate, lock)
  - Always enforce use of PIN-lock.
- One time password (OTP) theft/relay
  - Do not use OTP generators on same device as primary login (e.g., Google authenticator)
  - Ensure all antimalware measures are in place on primary and secondary device (e.g., personal computer and mobile phone)
- Malware on device
  - Take all possible measures to ensure malware does not reach the device (e.g., disallow jailbreak, use app-whitelist + pretest enterprise apps).
  - Use mobile device management software with jailbreak detection/other healthcheck support
  - Never store passwords in plain text—use salted hash

- Side channel attacks (e.g., smudge attack, accelerometer attack)
  - App and OS developers should block access to accelerometer during password entry
  - Use of PIN is more secure than pattern.
  - Use reverse patterns (covering the same digit more than once) where possible (although this is not allowed on Android), wipe screen regularly.
- Near-field communication authentication failure (e.g., relay attack)
  - Use time-bounding protocols to prevent relay attacks

User->Device specific attacks include:

- Biometric spoof
  - Do not use biometric device-lock or other biometric systems, which operate without any sophisticated liveness detection.
- No pin-lock
  - Enforce pin-lock
- Data not encrypted
  - Enforce disk encryption

General advice: Authentication strength inevitably involves a trade-off between security and usability or user cost, as well as deployment cost. You should weigh up the risk to the assets accessible via your mobile devices (this includes assets in the cloud) against the user cost involved. Try to minimize user involvement while providing an adequate level of security for the assets involved.

Index

Note: Page numbers followed by "b", "f" and "t" indicate boxes, figures, and tables respectively

Printed in the United States
By Bookmasters